James Ramsay Gibson Maitland

The History of Howietoun

James Ramsay Gibson Maitland

The History of Howietoun

ISBN/EAN: 9783337140069

Printed in Europe, USA, Canada, Australia, Japan

Cover: Foto ©ninafisch / pixelio.de

More available books at **www.hansebooks.com**

Waterfall on Loch Coulter Burn at Milnehome Hatching-house.

THE

HISTORY OF HOWIETOUN

CONTAINING A FULL DESCRIPTION

OF THE VARIOUS

HATCHING-HOUSES AND PONDS, AND OF EXPERIMENTS
WHICH HAVE BEEN UNDERTAKEN THERE,
FROM 1873 TO THE PRESENT TIME

AND ALSO OF

THE FISH-CULTURAL WORK

AND THE

MAGNIFICENT RESULTS ALREADY OBTAINED

BY

SIR J. RAMSAY GIBSON MAITLAND, Bart.
F.L.S., F.Z.S.
MEMBER OF THE FISHERY BOARD FOR SCOTLAND,
CORRESPONDING MEMBER OF THE AMERICAN FISH-CULTURAL ASSOCIATION,
ETC. ETC. ETC.

PUBLISHED BY

J. R. GUY, SECRETARY HOWIETOUN FISHERY,

STIRLING, N.B.

1887

EDINBURGH UNIVERSITY PRESS:
T. and A. CONSTABLE, Printers to Her Majesty.

TO
FRANCIS DAY
C.I.E., F.L.S., F.Z.S.,
Etc. Etc.

PREFACE.

THE Howietoun Fishery having now been just completed, after ten years of continuous constructive work, it seems to me unadvisable longer to delay publishing an account of the mode in which the design has been carried out, and of the results already obtained.

The object in view has been to prove, by actual experience, that the culture of the *Salmonidæ* can be made commercially a success, if set about in a business-like manner. At a very early period I realised that, in comparison with the numbers of live fish claimed to have been produced, the results of fish-culture as applied to the *Salmonidæ* were in general very meagre.

What the reasons were did not seem clear. At first I was inclined to attribute it principally to some want in the treatment of the ova. Now, with fuller knowledge, I only wonder that any results were obtained. At the head of the list stand out in strong relief over-statements, caused no doubt by anxiety to claim the best possible results, and the insuperable difficulty in counting the fry; next in order, the almost total ignorance of the habits and requirements of young fish; and the difficulty of transplanting them—for their mere conveyance alive to the destination is not sufficient: they must be carried in perfectly clean water, they must be perfectly prepared, the temperature of the transport-tank must be kept within a few degrees of that of the stream into which they are to be turned, and the stream itself must not only be suitable for fry, but the part of the stream where they are liberated must be skilfully selected.

Next in point of deadliness, the insane overcrowding of the ova, and afterwards of the fry in the trays. This was supposed to be the sovereign remedy for the admittedly meagre results. Do not waste money over your hatching-house. Only lay down enough eggs, and a few inches thick, if possible, and a very few pounds will suffice to stock all the waters in the country! The ova were laid down in this manner at first by hundreds of thousands, afterwards by millions. Tens of thousands of pounds sterling have been spent—wasted, if you like,—and to-day we are still asking, Where is the result? Where?

But there is a yet more fatal cause of failure, a cause so hidden that never was it suspected until the Howietoun experiments placed it beyond a doubt. *The maturity of the parents is of paramount importance in determining the chance of the offspring in the struggle for existence.* Old spawners produce strong and healthy fry; young spawners, though comparatively more prolific, produce weaker offspring, with a much smaller chance of holding their own in the waste of waters. The problem is now solved. The culture of the *Salmonidæ* is now an achieved success. And in the hope that the methods followed may prove of use to those working on the still larger question of our sea-fisheries, I will endeavour to bring the experimental part of the work, in which I have been largely helped by F. Day, C.I.E., F.L.S., down to the hour of publication.

I take this opportunity of acknowledging the great assistance I have received from my wife, to whose untiring energy the Fishery owes much of its present prosperity, and this book its existence.

J. R. G. MAITLAND.

STIRLING, N.B., *October* 1886.

CONTENTS.

CHAPTER I.

INTRODUCTORY.

The pre-eminence of Great Britain in matters pertaining to Fisheries—Government brand for cured herring—The Fishery Board for Scotland—District Fishery Boards—The period in the life-history of fish at which loss occurs—Legislative protection and commercial fish-culture—Salmon in fresh water—Work at Howietoun—Table of stock at Howietoun on 1st September 1886—Transportation of ova to the Antipodes—Shipments by Mr. Youl, 1860-79—Shipments from Howietoun to New Zealand—Shipments of ova from Howietoun to America—Shipments to New Zealand in 1886, . . . 1

CHAPTER II.

THE EGG HARVEST.

Time of spawning can be advanced or retarded—Method of spawning—Milting the ova—Collecting ova of salmon—of wild trout, . 23

CHAPTER III.

PACKING THE TROUT OVA.

Selection of the eggs to be packed—The sink used in packing—The packing-room—*Modus operandi*—Packing for abroad—Boxes for ova—Felted moss—Class of ova—Age of embryo at the date of packing—Temperature, ... 31

CHAPTER IV.

WORK IN THE HATCHING-HOUSE.

Preparations for the reception of the eggs—Laying down the eggs—The egg account—Hatching—Stages through which the ova passes: 1. The mulberry stage; 2. The spectacle stage; 3. The eye stage;

4. First appearance of red blood; 5. Completion of the embryonic circle—A co-operative breathing society—Daily work in the hatching-house—Feeding the fry—The short feeding-spoon—Despatching fry—Preparing fry for travelling—Fry travelling-tanks—Carboys—Temperature for travelling—Length of journey—Profit on sale of fry—Transplantation of fry, ... 48

CHAPTER V.

REARING YEARLING AND TWO-YEAR-OLD TROUT.

Teaching the fry to collect for feeding—Feeding—The two-year-olds, 71

CHAPTER VI.

DESPATCHING LIVE TROUT.

Water for travelling—Tanks—Preparation of yearlings—Of two-year-olds—Of large trout—Despatching live trout, . . . 75

CHAPTER VII.

BREEDERS.

Value of breeders—Segregation of sexes—*Salmo fontinalis* as breeders—Selection, ... 86

CHAPTER VIII.

SEASON 1873-74.

Construction: Middlethird.—The Francis box—Slate trays—The 9-feet plank pond—Safety-screen—Ova-extractor, . . . 91
Fish-Culture.—First experience of—Hill burn-trout—Hatching in the Francis box compared with hatching under natural circumstances—Great lake trout eggs purchased—Disaster from flooding—Value of water-cress in fish-culture—Danger of showing fish to visitors—First experiment in carrying fry—Fry turned into Loch Coulter, . . 99

CHAPTER IX.

SEASON 1874-75.

Construction: Middlethird Hatching-house.—Building the house. *Middlethird Dam*—A V-shaped spout—Overflow sluice—Leaf-screen. *Filters.*—

xiv   CONTENTS.

Plank filter—Slate filter—Wood filter. "Theory of waste"—Slate trays and hatching-boxes—Exudance of gas by ova—Sediment—Safety-screen—Protection of the ova from : 1, mice; 2, light; 3, fungus—Charring the boxes—Description of the original Howietoun hatching-box—Glass grilles—Manner of introducing the water into the hatching-boxes—Inlet screens—Breakwater—The E-spout—The rearing-boxes—Drains, ...   103

CHAPTER X.

SEASON 1874-75.

Construction: Craigend Dam.—Intake works—Leaf-screen—Sluice—Safety-screen—Distributing spout—A summer spate. *Craigend Hatching-room.*—Slate cistern—Slate and glass grille—Rearing trough,   .   135

CHAPTER XI.

SEASON 1874-75.

Construction : Howietoun.—Description of Howietoun—Location of ponds—Site selected. *Intake works: Plank ponds.*—Method of introducing the water—Gravel : Disadvantages of. *Small larder at Craigend.*—Removal of fish into the plank ponds,   .   .   .   150

CHAPTER XII.

SEASON 1874-75.

Experimental Work.—(1.) Loch Leven eggs milted by a burn-trout male; milt bottled six hours before using. (2.) Loch Leven eggs milted by a burn-trout male; same as No. 1, but males transported alive. (3.) Loch Leven eggs milted by a burn-trout male; the male immature, and quantity of milt small. (4.) Burn-trout eggs milted by a Loch Leven male; milt bottled twenty hours before using. (5.) Loch Leven eggs milted by a burn-trout male; eggs bottled twenty hours before using. (6.) Loch Leven eggs milted by a Loch Leven male pure; eggs with red liquid. (7.) Sea-trout eggs milted by a burn-trout male; male very small. (8.) Loch Leven eggs milted by a sea-trout male. (9.) Sea-trout eggs milted by a Loch Leven male. (10.) Burn-trout eggs milted by a burn-trout male; ova cut out of a dead female. (11.) Burn-trout eggs milted by a sea-trout male,   .   .   .   162

CONTENTS. xv

CHAPTER XIII.

SEASON 1874-75.

Fish-Culture.—Collecting breeders—History of the breeders—Fry—Travelling tank—Table of ova for the Season, ... 170

CHAPTER XIV.

SEASON 1875-76.

Construction: Middlethird Hatching-house.—It is devoted solely to hatching—Distributing spout—Downfall spout—Cutting bit, with adjustable cutter, ... 180
Craigend.—Construction of the ponds—Leaf-screen, . . . 185
Howietoun.—The sluice at the intake—New 20-foot plank ponds—The 60-foot pond, ... 187
Experimental Work.—Work of the season—Tables of temperatures and of incubation, ... 201
Fish-Culture.—Advantages of keeping breeders—Trout spawned—Fry turned out—Loss of trout at Craigend—Collection of fry for feeding—Depth and aspect of ponds for fry—Table of ova spawned in the Season, ... 207

CHAPTER XV.

SEASON 1876-77.

Construction.—Howietoun Hatching-house—Fence round the ponds—Larder—The 130-foot ponds—Dividing-box—Screens—The octagonal pond at Craigend, ... 216
Experimental Work.—Experiments suggested by Frank Buckland—Answers to his queries, ... 226
Fish-Culture.—Stock in hand at the beginning of the Season—Removals during the Season—Table of ova spawned—Fry sent to Loch Leven—Stock on January 1st 1877, ... 228

CHAPTER XVI.

SEASON 1877-78.

Construction: Howietoun.—Completion of the 130-foot ponds—The carriers or leads—Concrete for sides of water-courses—Apparatus for letting off the water—Bevel for dressing slopes—New mincing-house—Food for fish—Drain for new ponds at Howietoun, . . . 233

Craigend.—Drain for emptying the ponds—Dangers to fry from yearlings —From starvation—Turfing pond-sides—Spigot and Faucet pipe put in below leaf-screen—Method of working the Craigend ponds— Alterations to the octagon pond—The wells—Taking the fish out of the ponds, ... 237
Experimental Work.—Development of yellow spots by *S. levenensis*, . 246
Fish-Culture.—The 1875 Lochlevens—Water supply for 130-foot ponds —Removals of fish—Ova obtained for the first time from fish reared from eggs hatched at the Fishery—The Season's ova—Further stocking of Lochleven—Loss of fry through crowding when travelling—Statement of stock on 31st December 1877, . . 248

CHAPTER XVII.

SEASON 1878-79.

Construction: Howietoun.—The 300-foot ponds—Outlet-screen—Valves— Mode of emptying—Size of fish must be proportionate to the depth of the ponds—Well—Short arm at upper end of the ponds used in netting—Apparatus for mechanically feeding the fry in the 20-foot ponds—Water-cress, ... 253
Experimental Work.—Economising space in hatching—Deep hatching-tray —Quadruple hatching-box—Glass grilles—Experiment not satisfactory—Reasons—Zinc for screens—Quantity of water required to carry trout—The first important consignment of trout sent from Howietoun—Experiments in transporting yearlings, . . 265
Fish-Culture.—Notes of the Season—*S. fontinalis* ova purchased—Sale of ova—Herons troublesome—Table of ova spawned Season 1878-79— Statement of stock on 31st December 1878, . . . 273

LIST OF ILLUSTRATIONS.

Frontispiece.—Waterfall on the Loch Coulter Burn at the Milneholme Hatching-house.

FIG.		PAGE
1.	Plan of the Ponds at Howietoun,	10

PACKING THE OVA.

2.	Lead Basin used in packing, section	32
3.	,, ,, ,, plan	32
4.	Operator receiving a Grille of Ova,	33
5.	,, reversing the Grille,	33
6.	,, handing away the Empty Grille,	34
7.	Frame for isolating the Ova,	35
8.	,, ,, ,, section,	35
9.	,, ,, ,, side-view,	35
10.	Covering the Ova with Swan's Down,	37
11.	Laying the Ova in the Tray,	37
12.	Tray in which Ova are packed,	40
13.	,, ,, ,, ,, section,	40
14.	Plan of Ova Packing-case, with the Lid detached,	41
15.	Elevation of Ova Packing-case, with part of the Side removed, showing the Ova in position,	41
16.	Elevation of Foreign Packing-case for Ova, with part of the Side removed, showing the Ice-tray and the Ova in position,	42
17.	Top view of ditto, with Lid open,	42
18.	Moss-felting Machine, section,	43
19.	,, ,, ,, top view,	43

FEEDING THE FRY.

20.	Fry Feeding-spoon, section,	63
21.	,, ,, plan,	63
22.	The Short Feeding-spoon,	64
23.	The Long-handled Feeding-spoon,	72
24.	A Feeding-pail,	74

LIST OF ILLUSTRATIONS.

DESPATCHING LIVE TROUT.

FIG.		PAGE
25. Travelling Tank for Yearlings,		77
26. Travelling Tank for Two-year-olds, side view,		78
27. ,, ,, ,, end view,		78
28. *View of the Despatching-house, Howietoun*,		82
29. Despatching Yearling Trout,		84

MIDDLETHIRD.

30. The Francis Box,	91
31. ,, ,, longitudinal section,	92
32. ,, ,, transverse section,	92
33. A Slate Tray,	93
34. Section of ditto,	93
35. Transverse section of ditto,	93
36. Nine-feet Plank-pond, section,	94
37. ,, ,, ,, plan,	94
38. ,, ,, ,, end elevation,	94
39. ,, ,, ,, longitudinal section,	95
40. The Safety-screen,	95
41. *The Ova-Extractor*,	98
42. Section of ditto,	98

MIDDLETHIRD DAM.

43. Plan, showing the Filters,	105
44. The V-shaped Spout,	106
45. Section of the V-shaped Spout in position,	106
46. Transverse section of the V-shaped Spout,	107
47. Overflow Sluice, section,	108
48. ,, ,, front elevation,	108
49. Leaf-screen,	108
50. ,, section,	109
51. Sluice used in connection with the Leaf-screen,	109
52. Diagram showing a longitudinal section of the Leaf-screen, Sluice, Aqueduct, and their connection with the Filters,	110
53. A set of Sluices,	111
54. *The Plank Filter*,	111
55. Transverse section of ditto,	112
56. Longitudinal section of ditto, showing the Screens in position,	112
57. *Ground-plan of Middlethird, showing the Water-courses*,	113
58. *Slate Filter*,	114
59. Longitudinal section of ditto,	114

LIST OF ILLUSTRATIONS. xix

FIG.   PAGE
60. Transverse section of *Slate Filter*,   114
61. *Old Wood Filter*,   115
62. Transverse section of ditto,   115
63. Longitudinal section of ditto,   116
64. *Plan of Middlethird Hatching-house in* 1874-75,   118

HATCHING-BOXES.

65. Original Howietoun Hatching-box,   124
66. Transverse section of ditto,   125
67. Longitudinal section of ditto,   125
68. Portion of longitudinal section of a Glass Grille, showing the perforated zinc,   127
69. Portion of a Glass Grille,   127
70. Transverse section of a Glass Grille, showing the mode of attachment,   128
71. Inlet-screen for Hatching-box. First form (now obsolete) shown in section,   128
72. Front of ditto,   128
73. Plan of ditto,   128
74. Section of a Hatching-box, showing second form of Inlet-screen in position (also obsolete),   128
75. Longitudinal section of ditto,   128
76. Breakwater as at present used instead of an Inlet-screen,   129
77. Longitudinal Section of Hatching-box, showing Breakwater and Safety-screen in position,   129

MIDDLETHIRD HATCHING-HOUSE.

78. Longitudinal Section of a Portion of the House showing E-spout,   130
79. Transverse Section of the E-spout,   130
80. Plan of the E-spout, showing its connection with the Aqueduct and Distributing-spout,   130
81. Elevation of Stand with Rearing-boxes, showing the Distributing-spout and connections in section,   131
82. Cross-section of Distributing-spout, showing one of the Distributors in elevation,   131
83. Cross-section of Distributing-spout, showing one of the Distributors in section,   131
84. Plan of the Distributing-spout, showing connections,   132
85. Transverse Section of a Rearing-box and Lid,   132
86. The Lid of a Rearing-box,   132
87. Longitudinal Section of a Rearing-Box and Lid,   133

xx   LIST OF ILLUSTRATIONS.

CRAIGEND DAM.

FIG.   PAGE
88. Intake Works, elevation,   136
89.   ,,   ,,   section,   137
90. Leaf-screen, plan,   .   .   .   137
91.   ,,   longitudinal section,   .   138
92.   ,,   transverse section,   .   .   138
93. Plan of Intake Works, showing Water-courses,   .   .   139
94. The Sluice, section, ...   140
95. Plan of the Sluice, showing the Safety-screen and Distributing-
       spout for subsidiary Boxes, ...   141
96. The Safety-screen in position, elevation,   .   .   .   141
97. Stonework with Sluice and Wire-screen, elevation, .   .   .   142
98.   ,,   ,,   ,,   section, .   .   .   142
99. Distributing-spout to subsidiary Boxes, showing Overflow in elevation,   143
100.   ,,   ,,   ,,   plan, .   .   .   143
101. Plan of the Dam and Waste-water Course, .   .   144

CRAIGEND HATCHING-ROOM.

102. Craigend—Small Slate Cistern, plan, .   .   .   145
103.   ,,   ,,   ,,   transverse section, .   .   146
104. Longitudinal section of the Small Slate Cistern, showing the Supply-
       and Waste-pipes, ...   146
105. Slate and Glass Grille, plan, ...   147
106.   ,,   ,,   transverse section,   .   147
107.   ,,   ,,   longitudinal section, .   .   147
108. Slate Rearing-trough, transverse section,   .   .   147
109.   ,,   ,,   plan, showing Overflow-pipe, .   147
110.   ,,   ,,   elevation, .   .   147
111.   ,,   ,,   longitudinal section, .   .   147
112. Stand with Slate Trays, Slate Filter, and Cistern in section, .   148
113. Plan of Hatching-room, ...   149

HOWIETOUN.

114. Intake Works, first system; section, showing Leaf-screen and Regulat-
       ing-sluice, ...   153
115. Intake Works, first system, plan, ...   154
116.   ,,   ,,   transverse section,   .   .   .   155
117. 20-feet Plank-pond, plan, ...   156
118.   ,,   ,,   end elevation, ...   156
119.   ,,   ,,   longitudinal section, showing Safety-screen,   .   157
120.   ,,   ,,   transverse section,   .   .   157

LIST OF ILLUSTRATIONS. xxi

FIG.   PAGE
121. Small Larder, section, .   160
122.   ,,   ,,   elevation, .   160
123. Fry Transporting-tank (first form), section, .   177
124.   ,,   ,,   ,,   elevation,   177

MIDDLETHIRD HATCHING-HOUSE.

125. Part of Distributing-spout, longitudinal section, . 180
126.   ,,   ,,   plan, ... 180
127. Distributing-spout, transverse section, showing one of the Distributors in section, ... 181
128. Distributing-spout, transverse section, showing one of the Distributors in elevation, ... 181
129. Transverse section of Downfall-spout, . . . 181
130. Section through part of House, showing Downfall-spout, Main Drain, and part of Hatching-box, ... 181
131. Elevation of two Hatching-boxes, showing Main Drain in section, . 182
132. *Plan of Middlethird Hatching-house in 1875-76*, . . . 183

CRAIGEND.

133. American Cutter Bit, . . . 184
134. Section of Leaf-screen at Craigend, ... 185
135. Leaf-screen at Craigend, longitudinal section, showing the Regulators, Sluice, and Connections, ... 186
136. Leaf-screen at Craigend, plan, showing the Regulators, Sluice, and Connections, ... 186

HOWIETOUN INTAKE WORKS.

137. Longitudinal Section through the Apron of the Overflow, . 187
138. Plan, ... 188
139. Transverse Section, ... 189
140. Transverse Section, showing the Coffer-dam, . . . 189
141. Longitudinal Section through one of the Distributing Compartments, 190

HOWIETOUN PONDS.

142. Plan of the 20-feet Plank Ponds, ... 193
143. End Elevation of the 20-feet Plank-ponds, Nos. 1 and 2, showing the Main Aqueduct, Collecting-box, and Waste-pipe in Section, 194
144. Section through the 20-feet Plank-ponds, Nos. 1, 2, and 3, showing the Main Aqueduct, ... 194
145. Plan of part of the 20-feet Ponds, Nos. 1, 2, and 3, showing Outlets, 195
146.   ,,   ,,   ,,   ,,   195

LIST OF ILLUSTRATIONS.

FIG.		PAGE
147.	Longitudinal section of the 20-feet Pond, No. 2, showing Collecting-box and Water-drain,	196
148.	Longitudinal section of 60-feet Pond,	197
149.	Transverse section of 60-feet Pond,	197
150.	Plan of 60-feet Pond,	198
151.	*Plan of the Howietoun Hatching-house,*	218

HOWIETOUN 130-FEET PONDS.

152.	Dividing-box, plan,	221
153.	,, ,, transverse section, showing Waste-pipe,	222
154.	,, ,, longitudinal section,	222
155.	,, ,, transverse section, showing Supply-pipe,	223
156.	Inlet-screen Box, longitudinal section,	224
157.	,, ,, plan,	224
158.	Transverse section of the Ponds, showing Scour-pipe,	225
159.	,, ,, Trap-box, showing Scour-pipe,	234
160.	Section of Guard and Valve, showing Scour-pipe,	235
161.	Bevel for dressing slopes,	236

CRAIGEND PONDS.

162.	The Discharge-pipe,	238
163.	Section of ditto,	238
164.	Clay Valve-box in the Supply-pipe, longitudinal section,	240
165.	,, ,, ,, plan,	240
166.	,, ,, ,, transverse section,	240
167.	Plan of the Ponds, showing the connection,	241
168.	,, Well,	244
169.	Section of the Well,	244
170.	Transverse section of the Well, showing Catch-screen in position,	245

HOWIETOUN 300-FEET PONDS.

171.	Outlet, plan,	254
172.	,, section,	254
173.	,, elevation,	255
174.	Valve of Discharge-pipe, plan,	255
175.	,, ,, ,, section,	256
176.	,, ,, ,, transverse section,	256
177.	Well, section,	257
178.	,, plan,	257
179.	,, transverse section,	258

LIST OF ILLUSTRATIONS. xxiii

FIG.		PAGE
180.	Inlet, elevation,	258
181.	,, section,	258
182.	,, plan,	259
183.	Plan of the Watercourses connecting the 300-feet Ponds with the 130-feet Ponds,	260

THE MECHANICAL FEEDING APPARATUS IN THE 20-FEET PONDS, HOWIETOUN.

184.	Front and Side Elevation of Driving-pulley and Eccentric,	261
185.	Sketch showing Power-wheel working in the Main Aqueduct, with connections and detail,	262
186.	Diagram explanatory of the working of the Apparatus,	263
187.	The Feeding-spoon,	264

DEEP HATCHING-TRAY.

188.	Transverse section,	266
189.	Plan in position,	266
190.	End elevation,	267

QUADRUPLE HATCHING-BOX.

191.	Plan,	268
192.	Longitudinal section,	268
193.	Transverse section,	268
194.	Grille used in the Box, longitudinal section,	269
195.	,, ,, transverse section,	269
196.	,, ,, plan of part,	269

NOTE.

The remaining Chapters of the HISTORY OF HOWIETOUN, down to January 1st, 1887, a Chapter on the Construction of Redds, and Chapters on British and Foreign Fish-Culture, etc., and a voluminous Appendix, are in an advanced state of preparation, and will be issued shortly.

HISTORY OF HOWIETOUN.

CHAPTER I.

INTRODUCTORY.

THE great success of Howietoun as a trout farm, and the very prevalent idea that Great Britain as a nation is behind the rest of the world in the matter of its fisheries, has induced me to write this book in the form of an annual record of the work done from the commencement in 1873 to the present date, prefaced by a short account of the different processes in carrying on the work of the trout farm—from harvesting the eggs to the production of the oldest and best breeding fish.

It is most extraordinary, in these days of newspapers and voluminous departmental Government reports, that the pre-eminence of Great Britain in all matters pertaining to fisheries is in Great Britain itself but vaguely recognised. For a number of years the Scotch white fisheries have been under the care of a Government Board. Cured herrings are sold all over the world under the guarantee of a Government brand. The brand itself is a guarantee that the herring have been cured within a very few hours of capture, and that they are of the quality (matties, fulls, or spents) indicated by the brand, and that they are properly packed in efficient barrels, containing a specified quantity. A small fee is charged for affixing the brand, and the surplus, after defraying the cost—a few thousands annually—is applied in improving the harbour accommodation along the coast, a matter the urgency of which has been much increased by the larger boats now in use. In this manner the brand is directly beneficial to every man, woman, and child employed in the fishing industries. It is true the English sea fisheries have not received the same attention as those off the Scotch coast, but the northern portions of them were, until 1881, under the jurisdiction of the Scotch Board.

It is difficult to persuade the public that the harvest of the waters is won by very similar means to the harvest of the land. Harbours and submarine cables occupy the same position with regard to fisheries as farm buildings and roads to the land farm; and in improving harbour accommodation and promoting the extension of telegraphic communication (in order that supplies of salt may be sufficient for curing at every station, and that the boats may have the earliest information of the movements of the shoals of fish) the Fishery Board for Scotland is a fish-cultural department in the fullest sense of the word. Fish-culture means increasing the food of the people, and it has been cruelly wronged by the attempts so frequently made to persuade the world that a little ingenious apparatus, and a few buckets of water, are its principal essentials. It is impossible to separate entirely sea fisheries from those of fresh water, since the sea is the pasture of the most important *Salmonina*, namely, the *S. salar*, the *S. trutta*, and the *Osmerus eperlanus*. The life-history of the two former is probably intimately connected with the movements of *Clupeidæ*.

To the useful work performed by the old Board of white fisheries on the national farm of our sea fisheries—which is none the less a farm requiring careful attention and constant supervision, because the rich pastures of the North Sea are tenanted in common with other nations—the present Fishery Board for Scotland has added an improved system for the collection of the most exhaustive statistics. It has undertaken a carefully considered scheme for determining by actual experiment the effect of trawling on different portions of the coast; the portions reserved for experiment being sufficiently large to give approximately accurate results without interfering needlessly with the trawling industry.

INTRODUCTORY. 3

It is also conducting scientific investigations with a view of increasing the supply of bait, and determining the movements and life-history of food fishes, and the conditions which are favourable or the reverse to their increase.

The principal inland fisheries of the country are under the control of district Fishery Boards, but these, with one or two brilliant exceptions, have hitherto held that the principal duties required of them were to police their district. If the History of Howietoun persuade district Fishery Boards that their sphere of usefulness is wider than they have hitherto held, I shall be amply rewarded.

But whether we take our sea fisheries or our inland district Fishery Boards, no country in the world can show the same intelligent care of their fisheries, or the same substantial development within the last twenty years, and we have every reason to expect that the next twenty years will see the still greater advance.

The experiments at Howietoun have demonstrated that the first point to ascertain before any improvement of the fisheries can be successfully undertaken, is at what period in the life-history of the fish the greatest loss occurs.

That loss does occur may be inferred from the large number of eggs most fish produce, a number so large that, were it not for the loss, a very few seasons would suffice to overstock the waters. There are three periods at which this loss may be conceived to occur. At the time of extrusion impregnation may be deficient. This probably causes a great proportion of the loss in large-ovaed *Salmonidæ*, but does not seem likely to be a source of loss with fish which congregate in shoals for spawning purposes, as the herring, especially when the gelatinous nature of the envelope of the ovum is taken into consideration.

The period of incubation of the ovum forms the second period at which loss may be conceived to occur. With the large ova of salmon, the proportion of loss here is probably greater than at the first period, the duration of incubation extending over several months; while, in the case of herring, especially when spawning in summer, the duration of this period is so short, that in spite of the fact that the spawning beds of the herring are a resort of many and ravenous fishes, I do not feel inclined to attribute any serious proportion of loss. The third period is that immediately succeeding the absorption of the umbilical vesicle. The ova of *Salmones*, and most of the ova of *Salvelini* hatching in running water, the young fry are nursed by the current which bears particles forming their food more or less constantly past their resting-places, and as they are hatched out generally in the natural streams so late in the spring, that by the time the yolk sac is absorbed there is an abundance of animalculæ in the water, the loss at this period is probably less than at either of the preceding; but with herring, in a great number of instances, it is easily conceivable that it is precisely at this period myriads of the young fish perish. The yolk vesicle probably contains little more nourishment than suffices to supply the young fish on their journey from the bottom to the surface of the water, and their future existence depends on the quantity of microscopic larval life they find on their arrival at the surface. The conditions which determine the quantity of these forms are as yet very imperfectly understood, but it is probable that atmospheric conditions, temperature, and, above all, storms, must be important factors.

Should further research bear out these probabilities, the culture of such fish as herring will differ from the culture of large-ovaed *Salmonidæ* in this, that the quantities of the latter will be increased by piscifacture,[1] and of the former by legislative enactments framed with a view to secure natural reproduction, when and where the conditions (now being investigated by the Fishery Board for Scotland) most favourable to the survival of the myriad brood exist. Perhaps I may make the point plainer if I assume a purely hypothetical case.

Suppose the various shoals of herring to be more or less local races imperfectly localised, but still sufficiently periodic in their migrations to enable these to be mapped with tolerable accuracy;

Suppose, secondly, investigation shows that the resulting brood from spawn deposited in certain places, and at certain

[1] Bulletin de Ministère d'Agriculture.

seasons of the year, is more abundant than that from spawn deposited in other places, or at other times; and

Suppose, finally, that a connection can be shown between certain local races and certain spawning grounds, or suppose it can be shown that various local races use the same spawning ground at different seasons,—

Then the spawning ground would become a known factor in the abundance of the fishing in certain districts, and its management in the interest of the fisheries would constitute legislative fish-culture.

In this supposititious case set forth above very great good to the fishermen at large may result from a very slight interference with local uses. Had the sea fisheries been subjected to the harassing legislation inflicted at frequent intervals on our salmon fisheries, the harvest of the North Sea would have been almost entirely reaped by foreigners; and yet it is principally by regulation that our share of the harvest of the sea can be increased. But such regulations must be either limited, and merely for experimental purposes, in carefully restricted areas, or follow on known facts.

Almost the reverse is the case with the large-ovaed *Salmonidæ*. Commercial fish-culture, as distinguished from legislative fish-culture, can here secure great abundance without the assistance of the heavy penalties at present in force, which seem to be directed more by the greed of a few proprietors than by any intelligent desire to increase the number of fish. A law which makes no distinction between the destruction of the hungry wolves and the capture of the ripe hen-salmon heavy with 20,000 future possibilities, most of which will merely form delicious mouthfuls for some over-preserved kelt, can hardly be considered a law in the public interest. No doubt many will say, "But kelts do not feed in fresh water." The answer I gave in my paper on the Culture of *Salmonidæ* and the Acclimatisation of Fish, read at the Conference at the International Fisheries Exhibition in London, 1883, is probably still the shortest and clearest that can be given, viz., "If salmon never fed in fresh water a well-mended kelt would be a superfluous expression in the parlance of fishermen." But the fact that salmon reared from the eggs of wild fish have bred for two consecutive seasons at Howietoun shows that they will not only feed in fresh water, but that they will feed and fatten in fresh water under artificial conditions.

In the autumn of 1874 I placed a male sea-trout kelt in a Francis box in the wood at Craigend, and fed the fish on liver and worms. It rapidly improved in condition, and I regret I did not weigh the fish before and after the experiment. It eventually met its death from the hardness of the winter through the water in the box freezing solid; but the fattening of a sea-trout kelt in a confined stew in the middle of a severe winter proved absolutely that *S. trutta* at least had no disinclination to feed in fresh water after spawning.

In the case of the Howietoun experiments with *S. salar* it is open to argument that the fish, never having been to the sea, were under conditions so artificial that the fact of their spawning two successive seasons proves nothing conclusively as regards wild fish; but the answer is, it is far stronger evidence than any hitherto adduced by the other side, and it is hoped to carry out a set of experiments with large salmon kelts during next season which will set the question at rest for all time coming.

These experiments are very costly, and until the Fishery was completed it was not thought advisable to incur an expenditure of between £100 and £200 to set at rest what former experiments had reduced to a purely academic question.

The experiments in hybridism and embryology which have been conducted at Howietoun will be fully considered in the latter portion of this work, and from their scientific nature cannot be properly discussed in this introductory chapter. The creation of the fishery, as it proceeded from year to year, is minutely recorded in the ensuing chapters. Woodcuts, carefully drawn to scale, are given, showing plans and sections of most of the apparatus used, and of the various buildings and ponds, so that the conditions under which the Fishery has been carried on may be easily understood.

Woodcuts of apparatus which have been found unsuccessful are also given, so that the conditions may be studied, and the apparatus either be improved or avoided altogether.

The materials principally used consisted of wood, brick, and concrete. Concrete has been found the best material for roofing, as it is absolutely frost-proof, but it is not water-tight, and where this is a consideration it requires to be covered with asphalte or corrugated iron, but the preference must be given to asphalte, as the roof has not usually sufficient fall to ensure corrugated iron being water-tight.

Brick has been found the best material for inlets and outlets of ponds, a wooden frame being built in which to fix the screens. It is also the best material for building valves in the aqueducts or lines of pipe. Wood is probably the most important of all materials used in fish-culture. The best foreign pine should always be used. Home-grown timber does not last sufficiently well for the purpose, and hardwood is very liable to become coated with *saprolegneiæ*. The earth work is very important, and must be constructed under the supervision of a first-class engineer, who should be previously instructed that ponds suitable for fish-culture are required, and not mere dams to hold water. As the latter will probably be the only ponds the engineer has had any experience of, this caution must be given before the estimates are calculated. The expense per cubic yard is greater in a pond suited for fish-culture than in an ordinary reservoir, and it must never be forgotten that an ordinary reservoir is anything but suited for fish-culture. The principal difference being that a reservoir is usually deepest at the outlet, and a pond for fish-culture should be deepest at a point about one-third of its length from the inlet, and under no circumstances must the deepest part be nearer the outlet than the centre of the pond.

This principle has been carefully followed at Howietoun, and the success may be estimated by the annual increase in the production of the Fishery from laying down 25,205 trout ova in the autumn of 1874, to containing a stock of 282,672 fish in August 1886.

The stock are distributed as shown in the following table, and a plan of the ponds at Howietoun is given on page 10 for reference:—

TABLE OF STOCK AT THE HOWIETOUN TROUT FARM ON 1ST SEPTEMBER 1886.

Pond.	Species.	Age.		Number.
	HOWIETOUN.	Years.	Months.	
1.	*S. levenensis,*	0	6	3,000
2.	*Do.,*	0	6	3,000
3.	*S. fario,*	0	6	2,000
	S. salar (Tay),	0	6	400
4.	*S. salar* × *S. levenensis*♂,	1	6	1,250
5.	*S. fontinalis* × *S. struanensis*♂,	3	6	50
	S. fontinalis × *S. struanensis*♂,	2	6	600
	S. levenensis × *S. fontinalis*♂,	3	6	125
6.	*S. sebago,*	2	3	700
	S. irideus,	1	4	824
7.	*S. salar* (Howietoun),	1	6	450
	S. levenensis × (*S. fontinalis* × *S. struanensis*♂)♂,	1	6	225
8.	*S. levenensis* × *S. salar* (Howietoun)♂,	1	6	1,250
9.	*S. levenensis,*	1	6	5,200
10.	*S. salar,*	5	6	30
	S. levenensis,	3	6	4,500
11.	*Do.,*	9	6	1,100
12.	*Do.,*	8	6	2,000
13.	*Do.,*	2	6	15,000
	S. salar (Tay),	2	6	35
14.	*S. levenensis,*	2	6	1,600
	S. levenensis × *S. fontinalis*♂,	2	6	130
15.				
16.	*S. fontinalis* × *S. levenensis*♂,	3	6	9
	S. fontinalis,	4	6	500
	Do.,	3	6	400
	Do.,	2	6	700
	S. levenensis × *S. salar* (parr)♂,	2	6	24
17.	*S. levenensis,*	0	6	10,000
18.	*Do.,*	0	6	10,000
19.	*Do.,*	0	6	10,000
20.	*Do.,*	0	6	10,000
21.	*Do.,*	0	6	10,000
22.	*Do.,*	0	6	10,000
23.	*S. salar* (Howietoun),	0	6	5,000
24.	*S. levenensis,*	1	6	12,000
25.	*S. levenensis,*	0	6	15,000
26.	*Do.,*	0	6	15,000
27.	*Do.,*	0	6	15,000
28.	*Do.,*	0	6	15,000
29.	*Do.,*	0	6	15,000
30.	*Do.,*	0	6	15,000
31.	*Do.,*	0	6	15,000
32.	*S. fontinalis,*	1	6	1,800
				228,902

Pond.	Species.	Age.		Number.
	CRAIGEND.	Years.	Months.	
1.	*S. levenensis,*	0	6	15,000
2.	Do.,	0	6	15,000
3.				
				30,000
	MILNEHOLME.			
1.	*S. levenensis,*	0	4	8,000
2.	*S. fontinalis,*	0	6	450
3.	(*S. fontinalis* × *S. struanensis*♂) × (*S. fontinalis* × *S. struanensis*♂)♂,	0	6	680
4.	*S. levenensis* × *S. Willoughbii*♂,	0	6	20
5.	*S. levenensis* × (*S. fontinalis* × *S. struanensis*♂)♂,	0	6	620
6.	*S. levenensis,*	0	4	8,000
7, 8, 9.				
10.	Do.,	0	4	2,000
11.	Do.,	0	4	2,000
12.	Do.,	0	4	2,000
				23,770

It will be noticed that the oldest salmon—those in pond 10—are now five years and a half; they are much dwarfed, the largest being probably not over 3 lbs.; but the young salmon fry in pond 23, reared from the eggs obtained from these fish last winter, have thriven better, and are much larger than the salmon fry in pond 3, hatched from eggs obtained from the river Tay. From this it seems probable that the second generation of landlocked salmon will thrive better, and attain a larger size, than the direct produce of wild fish. Should this turn out to be the case, their ova would prove more valuable than the ova of wild fish for stocking the waters of the antipodes, since they would be easily retained in fresh water until they multiplied sufficiently to overcome, by sheer numbers, the dangers of an antipodal andromadous existence.

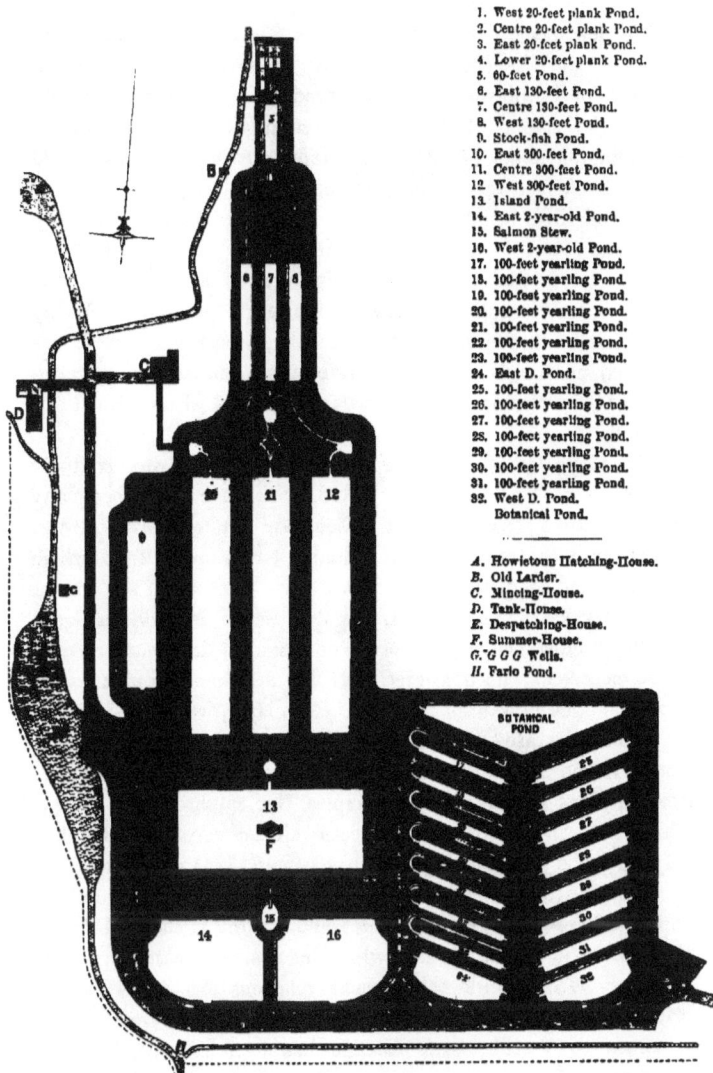

1. West 20-feet plank Pond.
2. Centre 20-feet plank Pond.
3. East 20-feet plank Pond.
4. Lower 20-feet plank Pond.
5. 60-feet Pond.
6. East 130-feet Pond.
7. Centre 130-feet Pond.
8. West 130-feet Pond.
9. Stock-fish Pond.
10. East 300-feet Pond.
11. Centre 300-feet Pond.
12. West 300-feet Pond.
13. Island Pond.
14. East 2-year-old Pond.
15. Salmon Stew.
16. West 2-year-old Pond.
17. 100-feet yearling Pond.
18. 100-feet yearling Pond.
19. 100-feet yearling Pond.
20. 100-feet yearling Pond.
21. 100-feet yearling Pond.
22. 100-feet yearling Pond.
23. 100-feet yearling Pond.
24. East D. Pond.
25. 100-feet yearling Pond.
26. 100-feet yearling Pond.
27. 100-feet yearling Pond.
28. 100-feet yearling Pond.
29. 100-feet yearling Pond.
30. 100-feet yearling Pond.
31. 100-feet yearling Pond.
32. West D. Pond.
   Botanical Pond.

A. Howietoun Hatching-House.
B. Old Larder.
C. Mincing-House.
D. Tank-House.
E. Despatching-House.
F. Summer-House.
G. G G G Wells.
H. Fario Pond.

Fig. 1—scale $\frac{1}{1870}$.
PONDS AT HOWIETOUN.

INTRODUCTORY.

The demand for the produce of the Fishery has also steadily increased, and the enormous quantity of seventy-nine boxes of eyed ova of Lochleven trout (the produce of the Fishery) were sold in the season 1885-6; the boxes running 15,000 nominal, and averaging about 17,500. This represents a sale of 1,382,500 eggs of Lochleven trout alone, while the eyed eggs of *salar, fontinalis,* and *fario* bring up the total despatched from the Fishery during the season to close on two millions.

Almost an equal number of eggs were, in addition to these, hatched into fry at the Fishery, and a large quantity of freshly impregnated ova was used experimentally, a portion of which was incubated at the University of Edinburgh, under the superintendence of Professor Cossar Ewart of the Fishery Board for Scotland.

The steps by which the Fishery has risen are very gradual; there have been no leaps and bounds, nor have there been any serious checks; losses have occurred, but I have always endeavoured to treat them as valuable experiments from which to deduce the conditions of success.

Twenty years ago, when Livingston Stone asked Seth Green in 1866 "How many of those who engaged in trout-breeding would succeed?" he answered with his well-known quickness of manner, "One in a million." Six years later, when Stone wrote his book, he states : "The whole aspect of the matter has been changed, and the care and study bestowed on the subject have evolved a set of rules and principles, the careful observance of which will render a degree of success almost certain. I think it may safely be said that the time has come (1873) when trout can be hatched, reared, and brought to maturity in great numbers, and with comparatively little loss; and I think it also safe to say that success in raising the fish will of necessity be accompanied by pecuniary success while the present relations exist between the prices of trout and the cost of the food on which they are reared."[1]

Since 1873 still greater change has been effected in trout-breeding. There is no longer any question as to how the fish are

[1] *Domesticated Trout,* page 3.

to be hatched, and under what conditions they can be grown. The questions in trout-culture are now precisely the same as those which demand solution in breeding cattle, namely, how to breed so as to produce the most desirable and suitable characteristics for the district where they are to be reared.

The Howietoun Fishery has proved that age and selection are two great factors in varying the characteristics of trout, and with a little skill and knowledge this can be done to adapt them to almost every situation. But by greater steps the successful transportation of ova has advanced, especially to the Antipodes. For several seasons the Howietoun Fishery has forwarded successfully consignments of salmon and trout ova, and the result obtained by the machine-packing designed by myself has been most satisfactory; so long as the eggs themselves are not disturbed on board ship, and ordinary attention given to the ice in the ice-tray and ice-chamber, they incur no more risk during the voyage than in the hatching-house, only, of course, the same vitality cannot be developed in the embryo. Nicols, in his *Acclimatisation of the Salmonidæ at the Antipodes*, gives a list of the shipments made by Youl, as under :—

SHIPMENTS OF SALMON, SALMON TROUT, AND BROWN TROUT OVA, MADE BY MR. JAMES A. YOUL TO THE ANTIPODES.

1. *February* 1860.—By *Sarah Curling*, from Liverpool to Melbourne. Salmon ova, 25,000.
2. *March* 4, 1862.—By *Beautiful Star*, from London to Hobart Town. Salmon ova, 80,000.
3. *January* 21, 1864.—By *Norfolk*, from London to Melbourne and Tasmania. Salmon ova, 118,000. Present from Admiral Keppel, through Mr. Frank Buckland, brown trout ova, 1,200. Present from Mr. Francis Francis, brown trout ova, 1,500.
4. *January* 20, 1866.—By *Lincolnshire*, from London to Melbourne and Tasmania. Salmon ova, 93,000; salmon trout ova, 15,000; brown trout ova, 500.
5. *January* 1868.—By *Celestial Queen*, from London to Otago, New Zealand. Salmon ova, 120,000; salmon trout ova, 4000. From Bavaria, *Salmo umbla* ova, 9000. Present from Lord Essex, through Mr. Frank Buckland, brook trout ova, 1500.
6. *January* 1869.—By *Mindora*, from London to Otago, New Zealand. Salmon ova, 110,000; taken by Mr. Frank Buckland, salmon trout ova, 5000.

INTRODUCTORY. 13

7. *January* 1873.—By *Oberon*, from London to Otago, New Zealand. Salmon ova, 120,000.
8. *January* 1876.—By S.S. *Durham*, from London to Melbourne and New Zealand, joint shipment. Mr. J. A. Youl, salmon ova, 90,000 ; Mr. Frank Buckland, salmon ova, 85,000.
9. *January* 1878.—By S.S. *Chimborazo*, from London to New Zealand, joint shipment. Mr. J. A. Youl, salmon ova, 24,000 ; Mr. Frank Buckland, salmon ova, 20,000.
10. *January* 1879.—By P. & O. S.S. and Orient Line S.S. *Cuzco*, five boxes brook trout, about 5000.

These ten shipments seem all to have been made under the superintendence of Mr. Youl, and it is probable that other consignments may have been made privately, of which there is no record.

Mr. Charles C. Capel made a shipment by the *John Elder*, January 1882, of 130,000 salmon ova. In the previous month, namely, on the 27th December 1881, we made our first consignment to the Otago Acclimatisation Society, Mr. Arthur having written to Mr. Handyside to procure some Lochleven trout ova.[1]

He communicated with me, and the result was that 10,000 Lochleven trout eggs were sent as an experiment to test the journey, and the suitability of our mode of packing. They were carried by the *Potosi*, with the simple instruction that it was requested the box should not be opened until it reached its desti-

[1] OTAGO ACCLIMATISATION SOCIETY,
DUNEDIN, *June* 23*d*, 1881.

DEAR HANDYSIDE,—As I see a mail goes to-day *via* Melbourne, I hasten to instruct you re the Lochleven trout ova. At our Council meeting on April 20th it was determined to try to get out some ova of the Lochleven trout, and I have now, on behalf of our Society, to ask you to be so good as to take the necessary steps to procure for us 10,000 ova (more or less) from Sir James G. Maitland, or any other person who can guarantee them to you. By more or less of course I mean 20,000, if we can get them, or it may be a few short of the lesser number. I have already instructed Mr. Capel of Foot's Cray, Kent, about the sea trout and salmon ova. *If* you can arrange for both lots, or all three (as perhaps I should write) to come by one steamer, so much the better. Only, as sea trout are said to spawn in October, salmon in December, and Lochleven trout in January and February, I fear they cannot all be sent at once. We will pay any expenses, and send Deans to Melbourne to meet the steamer if one direct to Lyttleton or Otago cannot be got. I fear that no steamer to N. Z. would have an ice-house, on which we must rely for the success of the venture mainly. I would like if you could also procure for us heads of, say the Tay salmon, male and female of a good big sea trout, both sexes of Lochleven trout and common burn trout.—Hoping you have had a good voyage, and found everybody well, I am yours faithfully, W. ARTHUR, *Hon. Sec.*
T. S. Handyside, Esq., Edinburgh.

nation. Unfortunately the consignment perished : but from Mr. Arthur's letter annexed,[1] describing the removal of the inner case, which contained the eggs, at Melbourne, and its trans-shipment to Dunedin in the *Rotomahana*, and from the advanced development of the ova, and the condition of the moss, it is quite clear that the eggs were suffocated through exposure to too high a temperature, probably during trans-shipment from Melbourne.

[1] OTAGO ACCLIMATISATION SOCIETY,
DUNEDIN, *March* 16*th*, 1882.

SIR,—You will be sorry to hear that the 10,000 Lochleven trout ova you so kindly sent to our Society were found on their arrival here to be all dead. Of this I sent a short intimation already, and having seen Mr. Handyside (who himself was quarantined at Melbourne), I can now supply some information regarding the shipment from London to Melbourne, and subsequently. 1st. On Mr. H. getting on board the *Potosi* at Plymouth, the box of ova could not be found. After much search it was discovered among the luggage "not wanted on voyage," and was lying on its side! It was too large to go into the ice-house, but Mr. H. succeeded in persuading the officers to enlarge the door, by which means it was got in, and packed round about with ice. The *Potosi* reached Melbourne on February 15, 1882, and the ova box was at once transhipped to the *Rotomahana*, and arrived here on the 21st February. The door of ice-house in this steamer was too small also, so the box had to be opened, and the inner one was then placed in the ice, and so came on. No fresh ice was put in the tray, but from your letter to Handyside that did not seem to be an essential. 2d. On the box being opened here the eggs were all dead, and were somewhat opaque. But the *form* and *eye* of the fish were quite visible, so that development had advanced very much. The ice-tray was empty, but the moss in the egg-trays was fresh and damp—at least so much as I examined was.

Without pronouncing any opinion on the merits or otherwise of your system of packing and shipping through the Tropics, I would like to point out that we have received several shipments of ova from America in years past—*S. quinnat* and *Coregonus albus* (whitefish)—which were mostly a success. For instance, 50,000 *S. quinnat* eggs came enclosed by an outer box considerably smaller than yours. Of these about 90 per cent. were good and healthy on arrival, and a large percentage hatched out, and were liberated in our rivers. I believe the packing was done by Mr. L. Stone, or under his directions. Sawdust in quilted bags was packed between case and ova box, and the lid and bottom of case or outer box, also of ova box, were perforated with a few auger-holes to allow the melting ice, which was piled on top of case, to percolate freely through. The ova box was arranged thus: layer of moss at bottom, two layers of gauze enclosing one of eggs, next layer of moss, and so on, about ten of each being in the box, resting on top of one another. Although, as I say, they arrived safely, and in healthy condition, about five per cent. were bad, which might perhaps have been avoided by having each layer supported by a tray. On the other hand, trays with metallic bottoms are liable to induce rust (oxide of iron), which I found present on your trays, due to the iron screws.

Judging from the success of the American plan, as applied to eggs having to run the gauntlet of the Tropics, it seems to me that the free passage of ice-water through the eggs is, in the present state of our knowledge, an essential.

The Council of the Society desires to send you its sincere thanks for the liberal gift of Lochleven trout ova, and will be very glad to pay any expenses of this or any future shipment which you might be good enough to grant us.—I am, Sir, yours obediently,

W. ARTHUR, *Hon. Secy.*

P.S.—I have preserved a few of the ova in glycerine and water.

I then offered to forward another consignment the following season.[1]

Neither of these consignments was successful, nor was the consignment of salmon ova from Mr. Capel by the same vessel, as appears from Mr. Arthur's letters.[2]

[1]
3d *July* 1882.

SIR,—I beg to acknowledge yours of March 16th, and also the *New Zealand Saturday Advertiser* of 8th April, with Mr. Deans' report, and I quite understand what has occurred. The swan's-skin cloth has shrunk up too close, and stopped ventilation, and stifled the eggs. Had it been otherwise, the ova would have *hatched en route*, not died, ten or twelve days after the ice was exhausted. I think next time a refrigerator should be constructed small enough to go into the ice-house, and broken ice and sawdust filled in *en route*.

The weather was very mild here when the eggs were being packed, which probably accounts for the ice being insufficient, as, from my own experience here, the quantity of ice mixed with the sawdust was sufficient to have lasted three months. The zinc bottom of the trays I find very successful, having packed about two million ova in the last season. The iron screws were an oversight, brass ones being invariably used at the Fishery. So far as I remember, Mr. Handyside started a steamer earlier than was expected, and there was some little push getting the cases ready at the last moment.

From the development I expect we shall have no difficulty in succeeding another time, and I will be happy to offer you another box this season.

I have never seen the eggs of the *O. quinnat*, but as the fish itself differs so much in its nature from the true salmon, it is just possible that the eggs may bear transport better than those of the latter, just as we find the eggs of the *fontinalis* in this country much hardier than those of the *fario*.—Yours truly,   J. R. G. MAITLAND.

W. ARTHUR, Esq., *Hon. Sec.* Otago Acclimatisation Society, Dunedin.

OTAGO ACCLIMATISATION SOCIETY,
DUNEDIN, *Sept. 8th*, 1882.

DEAR SIR,—Your favour of July 3d has been received, and will be duly considered at the next meeting of the Council of this Society. But in order not to lose any time, I have deemed it better to write by the mail which goes to-morrow morning. So, having consulted our Chairman and Treasurer, I am directed to reply that the Society will feel exceedingly obliged if you will carry out your kind offer, and send us a fresh lot of Lochleven trout ova. Our representative in London is Mr. J. A. Ewen of Sargood, Sons, & Ewen, E.C., to whom the box should be consigned, with instructions to see it properly placed in ice-house, with holes for the ice-water to drip through and through, and to give it in charge of a responsible officer who will see that the ice supply is regularly placed on top during the voyage. Mr. Ewen also should wire us when ova is shipped, but I shall write him directions in good time. There will probably be a direct bi-monthly line of steamers to Port Chalmers soon, which will be an immense advantage for getting ova out safely.

As you have not got any *O. quinnat* ova, I shall send you a few by next mail, also a few of your own Lochleven trout ova, so that you may form your own opinion. The salmon ova I have in spirits, and the *S. levenensis* in glycerine.—Yours faithfully,

Sir J. G. MAITLAND, Bart.,   W. ARTHUR, *Hon. Secy.*
Craigend, Stirlingshire.

[2]
OTAGO ACCLIMATISATION SOCIETY,
DUNEDIN, *March* 21, 1883.

DEAR SIR,—You would be sorry to learn from Mr. Ewen (whom I wired at once) that the Lochleven trout ova you were so good as send us by the *Nizam* were found all dead on arrival of that steamer at Melbourne. Our Manager, Mr. Deans, was waiting at Melbourne for

The next consignment forwarded to New Zealand was sent by the S.S. *Aorangi* under the care of Mr. Stoddart, and consisted the steamer, and lost no time in taking delivery. I have posted you a newspaper with his report. It is just possible they may have been neglected at the most critical part of the voyage, and I also fear the water soaking through the *sawdust* must have been injurious. The only other thing I noticed was that the layers of moss had pressed tightly on each other, and most of the dead ova in the middle of the trays was squashed almost beyond recognition. The best-preserved eggs were at the sides, otherwise, so far as I can judge, the packing was admirable. I have got a few of the best eggs for you, and will send them next mail.

Deans has gone to Wellington to meet the S.S. *British King* with the next lot. She has arrived, but I have not heard how the ova is. As I am going out of town to-morrow, I shall wire him to write you.

Should you be writing Mr. Ewen, would you kindly say that I shall write him by Brindisi? We are exceedingly sorry all your trouble and kindness hitherto has been, so to speak, lost, but trust the present shipment is all right. Meantime, with the best thanks of the Society,—I am, dear Sir, yours faithfully, W. ARTHUR, *Hon. Sec.*

Sir J. G. MAITLAND, Bart., Craigend.

STIRLING, N.B., *12th April* 1883.

DEAR SIR,—I beg to acknowledge yours of 2d April, enclosing copy of Mr. Arthur's letter. I regret my absence from home has prevented my replying sooner. My consignment of ova by *British King* consisted of about 25,000 Lochleven and 6000 or 7000 salmon ova from the Teith, a river perfectly free from bull-trout.

The eggs were stripped on the 16th December by Mr. Napier, Inspector to the Forth District Board, and myself, and I hope they may have arrived safely. I put a test-box of Lochleven eggs under Mr. Carrington's care at the Aquarium, stripped about the same time, on the 2d February. The box was unpacked by Mr. Maun of Bishop-Stortford on (I think) 22d March, and the eggs hatched out remarkably well same day. Had the box been kept in the ice-house I have no doubt they would have kept for another month, as this practically narrows the success of our shipment to the temperature of the *British King*.—Yours sincerely,

JOHN A. EWEN, Esq. J. G. MAITLAND.

OTAGO ACCLIMATISATION SOCIETY,
DUNEDIN, *April 20th*, 1883.

DEAR SIR,—I am very sorry to tell you that the Lochleven trout ova by the S.S. *Nizam*, which reached Melbourne in February, were found to be all dead when our Manager went on board there and looked at them, as already reported to you. The other salmon and Lochleven trout ova by the S.S. *British King*, which reached Wellington about March 20th, were also found to be dead, and Capel's salmon ova were no better. As regards the packing, yours was as nearly perfect as possible,—in fact, it was a pleasure to examine the box and trays. As regards the ice-tray, however, we found that a great deal of sawdust had been put in it, which, with ice-water flowing through it, was very apt to neutralise the good effects of the charring. In using sawdust *above* the trays, it should be enclosed in a calico pad, which pad should rest on top of the ice. I am posting you a small package with specimens of the eggs: *Nizam's* ova, phial No. 43; *British King's*, No. 44; Sir J. Maitland's salmon ova, No. 45; Lochleven trout ova, ditto; No. 46, C. C. Capel's salmon ova. I shall be glad to hear that these reach you in safety.

If you read the enclosed copy of register of temperature of ova boxes per the *British King*, fortunately kept by the purser, and his letter in explanation, you will have no difficulty in understanding the cause of failure, viz., too high a temperature of the melting ice. How this should be the case in an ice-house I cannot very well see, unless it be the unfavourable of two boxes, which were a partial success.[1] This consignment threw great light upon the increased vitality of the ova of older spawners, and also for ever solved the problem of transporting ova to the antipodes, as the eggs had actually been carried on deck in a temporary cooling-box lined with felt.

The consignment also seems to have turned out much better than was at first anticipated, as, on the 23d May 1884,[2] 1700 young fish were doing splendidly at Dunedin, and about 1000 at Wellington. The next consignment to the Otago Association was sent December 3, 1884, and consisted of brown trout

position of the house on deck. I wonder how the refrigerating chamber would suit for the boxes, and the ice regularly put in boxes.

We can hardly expect you to trouble any more about sending ova, trout in any case. We are returning you the boxes, as they may be useful, and I must beg to thank you very heartily for doing so much for us. Please let Mr. Ewen know what expense you have been at, and we will gladly refund you.—Yours faithfully,   W. ARTHUR, *Hon. Secy.*

Sir J. G. MAITLAND, Bart., Howietoun Fishery.

[1]
OTAGO ACCLIMATISATION SOCIETY.
DUNEDIN, *April 25th*, 1884.

DEAR SIR,— . . . You will be glad to hear that the Lochleven trout sent out by *Aorangi* are thriving exceedingly well.—Yours faithfully,   W. ARTHUR, *Hon. Secy.*

Sir J. G. MAITLAND, Bart., of Sauchie, etc.

[2]
OTAGO ACCLIMATISATION SOCIETY,
DUNEDIN, *May 23d*, 1884.

DEAR SIR,—Your favour of 18th March has been received, and I am glad to hear that there can be no doubt about the ova being those of the Lochleven trout. As to which box had the most successful eggs, I have seen both our Manager and Mr. Stoddart. The latter unpacked the boxes at Wellington, and repacked all the good ova he could find, which, he says, were all the *largest* ova. Some of these were left at Wellington, and hatched out well, about 1000 in all, young alevins. The remainder of these large good eggs, along with a few smaller and doubtful-looking ones, were replaced into Box 45, and brought on here. The large eggs all hatched out (about 1700), and the young fish are doing splendidly, but the small light-coloured ones perished, excepting a very few which I believe hatched, but no more. This is all that our Manager, Deans, says: "The number of the box here is 45. It contained four trays, two of which contained eggs evidently much further advanced than the other, and which turned out best. The other two trays contained eggs, I think, of a smaller size, and almost all bad. The few transparent eggs that were to be found did not show the eyes of the young fish."

I should have mentioned that Stoddart thinks the large and good eggs were in No. 45, but he is not quite certain.

As we have got over 1000 young sea-trout of your late Government shipment from the Wallacetown Ponds, I should be glad of any information as to what trays contained the common *fario* eggs, and what those of the graylings, as there was nothing on the trays themselves to determine this. Already I hear doubt expressed as to the young being sea-trout or not. Of course I have seen those we got; they are long, and thinner than the *fario* of same age, and, unfortunately, a good many have died since we got them.—Yours faithfully,

Sir J. G. MAITLAND, Bart., Stirling.   W. ARTHUR, *Hon. Secy.*

eggs, and was eminently successful.[1] This consignment was carried in a refrigerating case, specially prepared to receive the box, with about 4 inches clear space for ice to be placed round it, in addition to the supply that was kept in the ice-tray of the box itself; and not solely to depend on the ice made on board, one and a half tons of Wenham Lake ice was placed in the refrigerating chamber of the *Ionic*. Mr. Ewen, of Sargood, Ewen, and Co., made all the arrangements, and personally saw the box placed on board the steamer, and in the hands of the chief engineer, who is an enthusiastic fisherman, and thoroughly understands the conditions under which ova can be safely carried. I had the pleasure of meeting this gentleman in the beginning of 1886, and he described to me a visit he had paid to the Otago Society's ponds on a subsequent voyage, and the magnificent progress the fry from this consignment had made. Prior to this I had undertaken one consignment of salmon and trout ova at the request of Sir Francis Dillon Bell, K.C.M.G. The salmon ova were collected in the Tweed district, near Peebles, on the 4th and 10th January 1884, and were rather too delicate to pack on the 22d January. It was therefore thought advisable to send two boxes of trout ova in different stages of incubation so as to test the proper stage at which to pack the ova.

A refrigerating case was built on deck to receive one box, and a chamber designed by Mr. Haslam was constructed between decks, through which a current of cold moist air was driven. One box of salmon ova was placed in the refrigerating case, and one box of salmon ova and two boxes of trout ova were placed in the Haslam chamber, the packing-trays being removed from the boxes, and

---

[1] 11 Bunhill Row, London, E.C., *March 10th*, 1885.

Dear Sir,—By letter just received this afternoon from W. Arthur, Esq., Hon. Secy. of the Otago Acclimatisation Society, I am informed that out of the last shipment of brown trout eggs they estimate that 8000 healthy eggs had arrived, and are now in their hatching-boxes, of which you will be glad to hear.

What the ultimate result may be I am unable to communicate, but we have occasion for congratulation as to result so far.

Any further information I may receive I shall at once communicate.—I am, yours faithfully, John A. Ewen,
Sir James Maitland, *Per* J. W.
Howietoun Fisheries, Stirling, N.B.

placed in a grating formed to receive them. The result was most satisfactory. The box placed in the refrigerating case was a total loss, the salmon eggs being too young when packed to stand the treatment. The salmon ova in the Haslam chamber stood the journey much better, although the loss was very great. With the Lochleven trout eggs there was no loss in transport, but a large number hatched, and so perished just before arrival at destination. Taking this shipment, together with the success of the consignment of trout ova per S.S. *Aorangi*, it became evident that perfect success could be ensured in future, and that I had found the key to the whole problem, namely, the precise period which should elapse between spawning and packing of the ova.

The next season the only consignment to New Zealand was the *fario* eggs purchased by the Otago Acclimatisation Society, referred to above, but 108,000 Lochleven trout ova were presented to the United States Commission of Fish and Fisheries. The eggs were carried in my ordinary foreign packing-boxes, and the success of the consignment may best be gathered from Mr. Spencer Baird's letters of 8th and 10th Jan. 1885, and Colonel Marshall Macdonald's of March 31st, 1885 :—

U.S. FISH COMMISSION, WASHINGTON, D.C., *Jan.* 8, 1885.

DEAR SIR,—I have much pleasure in acknowledging the arrival, in excellent condition, of the trout eggs sent by you per *Furnessia*. Some of these were transferred to Mr. Mather's station at Cold Spring Harbour, N.Y., and the remainder to the Whitefish station of the Commission, in charge of Mr. Frank N. Clark, at Northville, Michigan. Both gentlemen greatly admire the method in which the eggs were packed, and the perfect condition in which they came to hand. I will keep you further advised in the matter. Thanking you for this courtesy,—I remain, yours truly, SPENCER F. BAIRD, *Comr.*

Sir JAMES G. MAITLAND,
    Craigend, Stirling, Scotland.

U.S. COMMISSION OF FISH AND FISHERIES,
WASHINGTON, D.C., *Jany.* 10, 1885.

DEAR SIR,—I have much pleasure in enclosing herewith a report[1] by Mr.

---

[1] U.S. COMMISSION OF FISH AND FISHERIES,
COLD SPRING HARBOUR, N Y., *Jan.* 7, 1885.

DEAR SIR,—In the matter of the Lochleven trout eggs, which I have already reported to you as having arrived in good order and repacked and shipped, I will say: There were 570 dead eggs, only one of which had a trace of fungus. There were perhaps as many more indented

Mather in regard to the Lochleven trout. He speaks very highly of the manner of packing adopted by you.—Yours truly,

S. F. BAIRD.

Sir JAMES MAITLAND,
Craigend, Stirling, Scotland.

U.S. COMMISSION OF FISHING AND FISHERIES.
WASHINGTON, D.C., *March* 31, 1885.

DEAR SIR,—The 100,000 Lochleven trout eggs so kindly donated by you to the U.S. Fish Commission reached destination in first-class condition. Ten thousand of them were retained at the hatching-station at Cold Spring Harbour, Long Island, New York, for planting in waters in the Adirondack region, and the balance were sent to Northville station, Mich. These were subsequently assigned as follows :—

E. B. Hodge, for a lake in New Hampshire presenting special adaptations, 5,000
A. W. Aldrich, for planting in suitable streams in North-eastern Iowa, 20,000
R. O. Sweeny, for lakes in Minnesota, ... 20,000
C. G. Atkins at Grand Lake Stream, for suitable lakes in Maine, . 10,000

We anticipate important results from this distribution, and propose to keep all of the plants under close observation, so as to be informed of the results in each case.

In connection with the introduction of this species into American waters, it is proposed to publish in our Annual Report a figure and description of the species, with a full account of its habits and habitat, and I am directed by the Commis-

ones. The latter I did not remove, but the wetting given them may restore many. In no book or paper on Fish-culture have I seen mention of injury to the embryo by the lack of moisture, which shows itself by indentation. As you are aware, I have received many millions of eggs that have come on long journeys, both from California and Europe, and I have found that the mortality in eggs that have been indented is so great as to be nearly total. In moss packing it happens that a few eggs will be protected from the drip of ice by some arrangement of the fibres of moss and will get dry.

Mr. Maitland's eggs were most thoroughly packed in boxes with a lining and a five-inch space between. This space may or may not be filled, I cannot see. The lining is charred, and a box, some three feet long, two feet wide, and two feet high (I guess at measures, writing at home), held six boxes, each about eight inches square, and five inches deep. We get more eggs in such-sized packages, and do not put on as much labour and expense.

I sent Mr. Clark's eggs in the box which brought me 1,000,000 white-fish eggs a few days before, and believe they will go in good order.

I will use Mr. Maitland's boxes, as far as they will go, for the shipments to Germany and Switzerland next week. I saw Mr. Maitland's instructions not to repack the eggs, but believe that they are better for the drink they had before going on.

Unless you telegraph me to do differently, I will ask the Cunard Line to take the eggs for England next week. They will arrive here about Friday or Saturday, 9th or 10th, and I see that there is no Bremen ship to go on Wednesday the 14th, so I will ice and keep the German eggs until then, and pick them over again before they start.

Mr. Emil Frey, Minister from Switzerland, requested me to correspond with the Swiss Consul in New York, as he had arranged with the Compagnie Générale Transatlantique. I wrote him some days ago, but have no reply.—Very truly yours,

F. MATHER.

Prof. S. F. BAIRD, Washington, D.C.

sioner to say that he will be greatly obliged for any data that will add interest to the proposed publication. If good plates of the species have already been published, will you be kind enough to indicate where and how they may be procured for use? If not, could you not place us under further obligation by sending, preserved, two or three good specimens, from which we may figure and describe the species?

You have received, I presume, the notice that we propose to send you, from our Northville station, 10,000 eggs of the California trout. The fish at that station are just now spawning, and as their development is more rapid than that of the ordinary brook trout, it is probable they will go forward in the next few weeks. In the absence of other instructions, Mr. Mather, who has charge of the foreign shipments, is directed to send them by one of the Anchor Line Glasgow steamers.—Very truly yours, M. MACDONALD, *Chief Div. of Dist.*

Sir JAMES MAITLAND, Stirling, Scotland.

This season the principal foreign consignment consisted of over 200,000 salmon ova and 30,000 Lochleven trout ova to the New Zealand Government. The trout ova were placed in the refrigerator, as it was desired to test that mode of transport, and I was very unwilling that any of the salmon ova should be subjected to what appeared to me to be certain death. Eight boxes of salmon ova were placed in a cold chamber, which I designed for the purpose, but the ninth had to be carried on deck for want of space.

The eight boxes in the chamber have been pronounced in the papers presented to the New Zealand Parliament this session the most successful consignment there has ever been. But the New Zealand Government had not heard of a consignment of 100,000 Lochleven trout ova, which was forwarded from Howietoun Fishery December 1885 to St. John's, Newfoundland, in which the loss was only 50 eggs on arrival, and the whole loss after hatching amounted to about 5 per cent.[1]

---

[1] ST. JOHN'S, *June 8th*, 1886.

MY DEAR SIR,—I am glad to say the Lochleven trout ova has done well—in fact, I may say, it was a perfect success, not five per cent. of loss on the whole lot. In fact, all the ova I got from you was the same—no loss worth speaking of. The first I got is three years old now, and fine fish. They spawned last Oct., at the end of the month. I could have taken ova from them, but was from home at the time, so it was too late when I got home. The two-years'-old lot is also fine fish. I think they spawn this year, as they are the size of herring now, and very fat.

The water-supply for my new hatchery is first-class, and plenty of it, so that is the main thing. I hatched 900,000 last winter, and all did well with me.—Yours truly,

J. MARTIN.

J. R. GUY, Esq., Howietoun, Stirling.

There have been many other successful foreign consignments from the Fishery, some of which will be referred to hereafter.

I will now describe the general work at the Howietoun Fishery, commencing with obtaining the eggs, and describing the mode of packing, the work in the hatching-house, rearing of yearlings and two-year-olds, the preparation and transplanting of large trout, and the raising and selection of the breeding fish.

I will then give a short account, year by year, of the construction of the Howietoun Fishery, of fish-culture, and the experimental work carried on there; and conclude by a few chapters giving the principal results of fish-culture at Howietoun, of the experiments, etc.

CHAPTER II.

THE EGG HARVEST.

THE harvesting of the eggs at Howietoun commences in the last week of October, and continues until the second week of January. Trout even of the same age and in the same pond vary considerably in their date of spawning. Fish seem to ripen naturally 360 days after their last spawning, but it does not follow from this they become five days earlier each year as they grow older.

In spite of the very general opinion that, on account of the absence of the sphincter muscle, spawners must shed their ova so soon as ripe, Howietoun experiments have proved conclusively that *trout, so long as they abstain from food, retain their ova*, and a single hearty meal will, by distending the stomach, cause the expulsion of the ripe eggs. This fact goes a long way to explain the frequent absence of food in the stomachs of unspawned salmon. I do not suppose that any one now seriously contends kelts to be at all abstemious.

The general time of spawning for any particular pond can be advanced to the first week in November, or retarded to the third week in December, by conditioning the fish earlier or later in spring. By commencing to feed with clams (*pecten*) early in February, good condition is reached in April, and early maturity of the ova assured. It is however dangerous to have a large number of fish in condition in April, an epidemic of fungus frequently appearing in a pond of fish in high condition during that month; and though a generous supply of bay salt in the water is sufficient to ensure the safety of the fish, it is not convenient to add salt to the water in every pond, as, if the water is to be used afterwards to supply ponds containing younger fish, very unpleasant contingencies arise. I am not prepared to say the young fish themselves dislike saline water, but vegetable and infusorial life are apt to resent the intrusion; and if they have been introduced so as to obtain the best results in the ponds, the balance is overset in a manner more costly than pleasant.

A pond specially designed, and whose overflow is led directly out of the works as waste water, is therefore advisable for conditioning early spawners. At Howietoun, pond No. 9 was built for this purpose, and it is so deep in the centre that a stratum of saline water of a high density can be maintained for many weeks at a small expenditure of bay salt. As a general rule, it is best to arrange for the oldest fish to spawn earliest, as their produce is used for stocking the warmest localities, and for the youngest fish to spawn latest, the fry from their eggs being most suitable for high and cold situations.

Before spawning, two ponds are netted, one for males and the other for spawners, these latter thriving much better when segregated. The nets used are of 1-inch mesh from knot to knot, the small mesh being found in practice to injure fish less than a large one. The net with which the pond containing the spawners is drawn is in the form of a bag 20 feet long, the mouth of which exactly fits the cross-section of the pond at its deepest part. The bottom rope is lightly leaded, and the two lower guys are attached by short chains placed at the distance of the narrowest part of the bottom apart. The upper guys are attached so that the top rope of the net is pulled tight above the surface of the water. The end of the bag is floated open by means of bladders; a large float made of several pieces of cork is placed on the centre of the top rope, and serves as a mark to guide the men in drawing the net evenly, or, when the pond is covered with ice, a float to keep up the centre of the top rope.

The sides of the ponds at Howietoun being symmetrical, this net encloses every fish, and, when drawn, the lower part of the bag is taken on shore, and the top rope held back across the corner of the pond or the inlet to give the fish plenty of space. A large tub is placed near the net, into which a few selected males are placed. Between two and three dozen large milk-plates are arranged in several piles near the tub. Milk-plates are by far the best utensils in which to impregnate trout ova. Earthenware is more suitable than any other material, because, being a very bad conductor, the temperature of the water and ova placed in it is very slightly affected by that of the atmosphere. The importance of this is only appreciated by those who have used both metal and earthenware spawning-dishes during intense frost, and compared the results after the ova have hatched.

The next advantage of milk-plates is the large flat area of the bottom. Before an ovum can be impregnated it is necessary live milt be brought in contact with it, and when the very short time the zoosperms remain active after the milt is diluted is remembered, the facilities offered by a large flat surface over a small or concave one are manifest. It is highly improbable the spermatazoon can enter the micropyle without the aid of water, and the Howietoun experiments have shown the vitality of the milt is much impaired by exposure to low temperatures, or even to air and light. Therefore the custom prevalent among pisciculturists of mixing ova and milt in deep metal dishes, leaving them together for a considerable time, and then washing off the milt, and pouring out the eggs into the collecting-pail, is contrary to common sense, and produces a large percentage of insufficiently vitalised embryos. With milk-plates, 10,000 eggs can be perfectly impregnated by the milt of a single fish, and, although I have no substantial reason, I have a strong prejudice against stripping several males over one dish.

The operator at Howietoun wears a silk mackintosh apron, partly to keep his clothes dry and clean, but principally to avoid injuring the fish.

Some years ago it was noticed that large numbers of the spawners were blind of the right eye, and on careful investigation it was discovered that this was due to the eye being injured against the buttons of the waistcoat whilst the fish were being stripped. Since the introduction of the aprons no fresh cases have been found.

Two wisps of hay are laid on the ground in front of the net, on which the operator kneels. A large Turkish towel is spread in front of him, and the spawning-dish is placed with the spout touching his left knee. A large square landing-net is dipped by an attendant into the net, and about ten females lifted out. A second attendant carries about half that number of males from the net in their pond, and turns them into the tub. If this number is much exceeded, or if they are left long in the tub, they become sulky, and refuse to yield their milt.

The first attendant places the landing-net with the females on the grass so that its edge is about 6 inches above the Turkish towel. The operator tails the fish with his left hand, and, resting her head for a second on the towel, passes his right hand upwards over the belly until his thumb and fore-finger rest against the pectoral fins, three fingers being extended over the right operculum. If the fish is large—that is, from 6 lbs. to 9 lbs.—she is raised, and her back pressed against the right breast, the tail being held a few inches over the bottom of the spawning-dish, and pressed back to open the vent. If she is very ripe the eggs will flow in an unbroken stream until only a few hundred are left, which are quickly removed by passing the right hand downwards over the belly, taking care not to use pressure until past the vitals. If the fish is less than 5 lbs. she can be easily stripped by merely holding her over the plate in a similar position, and bending her slightly backwards. This is the proper way to strip a trout or grilse. No force is used, the handling reduced to a minimum, and the fingers only passed once over the belly to extrude the few remaining ova. Some fish, especially very old ones, are harder to strip than others, and occasionally it may be necessary to press the ova out by hand; but the operator should consider this a rare exception to the rule, and if he have sufficient skill, it will be so. However, I must admit I have great difficulty in teaching others to strip fish as gently and rapidly as I can do myself. When a novice attempts to spawn fish the chances are much in favour of her being dropped probably into the spawning-pan; but after he has learned to tail a fish properly with the left hand, it is as easy to manage as a well-bitted horse, and is generally so passive as to appear as if mesmerised. When about 10,000 eggs have been stripped into the pan, two or three males are laid by the second attendant on the towel, one of which is selected, and held with the abdomen in contact with the ova. How this affects the fish I do not know, but the result is that a large flow of milt is more easily obtained than by the old method, where the milter was treated almost precisely the same as the spawner. The head of the milt-sacs lie above, and almost immediately behind, the pectoral fins, and a slight pressure of the thumb and fore-finger must be used over these parts.

The operator should remember that the hand must never be passed downwards towards the vent, or some of the small vessels will be ruptured, and a flow of blood instead of milt will result. Males are frequently very sulky, and require very delicate manipulation. If the male does not give sufficient milt, the milk-plate should be turned round and a second fish used. They are then replaced in the net, and returned to the pond from which they came; if any on the towel are not required, they are returned to the tub. The use of the towel is to facilitate handling, as, if the fish get covered with mud and dirt, they become excessively slippery. Time, in this operation, is of great importance; absolute impregnation can only be secured when the males are stripped in the least possible time.

Immediately the ova is milted, a small tumbler of water is added to facilitate the distribution of the milt, the whole thoroughly stirred, and the plate removed, and an empty one substituted by a third attendant, whose duty it is to look after the plates and fill them up with water a few minutes after impregnation. The second plate then receives its 10,000 eggs, the spawned fish being thrown over the top of the net into the pond; and the same processes are repeated until all the plates are filled. By this time, if over two dozen plates have been used, the eggs in the first plates will have separated. Livingston Stone says: "*Allow the eggs ample time to separate.* It will do the eggs no harm if you leave them an hour in the pan with the milt, but it *will* do them harm to move them too soon. Some authorities say that thirty minutes is long enough to leave them, some say twenty minutes, and one late authority says one minute. I should rather leave them together forty-five minutes than less. It depends, however, very much on the temperature of the water, the adhesive period lengthening as the temperature decreases. You are more likely to err on the *safe* side by keeping them too long together than by not keeping them long enough."—(*Domesticated Trout*, p. 103.) And under the caution that it is quite possible to suffocate eggs by over-milting, I cordially indorse the above. The cause of the adhesion of the ovum is not clearly understood, but I incline to attribute it to suction. The shell of the egg is marked with a large number of contiguous round spots which I think are pores. The egg when first milted feels very soft to the touch, and assumes a remarkable bloom, which I am inclined to attribute to the action of the water. After the eggs have separated they feel firm and hard, and produce a sensation to the hands, when passed through them, similar to the feeling of stirring dried peas in a bowl. This must be due to increased tension of the shell, produced by water being absorbed by the contents of the egg; the micropyle is probably closed subsequent to the entrance of the spermatozoon, and the water absorbed through the pores of the shell. The adhesion is easily explained on the principle of a boy's leather sucker.

The bloom visible on the ovum is perhaps produced in the same manner. When ova are left for some time with undiluted milt, washed, and at once placed in the collecting-pails, without regard to the time of adhesion, white eggs picked out from the trays next morning frequently exceed 10 per cent. of the whole ova, while 1 per cent. would be considered an extraordinary loss at Howietoun. When the milk-plates are ready to pour, a collecting-pitcher—one which will hold three gallons of water is the most convenient size—is filled with water, and the ova poured over the spout of the milk-dish into the centre. The ova, being heavy, fall slowly to the bottom, while any empty shells are carried away by the overflow. When the pail is a little more than half full of ova it is immersed in one of the built inlets to the ponds, where the current removes the effete milt, and after five minutes the ova are ready for the hatching-house. When all the ripe fish in the net have been spawned, the remaining males are set free, and the nets hung up to dry. From twelve to twenty gallons of ova represent a good morning's work, eighteen gallons being the most I ever remember taking out of a single net full of females. Eighteen gallons of ova contain about 600,000 eggs. I myself have spawned twelve gallons of ova in an hour and a half, on the 24th December 1885. They filled twenty-five boxes, but, being taken from the largest trout, would only number some 350,000.

Collecting salmon eggs is a very different business, at least at present, and will remain so until fishery boards sufficiently understand the true interests of their districts, and build proper ponds in which to retain the gravid fish until ripe.

I have frequently had to arrange for the collection of salmon ova for the New Zealand Government, and for stocking the Forth district. 175,000 salmon ova were obtained for the New Zealand Government, and brought to Howietoun in Christmas week 1885. This was the whole produce of five days' netting at the mouth of the Almond and in the Earn. I believe it took twenty-two days' netting in the same district to fill the hatching-house at New Mill, which is now so successfully replacing Stormontfield (the house contains twenty hatching-boxes similar to those at Howietoun). This gives more than one day's netting to a box, although ova is more easily obtained in the Tay district than anywhere else in Scotland.

Over the five seasons I have obtained ova from the Forth district, I have not averaged more than a box per day. The time, trouble, and expense usually expended in obtaining salmon ova are very great, and blank days are of frequent occurrence, though of course occasionally, when the water is exactly right, and the last run of fish nicely ripened, 100,000 eggs may be obtained in a single day; but such a fortunate combination of circumstances rarely occurs.

In collecting the ova of wild trout even greater difficulties arise. There are no carefully-tended shots, with all stones and sticks removed, holes filled up, and jagged points of rocks covered over with gravel, as in a salmon river. As a rule, the nets brought are not suitable for the water, and beyond placing a trammel at one end of a likely spawning-ground, and sweeping a net down to it, little can be effected. In lakes where the spawning streams are deficient in size matters are much better, as, by constantly netting the lake near their mouths, a fair number of fish can be caught, and by placing those in a floating stew until ripe several gallons of ova can probably be obtained; but, except in lakes very favourably situated,—such as Lochleven, where the men are accustomed to the nets, and thoroughly acquainted with the shots, —the eggs, when all expenses are added together, will seldom be found to have cost less than 15s. per thousand.

At Howietoun, 20,000,000 trout ova can be produced annually at a cost of a little over £1000 a year; and when the demand has risen sufficiently to absorb this large quantity, eggs could be incubated, packed, and delivered in any part of the United Kingdom for £12, 10s. per 100,000, and yet leave a fair margin of profit.

CHAPTER III.

PACKING THE TROUT OVA.

A GREAT many people suppose that ova can be forwarded from any well-regulated piscicultural establishment within a few hours of the receipt of a telegram. At Howietoun, at least fifty-six hours are required between the receipt of the order and the despatch of the ova. Even supposing the customer's water is well known to the Fishery, and his mode of hatching clearly understood, it is still necessary for the Secretary to determine the age and quality of ova most suitable, and the boxes in the houses in which such ova is being incubated. The despatching-house note must then be filled up, to be forwarded along with others to the Manager; the departure and arrival of the trains must be ascertained, and the railway advice-note sent to Stirling Station, and the letter announcing the days of despatch and arrival posted to the customer. This occupies the first day. The following morning the Manager lifts out the grilles from the boxes selected, in order that the attendants may remove all clear ova, and any eggs containing pale-coloured or puny embryos. This weeding process requires good clear daylight, and in winter in Scotland only four hours, from ten to two, are available. In the afternoon the eggs are thrown off the grilles in a very simple and expeditious manner.

In the anteroom of the sunk floor of the principal hatching-house a sink is placed in the recess formed by the stone staircase; a 2-inch pipe, protected by a suitable brass grating, is led into the bottom of the centre of the sink; a valve, worked by a large wooden handle, passing through the face of the skirting, closes

PACKING THE TROUT OVA.

the pipe, and between this valve and the sink two other pipes are connected,—one being a cold-water supply, and the other a hot-water supply, for washing and cleaning. These pipes are also closed by valves worked by wooden handles outside the skirting,—one to the right and the other to the left of the handle of the valve on the 2-inch pipe. These three handles are all in a line, and placed a convenient distance above the floor to be easily controlled by the knee.

The sink itself is lined with lead, and a lead basin, of a peculiar shape, is placed within it (Figs. 2 and 3).

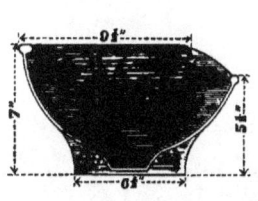

Fig. 2—scale ¼.

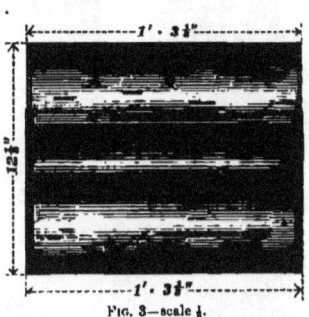

Fig. 3—scale ¼.

Immediately above the lead basin in the end of the sink an overflow is provided, from which the waste is conducted into the 2-inch pipe below the valve.

A wooden box, with a portion of one of its ends removed, and made a little larger than a glass grille, is also placed in the sink, one end resting on the inner edge of the lead basin, and retained in its position by a back-weight resting on the edge of the sink; the other end held, when the sink is full, by flotation, against a pin inserted in the elm framework that forms the top of the sink.

The *modus operandi* is as follows :—The valve on the hot-water supply is closed by turning the handle horizontal; the valve on the 2-inch pipe is also closed by turning the handle upwards to the perpendicular; the valve on the cold-water supply is opened by turning the handle upwards to the perpendicular. The sink rapidly fills, but the overflow prevents the water rising more than

3 inches in the wooden box. One of the picked grilles is then handed to the operator (Fig. 4), who reverses it in the wooden box (Fig. 5), and by a single movement of the wrist washes off the whole of the ova. An attendant, standing on the left (Fig. 6), receives the empty grille, and carries it away; the operator

Fig. 4.

Fig. 5.

then receives and reverses the next grille, and so on until the ova from twelve grilles have been deposited in the wooden box. The valve of the supply-pipe is then closed by a movement of the left knee, the back-weight steadying the wooden box removed, the box itself pressed gently forward until the end clears the pin, when it is raised and rested above the pin on the frame of the sink. The right knee then opens the valve on the 2-inch pipe, and, as the

34 PACKING THE TROUT OVA.

water leaves the sink, the ova are drawn into the lead basin. The wooden box is then removed, and the valve of the 2-inch pipe closed so soon as the water falls below the edge of the basin.

Several hundred frames, according to the number of eggs to be packed—one frame being provided for every thousand eggs,—are arranged in convenient piles on the right hand of the operator.

FIG. 6.

These frames are made of eight pieces of wood, arranged in two squares, with coarse peach netting stretched between. The squares are held and the netting stretched by brass screws, so that any required degree of tension can be easily adjusted. The frames (Figs. 7, 8, 9) are made so as to fit easily inside the travelling trays (Figs. 12, 13).

PACKING THE TROUT OVA.

One of these frames is floated in the sink, and a glass measure, which has beforehand been ascertained by actual count to contain about 10 per cent. over one thousand eggs—that is, about eleven hundred eggs,—is used to measure the eggs out of the lead basin on to the frame. One attendant immerses the frames in the sink,

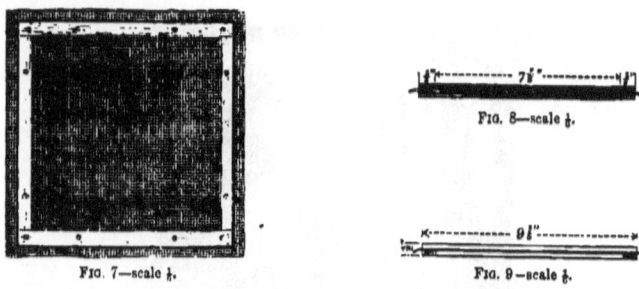

FIG. 7—scale ¼.   FIG. 8—scale ¼.   FIG. 9—scale ¼.

and another removes them as each receives its quota of ova. When the basin is nearly exhausted, the sink is refilled, and twelve more grilles emptied into the wooden box, and this is repeated until the whole of the consignments are filled. A quarter of a million of eggs are frequently thrown on the frames in the course of an afternoon.

After all are filled the basin is removed, and each frame immersed a second time in the sink, and the eggs spread by means of an undulatory motion. This is a very rapid process. The holes in the peach netting are very nearly as large as a salmon egg, so that without any manipulation the ova arrange themselves, one egg in each mesh. The frames are then removed and placed in the packing-room, on the shelf described in Chapter XIX., in piles, each pile containing frames equal to the number of layers of one thousand each (nominal), to be packed in the respective boxes.

A tray, with loose moss, is then placed above each pile, and a ticket with the number of the packing-box laid in the tray. Next morning the frames are carefully examined in case any puny embryo may have been overlooked; these are easily known by the appearance of the eye. In this process each pile becomes inverted, but the piles being examined separately, there is no danger of the frames from one pile becoming mixed with those of another. In the afternoon, so as to allow the best morning light for examining the frames, the eggs are packed in the trays, the time required being one hour for each hundred thousand ova for consignment to any part of the United Kingdom, and double that time for ova to be sent abroad.

The mode of packing is as follows :—Six trays are piled at one corner of the table, which is placed in front of the shelf in the packing-room. An attendant stands between the table and the shelf, and places six frames from one pile on the shelf on the table in line with the trays. She next takes a bundle of damp swan's down, cut into squares, from a pail on her left hand, and lays this over the other corner of the table in the same line.

A light frame, formed of a narrow packing-tray, with the zinc bottom protected by several squares of cotton flannel stretched and nailed over it, is reversed, and placed in front of the frames, and opposite this the operator stands, a large number of packing-trays, each containing a pad of felted moss, being arranged behind him. The attendant holds a square of swan's down by two contiguous corners, the operator grasps the other two corners, and the square, stretched to its full extent, is placed over the top frame. He then reverses the padded tray on the top of the swan's down, and inverts the frame by a rapid turn of the wrists. If this is done properly, every egg leaves the frame and rests on the swan's down in a position exactly corresponding to that it occupied on the frame.

The frame is lifted and placed on the table to the right of the operator, and he again grasps two corners of the swan's down, the attendant taking the other two. The square is then lifted, tightly stretched between its four corners, and laid in its top tray, when the attendant, releasing the top corners, gets the next square of swan's down ready; while the operator, leaving his forefingers in contact with the swan's down, grasps the tray by moving his thumbs over the top, and places it on the table on his left. His hands are now in position to grasp the lower corners of the next piece of swan's down, which is held up by the attendant,

PACKING THE TROUT OVA. 37

and to continue as before, until each tray has received one layer
of ova (Figs. 10, 11).

The trays are now all piled on the table at the operator's left
hand; the attendant removes the empty frames, and the padded
tray is pushed forward into the position the full frames formerly
occupied.

Fig. 10.   Fig. 11.

The operator half turns, and takes a tray from behind;
this he reverses smartly on the table, and the moss bottom leaves
the tray, and lies on the table in the form of a compact square of
felt. He then places the empty tray on his right hand, while the
attendant lightly introduces the fingers below the pad. The
operator does the same on his side, care being taken that the moss

is not grasped by the thumb, or it will break up. The square is then lifted and placed in the top tray, the attendant removing it from the pile to where the trays were first placed, and gently pressing the pad over the eggs, while the operator turns and selects the next one, and so on until all the eggs have been covered. The pile of trays now occupies its first position, ready to receive ova from the next set of frames, which are now placed on the table. As it is evidently impossible to make all the pads of felted moss of exactly the same thickness, it requires much practice and considerable delicacy of touch to ensure all the trays being filled up to exactly the proper height, so that, without any undue pressure on the eggs, they may be sufficiently packed to resist the many contingencies of a railway journey.

In packing eggs for abroad swan's down cannot be used, because after fifteen or twenty days it becomes so charged with carbonic acid as to partially suffocate the embryos. For American and Continental consignments unbleached lino is therefore substituted.

But when ova is packed for the antipodes even unbleached lino is undesirable, as, from the length of journey, the eggs are very far advanced on arrival, and it is absolutely necessary to remove the whole of the carbonic acid given off by the embryo. This can only be done by the immediate contact of live moss, and very great practical difficulties now intervene. If the moss is pressed in felting sufficiently to make the pad tolerably adhesive, much of it is crushed, and dies and blanches *en route*; if, on the other hand, the pad is so slightly felted as not to crush any sprigs of the moss, it is almost impossible to handle it sufficiently to lift the square after it has received the eggs from the frame into the tray. Perhaps the best plan is to use very thin pads, with a square of unbleached lino between them. In this way a thin pad of moss is thrown from a tray over the frame, a square of lino is then placed over the moss, and the whole reversed on the padded tray. The lino is then lifted in the same manner as the square of swan's down, and placed in the travelling tray; a very thin pad of moss is then thrown over the eggs in the tray, and another thin pad of moss thrown over the next frame, covered with lino, and the process continued as before. Packed in this way, a section would show:

PACKING THE TROUT OVA.

Perforated zinc bottom of tray.
Thin bottom of moss.
Unbleached lino.
Thin pad of moss.
Layer of ova.
Thin pad of moss.
Unbleached lino.

Thin pad of moss.
Layer of ova.
Thin pad of moss.
Unbleached lino.
Thin pad of moss.
Layer of ova.
Thick pad of moss.

One of the great advantages derived from the use of frames in the process of packing is that all handling of the ova is avoided, and also each ovum is isolated from all the others when transferred on to swan's down.

As the complement of trays for each box is completed, they are carried to the box-room. An empty tray to form an air-space is placed on the top of the pile, and a double strip of flannel passed round, and the trays lowered into the packing-box. The top is then screwed on, and covered with 2 inches of sawdust to the level of the top of the outer packing-case, whose lid is then fastened on with four screws, and the box placed in the cart. The address label is always pasted on the lids the previous day, when the eggs are removed for picking, and contains all the information necessary for the safe transit of ova.

LIVE TROUT OVA. *Per Express Passenger Trains.*

WITH CARE	To_____ _____ _____ Via_____		TO BE KEPT COOL
	FROM **HOWIETOUN FISHERY,** STIRLING.	_____S._____ *Spawned*_____	
	Date,_____	*Train*,_____	

PACKING THE TROUT OVA.

The trays in which ova are packed merely consist of a light wooden frame, 10 in. square, 2½ in. deep, bottomed with old perforated zinc, the older the better. At Howietoun the zinc screens are renewed periodically, and the old zinc removed and carefully put by for bottoming travelling trays, by which a double economy is effected, as, the screens being renewed before they are worn out, all risk of loss through a broken screen is avoided, and the perforated zinc is rendered by a year's immersion the most suitable and absolutely safe material for bottoming travelling trays (Fig. 12).

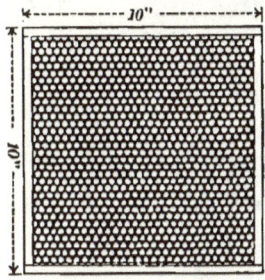

Fig. 12—scale ¼.

Fig. 13—scale ¼.

The ordinary packing-boxes consist of an inner box three-eighths of an inch larger than the frames, so that they can be easily lowered or raised by means of the flannel slip, without having sufficient room to shake about. The outer box is 4 inches deeper than the inner, and 3 inches wider, so that a sufficient quantity of sawdust can be packed between the two boxes, which serves not only as a protection against any frost likely to be encountered in this country, but also to act as a cushion, and minimise the effects of rough usage incidental to travel. And here I may say that the heavier the box the more care railways and steamships bestow on it. Rope handles are fitted to the outside box to facilitate handling, and the name of the Fishery painted on one side, with the number of the box on the other (Figs. 14, 15).

The foreign egg-boxes are constructed with a view to the supply of ice during the voyage, and an air-space surrounds the trays to secure an equal temperature to each. The boxes are 2 feet

PACKING THE TROUT OVA.

7 inches long, by 1 foot 6¼ inches wide, and 1 foot 8½ inches high, outside measurement. The inside box is sufficiently smaller, to

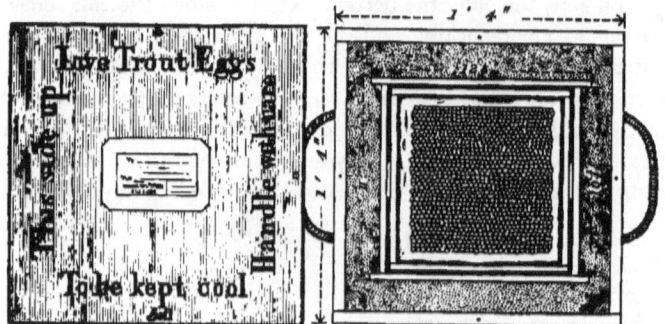

FIG. 14—scale ¼.

FIG. 15—scale ¼.

allow 2¾ inches of sawdust below and between the two boxes. Charred fillets are fitted into the inside box, which is also charred, to hold the trays half-an-inch clear. Only six trays are placed in the box, in two piles of three each, with a free air-space of about an inch between them. Twenty thousand salmon ova—that is, eighteen layers of one thousand each (nominal)—are packed in each box. Each tray has four holes cut in the sides to admit air freely to the moss and to facilitate adjusting between the fillets. A large ice-tray

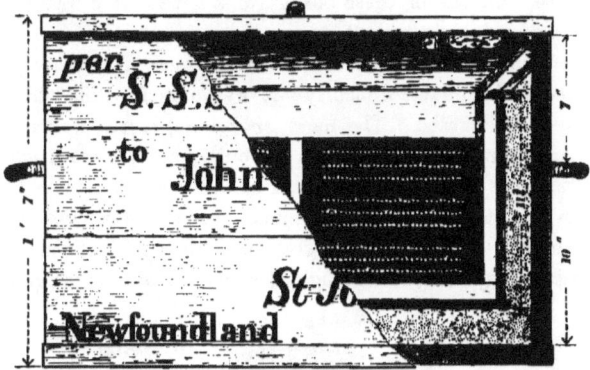

Fig. 16—scale ⅛.

rests on the top of the ova trays and is bevelled outwards so as to entirely close the inside of the outer box, the lid of which is merely

Fig. 17—scale ⅛.

fastened by a wooden pin passing through a staple, so that

crushed ice may be easily supplied as described. A cleverly designed drain is fitted in the bottom of the box to carry off the melted ice. In one of these boxes ova can be safely transported during a period of sixty days.

The manufacture of squares of felted moss for many years presented a formidable difficulty; it was only in 1883 that the process was perfected. The moss (*sphagnum*) is gathered on the moor early in winter and kept in a cool outhouse. Before it is used for felting it is carefully picked, and all dead pieces removed. A quantity is then placed in a common wooden wash-tub, across which the moss-felting machine stands. This machine is merely a board with many holes cut through it, connected with slight grooves

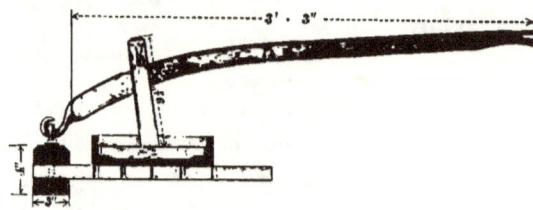

Fig. 18—scale $\frac{1}{17}$.

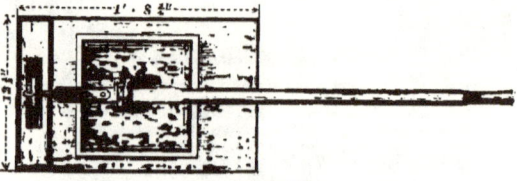

Fig. 19—scale $\frac{1}{17}$.

to drain the water away as quickly as possible (Figs. 18, 19). At one end of the board a lever is placed, carrying a cross-piece, which, when lowered, rests on the centre of the perforated portion. An empty travelling tray is next floated in the tub, and the quantity of moss proportioned to the thickness of pad desired thoroughly mixed in the tray, which is then placed on the board over the perforations, and pressed under a board, the edges of which have been bevelled off to the depth of a quarter of an inch, which is about the thickness of a layer of ova. So soon as the surplus water has been drained by force out of the moss, the pad is ready, and the trays, in lots of eighteen, are carried down to the egg-packing room.

The three great considerations in supplying ova satisfactorily are—the class of ova selected, the age of the embryo at the date of packing, and the temperature maintained during the whole time of transportation.

CLASS OF OVA.

By class of ova I mean, not only the locality from which the spawners were procured, but, and most particularly, the age of the spawners from which the ova was obtained. The Howietoun experiments have pretty conclusively proved that the individuality of a local race is very generally maintained in the offspring of the oldest parents, while the diversity common to the species is exhibited in a very large proportion of the fry, the produce of young fish. Therefore, while all trout are probably merely local races of *fario*, and the fry produced from young fish of any local race, if transported, rapidly become undistinguishable from the aborigines, the produce of old spawners retain so much of the characteristics of their parents as to become unsuited to the smaller and more rapid rivers and for many cold and barren highland lochs. Thus there is room for the exercise of great skill in the selection of ova according to the age of the parent fish and the nature of the water to be stocked. For ponds and lakes in England and the south of Scotland, it is desirable to introduce fry hatched from the ova of the oldest and largest parents. The same rule applies to large rivers, as the Thames below Oxford, and generally to all sluggish streams in the south and midland portion of England. On the other hand, when a small cold mountain stream is to be stocked, or a hill lake, where the chief advantage must arise from the introduction of fresh blood, fry from the ova of four-year-old fish should be selected. Between these extremes lies a vast and, as yet, little-trodden field of scientific pisciculture, it is therefore of great importance that the water be fully described to the pisciculturist from whom the stock is obtained.

AGE OF EMBRYO AT DATE OF PACKING OVA.

The percentage of incubation which the embryo has accomplished is of more importance in the success of the consignment than has hitherto been supposed.

As far better results can be obtained in large hatching-houses properly furnished with all the best appliances than in the hatching-trays at the command of most amateurs, as a general rule it is desirable to pack the eggs after 90 per cent. of the period of incubation has been accomplished; and where the ova is to be laid down in redds, we usually pack it when only 2 per cent. of the period of incubation remains, so that it would hatch out within a few hours of being laid down in the redd, thus avoiding all danger from sediment, which in some water would suffocate the ova in less than ten days. Muddy water seems to have no terrors for alevins, who, by herding together, keep portions of the redd clean, and, like other children, revel in a little dirt. If the journey is long, and the weather warm, a little snow or powdered ice mixed with moss placed in the air-tray obviates any danger of the eggs bursting before they are unpacked. Neither ice nor snow must be used without being well mixed with dry moss, powdered charcoal, or old white-wood sawdust, as, if the temperature rose in the box after the moss pads become saturated with melted water, embryos on the point of hatching would run much risk of suffocation. So long as the ice remains, the temperature in the trays is sufficiently low to check the exudation of carbonic acid from the ova, and the oxygen in the moss pads is amply sufficient for the requirements of the embryos. When eggs are packed ten days before they are due to hatch, there is little danger of suffocation, even if the moss become saturated. But the great secret of the successful transportation of ova is to keep the moss only damp—not wet, unless a low temperature can be ensured during the whole time of transportation. In packing ova to send to the antipodes, they need not be thrown on to the frames until one-third of the period of incubation has elapsed. If removed from the hatching-boxes before the formation of red blood, the loss in packing would be very great, generally sufficient to cause the loss of the whole consignment. Eggs, of course, can be packed with safety immediately after impregnation; but after the germ rises and segmentation commences they become more and more delicate, until about 17 per cent. of the period of incubation has been accomplished, when a very slight disturbance will cause death. After 25 per cent. of the period of incubation has been accomplished the ovum can be handled safely only when great care is exercised; but after 30 per cent. has been completed the embryo no longer resents handling,—in fact, at this stage, the ovum can frequently be dropped on to a wooden table from a height of 12 or 14 inches without sustaining any apparent injury. This, therefore, is a most favourable stage at which to pack ova for long voyages, especially as the remaining two-thirds of the period of incubation can be spread over sixty days without much injury to the future fry.

TEMPERATURE TO BE MAINTAINED DURING TRANSPORTATION.

In ordinary cases, where the ova is packed on damp swan's down between pads of tolerably dry moss, no precautions as to temperature are necessary, beyond a little care in filling the sawdust equally round the interior box; but if the ova are on the point of hatching, and the length of journey uncertain—as in the case of Ireland, and many parts of the Scotch Highlands—judgment must be exercised to determine whether the eggs should be retarded by means of ice filled into the air-tray. At a low temperature ova require very little air, but plenty of moisture; but in a temperature between 40° and 50° the ova require plenty of air and very little moisture. So long as the eggs are sufficiently backward to enable them to be packed in the dry method, the matter is very simple; but it is often necessary to stock redds in almost inaccessible positions, and, where it is highly important, the alevins are hatched immediately the eggs are laid in the redd. Pounded ice must be filled into the air-tray, and as it melts the moss becomes saturated. So long as the ice-water percolates through the pads there is no danger, but if the ice becomes exhausted, and the temperature rises, suffocation of the embryo will certainly ensue. Under these circumstances it is frequently advisable to send an attendant in charge of the consignment, with orders to replenish the ice according to circumstances. In the case of foreign journeys of short duration—as, for instance, to America or Newfoundland—ova may either be packed dry, in which case the air-tray is filled with sawdust to protect against frost or moisture, or the air-tray being filled with pieces of ice broken to the size of walnuts and rolled in sawdust, partly to prevent them rattling about, but principally to ensure the ice lasting the ten or fourteen days occupied on the journey.

Where eggs are to cross the equator, the foreign boxes require to be placed in an ice-house and the ice-tray kept full of crushed ice, so that the temperature of the moss may fall as closely as possible to 32°, while the temperature of the ice-house itself should be kept below 46°.

I do not think it judicious to freeze ova, as—although I have several times successfully hatched a few eggs which I had previously frozen in air—as a general rule, ova which have been once frozen are useless.

CHAPTER IV.

WORK IN THE HATCHING-HOUSE.

By the 20th October all the hatching boxes have been re-charred and carried back to be placed in the hatching-house. The carpenter attached to the Fishery then fixes the divisions, slips, cleats, and break-waters in the boxes, while the Manager himself scours all the pipes and the two large distributing-tanks—the successful working of the house for the next six months depending on these being in perfect order. It is of the utmost importance that no hammering and no workmen be permitted in the hatching-house from the time the first ova be laid down till the last pellet be hatched.

By the 25th October everything is ready for the reception of ova, with the exception of the grilles, which are laid down as required before each day's spawning. Grilles are placed in about forty boxes, this being the largest number hitherto filled in a single day's spawning. The collecting-pails are carried to the hatching-house, and the work of laying down the ova commenced. As the pails are carried into the house, the Manager receives them, and, pouring off all the water from one pail, proceeds to lay down the ova with a glass measure holding about one-sixteenth of a gallon. Two of these measures are poured on each grille, the mouth of the glass being partially closed by the fingers of the left hand, so that the ova is distributed in an evenly thick line across the centres of the glass tubes. With a little practice this can be done so accurately that, when all the boxes are charged, a very slight tilt given to each box in turn spreads the ova evenly over the grille, and the work of feathering is reduced to a minimum.

As the bulk of eggs varies according to the cube of the diameter, and the number a grille will contain varies inversely according to the diameter of the eggs, it is necessary to use different measures according to the age of the spawners. The number of eggs in a box (four grilles) varies from 14,000 of the finest salmon eggs to 30,000 *fontinalis* eggs. These latter are so small that special grilles are required containing a greater number of glass tubes of considerably less diameter.

After the boxes are all charged, the hatching-house attendants dress the eggs into rows by feathering. This operation is much better performed by girls, as it is difficult to prevent men touching the eggs with the feather. The proper method is to move the feather in front of the eggs towards the position they are wished to occupy; the eggs are carried by the slight current thus created after the feather, and the operation is both rapid and harmless. A trained girl should be able to dress ten boxes an hour, always supposing the Manager has laid down the eggs evenly at first. Ova should not be disturbed after the first twenty-four hours from spawning.

The next morning any shells which have not been removed in the washing are picked out, and after this the boxes are daily examined, and a record kept on a printed form, a facsimile of of which is given on next page, signed by the principal attendant. These forms are collected weekly by the Manager, and entered in a book, a page of which is reproduced, one-half size, in the Appendix.

Each box is entered, the number of eggs being written across the upper left corner, and the species marked across the upper right. The season and date of spawning are entered below the number of the box, and the dead eggs picked out are written in the space corresponding to the day of the month. The total of each month is entered opposite T., and the grand total is written in the lowest line below the month in which the eggs were sold or hatched.

When eggs are sold, and the box re-stocked, a new account is opened for it. In this manner a very large quantity of statistics have been collected, and the daily conduct of many a batch of eggs can be compared at a glance with that of any other batch of the same or the preceding seasons.

WORK IN THE HATCHING-HOUSE.

OLD HOUSE.			NEW HOUSE.			
1	1	21	41	61	81	101	121
2	2	22	42	62	82	102	122
3	3	23	43	63	83	103	123
4	4	24	44	64	84	104	124
5	5	25	45	65	85	105	125
6	6	26	46	66	86	106	126
7	7	27	47	67	87	107	127
8	8	28	48	68	88	108	128
9	9	29	49	69	89	109	129
10	10	30	50	70	90	110	130
11	11	31	51	71	91	111	131
12	12	32	52	72	92	112	132
13	13	33	53	73	93	113	133
14	14	34	54	74	94	114	134
15	15	35	55	75	95	115	135
16	16	36	56	76	96	116	136
17	17	37	57	77	97	117	137
18	18	38	58	78	98	118	138
19	19	39	59	79	99	119	139
20	20	40	60	80	100	120	140

Date,   188   *Int.*   *Howietoun Fishery.*

The daily care of the eggs in all the hatcheries at Howietoun occupies the time of two girls, but as they also assist in packing, and the annual number of eggs sold is little under two million actual count, the great advantage and economy of grilles is evident. The temperature of water in the hatching-house is so regular, the supply being obtained from deep springs, the date of hatching of any particular batch of ova can be accurately predicted, and boxes (cleared by sale beforehand) prepared for the reception of the alevins. This is done by removing the fittings and cleaning each box. The safety-screen is next placed in position, and held by a strip of flannel passed round it, pressing tightly against the sides and bottom of the box. Experience has shown that two grilles of ova hatched in a box produce stronger and earlier feeding-fry than a larger number, and as there are four grilles in a box, twice the number used for incubating are required for fry. The accommodation for fry at present at Howietoun is equal to 208 boxes, therefore 104 boxes of ova are sufficient to hatch. Additional accommodation, in the form of 20-feet ponds, has been provided, but the results are not so satisfactory as where fry are reared under cover, thus still further strengthening the reasons in favour of grilles, and defeating the argument advanced against them by foreigners, on the ground of the space they occupy.

A few hours after the egg is laid down the germ rises. The proportion of the germinal disc to the whole ovum is very small in trout eggs, while in herring eggs the disc may form as much as one-fifth of the whole. This will probably exercise a material bearing on the attempts now being made to transport the ova of the latter to New Zealand. The segmentation is meroblastic, and in the ova of salmon and trout the first furrows only penetrate for a certain depth through the germinal disc. "During the latter stages of segmentation one end of the blastoderm becomes thickened, and forms the embryotic swelling; and a cavity appears between the blastoderm and the yolk, which is eccentrically situated near the non-embryotic part of the blastoderm. This cavity is the true segmentation cavity.

"With the appearance of the segmentation cavity the portion of the blastoderm which forms the roof becomes thinned out, so that the whole blastoderm consists of (1) a thickened edge, especially prominent in one point where it forms the embryotic swelling; and (2) a thinner central portion. The changes which now take place result in the differentiation of the embryonic layers, and in the rapid extension of the blastoderm round the yolk, accompanied by a diminution of its thickness. The first differentiation consists in a single row of cells on the surface of the blastoderm becoming distinctly marked off as a special layer, which, however, does not constitute the whole epiblast, but only a small part of it, which will be spoken of as the epidermic layer.

"The complete differentiation of the epiblast is effected by the cells of the thickened edge of the blastoderm becoming divided into two strata. The upper stratum constitutes the epiblast. It is divided into two layers, viz., the external epidermic layer already mentioned, and an internal layer, known as the nervous layer, formed of several rows of vertically arranged cells. According to the unanimous testimony of investigators, the roof of the segmentation cavity is formed of epiblastic cells only. The lower stratum in the thickened rim of the blastoderm is several rows of cells deep, and corresponds with the lower-layer cells, or the primitive hypoblast in Elasmobranchii. It is continuous at the edge of the blastoderm with the nervous layer of the epiblast. . . . In the larger Teleostean eggs, such as those of the *Salmonidæ*, the hypoblast, as in Elasmobranchs, appears to be only partially formed from the nuclei of the granular layer. . . . The cells derived from the granular stratum give rise to a more or less complete cellular floor for the segmentation cavity. The segmentation cavity thus becomes enclosed between an hypoblastic floor and an epiblastic roof several cells deep; it becomes obliterated shortly after the appearance of the medullary plate.

"The first changes in the epiblast give rise to the central nervous system. The epiblast, consisting of the nervous and epidermic strata already indicated, becomes thickened along the axis of the embryo, and forms a keel projecting towards the yolk below. So great is the size of this keel in the front part of the embryo that it influences the form of the whole body, and causes the outline of the surface adjoining the yolk to form a strong ridge moulded on the keel of the epiblast. Along the dorsal line of the epiblast keel is placed the shallow medullary groove. The keel becomes gradually constricted off from the external epiblast, and then forms a *solid cord* below it. Subsequently there appears in this cord a median slit-like canal, which forms the permanent central canal of the cerebro-spinal cord. The separation of the solid nervous system from the epiblast takes place relatively very late, and before it has been completed the first traces of the auditory pits, of the optic vesicles, and of the olfactory pits are visible. The auditory pit arises as a solid thickening of the nervous layer of the epiblast at its point of junction with the medullary keel, and the optic vesicles spring as solid outgrowths from part of the keel itself; the olfactory pits are barely indicated as thickenings of the nervous layer of the epiblast.

"After its separation from the central nervous system, the remainder of the epiblast gives rise to the skin, etc., and most probably the epidermic stratum develops into the outer layer of the epidermis, and the nervous stratum into the mucous layer. The parts of the organs of special sense which arise from the epiblast are developed from the nervous layer. In the trout (*Œllachar*) both layers are continued over the yolk-sac." Certain cells in the median line of the embryo, underneath the medullary groove, give rise to the notochord. The mesoblast very soon forms two lateral plates, one on each side of the body, and between them is placed the notochord. " The general fate of the two mesoblastic plates is the same as in Elasmobranchs. They are at first quite solid, and exhibit relatively late a division into splanchnic and somatic layers, between which is placed the primitive body cavity. The dorsal part of the plates becomes transversely segmented in the region of the trunk, and thus gives rise to the mesoblastic somites, from which the muscle plates and the perichordal part of the vertebral column are developed; the ventral or outer part remains unsegmented. The cavity of the ventral section becomes the permanent body cavity. It is continued forward into the head (*Œllachar*), and part of it becomes separated off from the rest as the pericardial cavity. . . . The hinder end of the embryo, which is placed at the edge of the blastoderm, is somewhat prominent, and forms the caudal swelling; the axis of the embryo is marked by a shallow groove. The body now rapidly elongates, and at the same time becomes considerably narrower, while the groove along the axis becomes shallower and gradually disappears. . . . The trunk grows in the usual way by the addition of fresh somites behind. After the yolk has become completely enveloped by the blastoderm, the tail becomes folded off, and the same process takes place at the front end of the embryo." During the latter stages " the gill-clefts develop from before backwards. The first cleft is the hyomandibular, and behind this there are the hyobranchial and four branchial clefts. Simultaneously with the clefts there are developed the branchial arches. The post-oral arches formed are the mandibular, hyoid, and five branchial arches. . . . All these appear before hatching. The first cleft closes up . . . about the time of hatching, . . . and about the same time there springs a membraneous fold, the hyoid arch, which gradually grows backwards over the arches following, and gives rise to the operculum. There appear . . . shortly before hatching double rows of papillæ on the four anterior arches behind the hyoid; they are the rudiments of the branchiæ. They reach a considerable length before they are covered by the operculum membrane. . . . The unpaired fins arise as simple folds of the skin along the dorsal and ventral edges, continuous with each other round the end of the tail. The ventral fold ends anteriorly at the anus. The dorsal and anal fins are developed from this fold by local hypertrophy. The caudal fin, however, undergoes a more complicated metamorphosis. It is at first symmetrical, or nearly so, on the dorsal and ventral sides of the hinder end of the notochord. This symmetry is not long retained, but very soon the ventral part of the fin, with its fin rays, becomes much more developed than the dorsal part, and at the same time the posterior part of the notochord bends up towards the dorsal side. . . . Owing to the simultaneous appearance of a number of fin rays on the dorsal and ventral side of the notochord, the external symmetry of the tail is not interfered with. . . . The yolk-sac persists long after hatching, and is gradually absorbed. There is . . . just before hatching . . . a rich vascular development in the mesoblast of the yolk-sac. The blood is at first contained in lacunar spaces, but subsequently it becomes confined to definite channels."[1]

In practical fish-culture there are five stages which pre-eminently command attention. The first stage is sometimes called the

MULBERRY STAGE,

and occurs about the close of the segmentation. The round disc rises in all ova during the first twenty-four hours, but during the period of segmentation the disc, in properly fertilised eggs, becomes hard, and in unimpregnated eggs annular.

At about the close of the period of segmentation the disc in properly fertilised eggs enlarges, and has a soft appearance to the eye, so that it is perfectly easy to remove all ova likely to produce

[1] Abridged from Balfour's *Embryology*.

imperfect embryos at this stage. Eggs which are absolutely unimpregnated show a well-defined annular ring when one-third of the period of incubation has been accomplished. These eggs give no trouble whatever, and are easily removed before packing for transportation or laying down to hatch. It is a very different matter with the imperfectly fertilised ova. In this case the blastoderm, on account of imperfect segmentation, does not differentiate into well-marked embryonic layers. Blood is frequently formed in lacunar spaces at the opposite pole to the embryo, and this blood is very pale in colour. These are the eggs which occasion the principal part of the daily work in the hatching-house. It is true that an unimpregnated egg sometimes becomes opaque in the hatching-trays, especially if the water be subject to changes of temperature; and if shaken in water, or even disturbed, a large proportion of unimpregnated eggs will turn white; but in a well-managed hatchery nearly the whole of the unimpregnated eggs remain clear throughout the season. I strongly suspect, when they do turn white, the coagulation is caused by the penetration of water through the micropyle. Where imperfect segmentation has taken place, there is probably a passage of blastoderm between the yolk and the shell, and the latter, being porous, probably supplies more water than the puny embryo can absorb. The yolk will then coagulate and the egg become opaque. The Mulberry Stage affords an excellent test of impregnation in large pure-bred eggs, but it will be easily seen that it cannot be relied on in the case of eggs from young fish or with crossed fertilisation. The

SPECTACLE STAGE,

which is the second important stage, however, affords a test of the character of experimental work. This stage is marked by the appearance of a loop of globules anterior to the embryotic line. This loop gradually enlarges, and passes backwards over more than half the sphere, giving the egg at one time the appearance of a pair of spectacles, *minus* one eye, and a little later bears a striking resemblance to the three legs on a Manx coin. The left side of the eye of the spectacle stops in the position shortly to be occupied by the principal duct of the yolk-sac circulation, and the right side gradually disappears. From the early or late appearance of this triune, and by the rate of its passage round the hemisphere, the vitality of the embryo can be accurately presumed. The ova in this stage will bear very little handling, and should be examined without contact. A lucifer match placed close to the surface of the water is a good and expeditious way. The

EYE STAGE

marks a still further development, and although neither colour nor red blood are present, the eggs may be safely handled; this is the best time to pack ova for the antipodes. The tail is in this stage free, and, by holding the egg up to the light in a warm hand, it will move slightly—generally to its own right.

Breathing on the egg will cause the same effect, and is a convenient test when the hands are cold. It is, however, very important not to pack ova until the movement can be discerned in the tail. The next stage is marked by the

FIRST APPEARANCE OF RED BLOOD.

The eye-spots simultaneously show black colour, and the eggs will now stand any fair usage; they may even be dropped on the floor, and picked up again without injury. One half of the period of incubation is completed; all the unfertilised eggs show the annular disc clear and hard. A few of the imperfectly fertilised still show a disc with a hard centre, but these will turn white in transference from the trays, and even if a few survive, they are easily recognised. The only eggs which cause any anxiety are those nearly, but not quite sufficiently, fertilised, which are difficult to tell at this stage. They may be divided into two heads,—those with small and very black eyes, and those with ordinary-sized eyes but of a very red colour. However, as insufficient impregnation occurs almost solely in experimental work, or in the eggs of young trout, little inconvenience occurs from this cause in a well-regulated trout-farm. Eggs for America or the continent of Europe are packed at this stage, and so well do they travel that the loss in one consignment to Newfoundland of over one hundred thousand this season—1885-86—was under fifty eggs, or less than ·005 per cent. The

COMPLETION OF THE EMBRYONIC CIRCLE

immediately precedes hatching. The tail curls round generally to the right, and passes the nose. The body of the embryo has now become dark, the yolk globules have mostly collected immediately below the stomach. The yolk-sac circulation, though still lacunar in many parts, follows well-marked lines. In the case of twins it is common to both. The caudal pulse is well marked, and the motion of the pectoral fins easily discerned. A very slight rise in temperature will cause the eggs to hatch instantaneously. At Howietoun, when the eggs are washed off the grilles on to the bottom of the box, sometimes 90 per cent. will hatch in the first half-hour.

When a lot of eggs are ready to hatch, the grilles are taken out of the boxes, and all unimpregnated eggs and any puny embryos removed. The hatching-boxes are next stripped of their fittings, thoroughly cleaned, and the safety-screens fixed 13 inches above the outlet. If the ova is on the point of hatching it is then laid down on the wood. It is often convenient to prepare the boxes a few days before the eggs are due to hatch; and since, if the eggs remained many hours in the comparatively still water at the bottom, some of the embryos would be drowned, a small piece of tile is laid in the box, and a couple of grilles balanced on it until the hatch commences, when the tile is taken out, and the grilles reversed and removed. With 3 inches of water in the hatching-boxes there is no danger of the alevins becoming suffocated—a very common source of loss in badly constructed trays.

A CO-OPERATIVE BREATHING SOCIETY.

Shortly after hatching the alevins congregate together in dense masses in the corners and against the sides of the hatching-boxes. If the water over these masses be slightly discoloured so as to render visible the paths of the currents, small whirlpools will be noticed descending over the apex of each mass, while from the base the water radiates in a thin, swiftly-moving cloud.

On closer inspection it will be noticed the alevins are lying with their heads approximately towards the apex, and their paired pectoral fins working with remarkable rapidity; thus, instead of those lowest in the mass being in danger of suffocation, they really receive the strongest water currents. The mass is, in fact, a gigantic co-operative breathing association.

Very different is the fate of the unfortunate who finds a refuge beneath the sheet of glass so frequently used in the early days of trout-hatching to preserve the eggs from fungus. In a very few hours a pale lifeless form marks the grave of the suicide. Charred wood has abolished the necessity for linings of any sort, but the general public still delight in providing all sorts of death-traps, under the name of shelters.

After the fry have herded together for a few weeks, more or less, according to the temperature of the water, they are seized with a roaming and inquisitive spirit. At this stage the use of flannel in fixing the safety-screen becomes apparent. But it must be new flannel; old sodden stuff is certainly water-tight, but still they manage to burrow beneath it, and, although they cannot pass through, will manage to suffocate themselves in considerable numbers. New flannel is seldom water-tight, but this is of no consequence. Whether the fine hairs annoy them, or whether inherited instinct teaches them to dislike the manufactured product of the animal whose periodic washings have so frequently nauseated their ancestors, I know not; but it is nevertheless a fact that the alevins will test every joint in the box, but leave the flannel-protected joints of the safety-screen alone.

The only attention newly hatched alevins require is as to the strength of the current passing through the safety-screen. If the water is kept shallow, and the current equivalent to 2 gallons per minute through the ordinary Howietoun hatching-box, there is some danger, during the first few hours of the hatch, of so many of the holes of the perforated zinc of the safety-screen becoming clogged with cast-off shells as to make the current sufficiently strong through the remainder to catch and hold any unfortunate alevin passing. It is not safe to heighten the water in the hatching-box by placing flannel on the outlet screen before nine-tenths of the eggs are hatched, or the decreased current will cause partial suffocation of the embryos. And even when one-tenth of the eggs are left, they should be well separated with a feather before the water is deepened. If alevins get against the safety-screen, the pressure of the water gradually forces the yolk-sac, which is very elastic, through one of the perforations of the zinc. If No. 9 size is used, little harm accrues, as a strong alevin, so soon as he feels the process commence, can free himself by his struggles; and he takes care in future to avoid the screen. But with a smaller size matters are very different. The least portion of the yolk-sac slipping through—which it does the more easily, as the smaller the number of zinc the stronger the current—bulges out, and keys the fish on the reverse side of the safety-screen in such a manner that escape is impossible.

At Howietoun the eggs are laid down to hatch between nine and ten in the morning, and, unless the day is very cold, the hatch is completed by three in the afternoon, when the shells are skimmed off and the water in the box heightened. This is tedious work, and we do not care to hatch more than a quarter of a million in one day, although it is occasionally necessary to lay down a much larger number. After the shells are skimmed off and the water heightened in the boxes, the attention required is reduced to a minimum. As the fish get stronger the current is increased, the regulating tap being moved once a week through a space equivalent to 1 quart per minute per box. Hardly any alevins die except in experimental lots. The boxes themselves never require cleaning; the alevins are their own housemaids. They are constantly scouring over the bottom of the box, and keep the charred wood polished like a piece of dark mahogany. The current carries the dirt through the safety-screen, and it settles in the space of 13 inches between that and the outlet. The rough of this dirt is removed with a syphon every morning. Once a week the cork in the settling-tank is drawn, and the bottom of the box thoroughly cleaned with a brush.

The importance of exactly balancing the number of alevins to the box, and adjusting the proportions of the hatching-box to the current, are apparent. There is little danger of having too many alevins in a box, as the number put in is determined by the number of feeding-fry that can be properly reared; but if too few alevins are placed in the box, or if they have been improperly incubated and have not sufficient vitality, they will neither have strength nor activity to polish the bottom; and as—with due deference to the opinions of some—perfect cleanliness at this stage is absolutely essential to their future success in life, if they do not do their own housemaids' work it must be done for them at great trouble and expense. Up to this stage the

DAILY WORK IN THE HATCHING-HOUSE

is much the same for eggs and alevins. It is not advisable to begin too early in dark mornings; eight o'clock is quite soon enough to unlock the door. The Manager should always enter the house first, check the thermometers, and notice the overflows of the regulating-tanks. The girls then look over the hatching-boxes, pick out the opaque ova, and note the numbers on the printed form, page 50. The Manager gives the head attendant a list of the boxes from which all unimpregnated eggs are to be picked, for sale or before laying down to hatch. If it is a bright morning he sees that the swung shutters are tightly closed on the south side of the house. Direct sunlight is not only injurious to the embryos, but is apt to induce a cryptogamic growth on the shells of the eggs. The particular fungus I have not determined, its principal characteristic being the length and delicacy of its filaments.

When any eggs are near hatching, boxes which have been already emptied, for sale or otherwise, are prepared; if not, the Manager is free to go to the ponds. Should the following day be one on which ova are despatched, he returns in the afternoon to throw the eggs on to the frame; but on other days he merely looks round in the evening to receive the schedule of the dead ova

FEEDING THE FRY.

picked out, and to see generally that all is right. When the alevins are hatched, he has to attend to the depth of water in each box, which is increased by raising the flannel on the outlet screen, and to the weekly increase of the supply when the water is raised. He has also to see that a sufficient number of ova packing-boxes are prepared, with sawdust carefully filled between the inner and outer cases. In practice, it is found necessary to have at least twelve ordinary egg-packing-boxes and six foreign always ready in the box-room. He also requires to take stock of the quantity of swan's-down squares, and to check the amount of sphagnum moss in the cellar, where it keeps best.

It must always be remembered that, in the case of a heavy snow, it is impossible to get good moss sometimes for weeks together. If the stock runs short at these times, marshy places below springs are generally open, but the sphagnum is rank, soft, and the lower portion frequently bleached, and neither suitable for felting nor capable of living over a long sea voyage.

The Manager inspects the grilles removed the day previous, to see if they are in good condition and have been properly cleansed, after which he superintends their being placed on the rafters of a shed, where they remain dry and safe all summer.

When the fry begin to feed, the hatchery demands much more of the Manager's time. He requires to check the food left by the butcher, test the paste prepared for feeding the fry, and to specify the exact quantity of food each box requires.

FEEDING THE FRY.

The best and most economical food for trout fry costs about 1s. 4d. per lb., and, strange though it may appear, it is much cheaper than liver at 1d. per lb.,—that is to say, one pound of this paste goes far further, and produces much better results, than sixteen pounds of liver, because it is more nourishing, and there is no waste. The food is prepared by weighing several pounds of fillet of beef,—not beef-steak, which is too stringy, nor a piece off the surloin, which is generally too fat. Fillet of horse is equally suitable with fillet of beef, and surloin of horse, being generally very lean, is nearly as good. But as no establishment kills anything like a sufficient number of horses to supply the fry with the tit-bits, the butcher must necessarily be the chief purveyor. Mutton is not suitable. All the fat being carefully scraped off, and the meat being weighed, it is pounded in a large marble mortar, and passed through a coarse sieve. The yolks of hard-boiled eggs are then added, nine eggs being allowed to each pound of meat. The eggs should be several days old, as, if new-laid, it is impossible to boil the yolk until it is mealy. This can be easily arranged by buying foreign eggs from a wholesale dealer by the box, which runs from 120 to 150 dozen, and at Howietoun generally lasts about ten days. When the yolks of egg and meat have been thoroughly mixed in the mortar, they are passed through a fine wire sieve and kneaded into a stiff paste. This is rolled into the shape of a thick sausage, and cut and rolled into large pills, each sufficient to give one meal to five boxes. Theoretically, the weight of each pill should be checked, but in practice it is found that the eye is a sufficient guide. When the food is all prepared, it is taken into the hatching-house, and one pill placed on the edge of the fifth box in each row. One of the girls then goes round with a feeding-spoon, and, beginning at the bottom box, presses the food through the perforated zinc of the feeding-spoon, which reduces it into fine vermicelli. When the threads are about 2 inches long, they are shaken off into the water, and the current keeps them always in motion. The fry, having their attention attracted, seize on the moving filaments, and drag them all over the box, causing the greatest excitement, so that the fry eat quite as much out of jealousy as from hunger. I can compare it to nothing else than a pack of highly-bred hounds breaking up a fox. If the meat has been too fat, the filaments adhere, and lie in the bottom untouched. If, on the other hand, too little egg has been used, they break up into a thin soup, which very soon fouls the box. But when properly prepared, and the fry not over-fed, there is not one particle of waste.

The feeding-spoon is made out of elm by boring a large hole out of a 1-inch plank, and making a saw-drift through which to pass the perforated zinc. The hole is tightened up with a couple of brass screws. (See Fig. 21.)

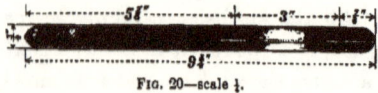

Fig. 20—scale ¼.

Nos. 8 and 9 zinc are the proper sizes. If the holes are smaller it is impossible to pass the prepared food through, and if larger, the filaments are too thick to be easily eaten by the fry, and get broken up. Should it be imperative to feed with liver, sheep's is better than bullock's, as it breaks up through the zinc into much larger particles, and, though more costly to buy, there being much less waste, is less expensive. Great care must be taken not to over-feed the fry on the prepared food, or they will stretch their stomachs to the size of the original yolk-sac, a condition which is generally followed by a suffusion of blood near the anus, and death.

After a fortnight's feeding on the prepared food, finely ground horse-flesh is substituted.

Fig. 21—scale ¼.

This is prepared by selecting the mash from the large chopping-machine with which the food of the older trout is prepared, pounding it in the mortar, and passing it through a very fine wire sieve. It is then fed out through No. 9 perforated zinc rolled round a circular base. This utensil we call the

SHORT FEEDING-SPOON.

It is found very useful, and obviates any danger of choking, as all particles too large for the fry to swallow are retained in the cylinder, and emptied out into a pail provided for the purpose, to be mixed with the food of the yearling trout (Fig. 22).

Many ingenious fry-feeding machines have been designed, but as this part of fish-culture demands constant attendance, and can only be successfully undertaken where the whole time of at least one person can be devoted to the trout, I think it unnecessary to refer to them here. The best and simplest is that used at Howietoun in the experimental tanks Nos. 1, 2, 3, and 4, p. 263.

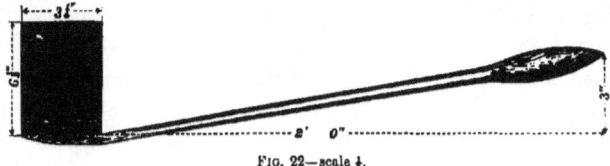

FIG. 22—scale ¼.

Amateur fish-culturists should, as a general rule, turn out their fry ten days before the yolk-sac is absorbed. It is a very common error to suppose fry will not feed until the absorption of the sac. Where they are deficient of vitality this may be so, but when the produce of properly selected breeders, and when the eggs have been so incubated as to induce great vitality in the embryos, and where the alevins had suitable depth of water and sufficient current, they come on the feed before the total absorption of the sac. Nature has, in fact, provided them with a large reserve of food, and, if vigorous, the hinder portion of the sac becomes separated by constriction, and drops off under ordinary circumstances, and it is only where there is an absence of vitality that the sac is totally absorbed.

The above does not apply to *fontinalis*, nor to the ova of young trout, or of grilse, and even with the largest salmon if hatched in water of a falling temperature, whereby the period of alevinage is much prolonged, when the whole nutriment contained in the sac becomes necessary to the life of the fish.

DESPATCHING FRY.

In the early days of trout-culture fry formed the principal sales; few cared for the trouble of hatching the ova. The carriage of yearlings was far too expensive; clearing-house rates were unknown; proper preparation not understood; nothing better than a carboy had been thought of for their transport. The water in which they were conveyed required to be frequently changed; air required to be supplied either by splashing the water or by bellows, and an attendant's constant anxiety frequently supplied an illustration of the proverb, "Care killed the cat,"—especially if he solaced himself with a pipe of tobacco during an extra long spell at the bellows. In those days fry were very costly, and, as a natural sequence, they were carefully counted before despatch. Now, if there is one thing more fatal to fry than another, it is catching and counting them; the least touch removes the mucous, and fungus follows. This was very early discovered at Howietoun, and many methods were tried to mitigate the evil. They were caught up on perforated zinc, counted, and washed off into a pail; they were skimmed up with a light muslin skimmer mounted on fine wire; they were spooned up with a soup-spoon; they were shovelled up in a miniature dust-pan (used for sanding birds' cages); they were poured into milk-plates, and counted as they passed over the spout into a pail; but none of these methods were satisfactory. The miniature dust-pan was, however, far the best and quickest of the lot.

After much consideration, and seeing that two grilles of ova were laid down to hatch in each box—which was always 7000 eggs, and frequently more than 8000,—it was decided to sell fry by the box, guaranteed to be not less than 5000. This left a margin of about 50 per cent., and the Fishery had the satisfaction of knowing that the fry despatched were uninjured; and although the price might appear high in comparison with that of ova, the results obtained were so satisfactory that the sale of fry has steadily increased every year.

PREPARING FRY.

The preparation of fry is a very difficult matter. It does not do to starve them, or they lose vitality, and cannot find their own food when turned adrift in strange waters. On the other hand, if they are fully fed, they travel uncommonly badly. We have found them travel best if fed on sheep's liver for a week before they start; but it makes a foul mess on the bottom of the box, which must be carefully cleaned before pouring the fry out, as, if the water in which they are transported is the least dirty, a large proportion of them will perish. If they are fed on the prepared food up to the day of starting, their stomachs are too distended, and inflammation would be the result. If fed on pounded horse-flesh, the matter they deposit is too gross, and the water becomes fouled.

Fry stand cold badly, and travel best in the daytime. They may be lightly fed over-night before starting, but not in the morning.

FRY TRAVELLING TANKS.

Fry will not stand much knocking about, and if the yearling tanks are used to transport them they must be filled until the water stands above the point of the perforated zinc cone, the wave rising and falling through the zinc is cushioned, and the motion at the bottom of the tank greatly modified.

The bottom of a tank used for transporting fry should be stiffened by cross-pieces soldered underneath, as, if it saggs at all, the fry soon get fatigued, possibly because the least spring from the bottom frightens them, and they exhaust their strength by frequent and aimless sallies through the water.

The old tank used to carry the fry from Middlethird to Loch Leven in 1875 answers the purpose well, but the area of the bottom is so small only a few thousand fry can be contained in it. It has, however, the advantage of being light, and can be placed on a dog-cart or the box of a four-wheeled cab, and is perhaps the handiest shape for amateur work. Pieces of wood carrying iron lugs have been bolted on to the side, so that it can be carried between two sticks. Ventilation is provided by little cylinders of perforated zinc soldered round an aperture in the lid and guarded by its handle. This in practice has been found sufficient.

CARBOYS

are used by some pisciculturists, and, when well filled with water, there is no jar; they keep a very equitable temperature, the thick glass being a bad conductor, besides which they are generally packed in a basket. The only objection I have to them is their weight, and the space they occupy in proportion to the number conveyed. Fry appear to travel by sea fairly well in carboys; while, in conical travelling tanks, they appear to suffer from the motion of the steamer. During the Edinburgh Exhibition of 1881, some thousand fry of *Coregoni* arrived in good condition from Russia. They were carried in a modified form of carboy packed in a square box lined with felt, air being admitted by a tube passing through a cork.

Conical tanks have one advantage in warm weather: if a jacket of coarse sacking be laced tightly over the tank, and the lid arranged so as to admit sufficient water to escape to keep it damp, the evaporation will so cool the tank that the temperature seldom rises above 45°. The

BEST TEMPERATURE FOR TRAVELLING FRY

is, I think, above 40°, and certainly below 50°. I do not think it ever advisable to reduce the temperature of the water in the travelling tank below that at which the fry are being reared, which is usually below 50°. I have never attempted to carry young fish above this degree. Although Sir Samuel Wilson in his *Salmon at the Antipodes* talks of a temperature of from 55° to 57°, and occasionally up to 60°, as successfully used by him in transporting and distributing the Californian salmon, he adds: "A lower temperature for salmon or trout is unnecessary in transit, and if too low it may even be dangerous, though higher than 60° should be avoided." It may be so in Australia, but in Great Britain I should certainly consider his minimum the proper maximum. I do not however care to transport fry in water below 40°, the temperature which is the maximum which can be profitably used in transporting yearlings, and 5° too high for two-year-olds.

LENGTH OF JOURNEY.

With care fry can be carried for twenty-four hours, but the result is not satisfactory if the journey be longer. They get weak from want of food, while it is impossible to feed them in the tank without fouling the water. Of course small quantities of fry can be sent much further and much easier than large. The re-aëration of the water with fry is a difficulty. It cannot be done automatically, as is the case with yearlings, because the motion the water acquires tires out the fry. In fact, the object of filling the tank well in to the cone of zinc is to check the very motion the tank is designed to produce, and the amount of which is determined by the diameter of the tank at the water-line. Within certain limits, the less water in the tank the greater the disturbance and the better the aëration. A skilled attendant is generally necessary, if fry are sent a long journey, to watch the temperature, especially at out-of-the-way junctions. All the stations on the usual routes are now accustomed to live fish-traffic, and invariably show the greatest consideration, but where tanks of live fish are a new thing, they are apt to be placed in the best light, *i.e.* the hot sun, and very considerably admired, which, however complimentary, is anything but beneficial.

PROFIT IN SALE OF FRY

must be much larger than in any other department, as the risks are much greater, and when redds are properly understood we expect to be able to drop them out of the price-list, or, at least, merely retain them as samples. The situations in which fry can be more profitably used for stocking than ova in redds are very limited; in fact, we consider four hours' journey from the hatching-house the practical limit. And in this case the fry should be turned out a week or ten days before commencing to feed. At this period they show a strong tendency to wander, and will take up what they consider suitable positions before the sac food is exhausted and they become faint with hunger. This pre-supposes that gravelly shallows are to be found in the stream which it is required to stock. Should this not be the case, fry should not be despatched until they have been artificially fed for about a month. So soon as they can take pounded horse-flesh they can stand starvation for twenty-four hours without much loss of energy, which will give them time to find some food in their new quarters. It must never be forgotten that fry of salmon and trout do not roam in search of food, but take up fixed positions, and snatch at particles carried past by the current ; and they do not forage like yearlings until they are three or four months old. Many of the failures in fish-culture are attributable to this habit being overlooked, although as early as 1873 it was noted by Livingston Stone, who says (*Domesticated Trout*, p. 171) :—

" As they continue to grow," they " increase their range, and by the first of September or a little later . . . they take their food like old trout."

The quotation however occurs in a passage in which Stone gives directions as to the size of the habitat to be provided for fry artificially reared, and it is not clear from the context that the immense importance of the converse in stocking natural waters was realised. Fry are useful for stocking artificial ponds fed by a long open canal without sufficient level to afford the slight fall required to construct redds. When in the hatching-house they have been thoroughly accustomed to pounded horse-flesh,

THE FRY ARE TRANSPLANTED

to Howietoun. This is always done before breakfast, when the water at Howietoun, which at this season is higher than that in the hatching-house, is coolest. The hatching-boxes are poured into pails provided with a large perforated zinc window immediately below the top rim, so that they always remain nearly full without running over. Through this precaution no fry are injured in transference. One box is poured into each pail and two pails into each conical yearling tank. These are filled ready on a cart outside the hatching-house. They are carried down to the ponds Nos. 17 to 32, and two tanks are emptied into the smaller ponds and three tanks into the larger. The ponds at Craigend receive three tanks each. In emptying the tanks a man stands, with one boot in the water, on the ledge of the pond opposite the centre, and at once pours the tank directly over the deepest part of the pond.

The depth of water spreads the fry before they reach the bottom. At first we used to place the fry in the shallowest water near the inlet of the pond, but they were so frightened they used to lie huddled together in masses. Probably the strong light affected them after the semi-darkness of the hatching-house, and instead of spreading they spent their time in trying to get under each other—a most unsatisfactory amusement, which generally ended in the suffocation of some of them. When poured into the deep water they instantly disperse, and in a few minutes have spread all over the pond in a lively and inquisitive spirit, *Mens sana in corpore sano.*

CHAPTER V.

REARING YEARLING AND TWO-YEAR-OLD TROUT.

THE fry, after being turned into the 100-feet ponds, are left to themselves for one day, during most of which time they are incessantly roaming about. By the following morning they have settled down considerably; and one of the most difficult processes of fish-culture, namely, teaching fry to collect for feeding, is begun.

If the 100-feet ponds have been filled for several weeks before they are stocked with fry, a certain amount of natural food is produced, which will be found of great assistance in strengthening the young fish. But it frequently happens that it is impossible to have the 100-feet ponds cleaned ready to be refilled with water sufficiently long beforehand to permit much natural production of food, and the success of the transplantation mainly depends on the skill of the attendant in collecting the young fry when they are fed. To do this successfully two things are necessary: (1) They must not be disturbed by strangers,—in fact, for the first few weeks it is highly important they see no one but the attendant told off to feed that set of ponds; (2) Each pond requires constant attention for about twenty minutes at a time at least three times a day. The attendant proceeds by throwing a little of the prepared food, in the form of vermicelli, on the surface of the water over the deepest portion of the pond, which, in all the 100-feet ponds, is about the centre. The artificial worms, having to fall through about 4 feet of water, occupy a perceptible interval of time in their descent, and one or two fry are sure to quarrel over the food. The disturbance they create attracts others; and when the food has disappeared a very small quantity of pounded horse-flesh is washed out of a long-handled spoon over the fish (Fig. 23). The smaller the quantity the better, as, should there be sufficient to give a shred to each fish, it would be quietly consumed; while, if the quantity

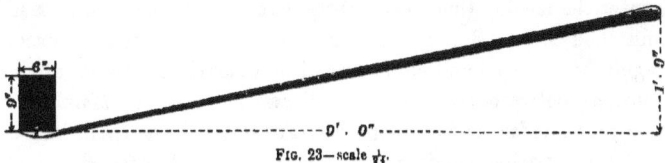

Fig. 23—scale 1/12.

is very small, prompted by jealousy, the fry will quarrel, and create a very considerable commotion, thus attracting many others. The process is then repeated, and if care is used never to wash out too much at a time, in about seven minutes all the fry within a distance of 15 feet, if the water be clear, are attracted. The long-handled spoon can then be strongly shaken in the water, and the fish fed. The attendant then divides the distance between the centre of the pond and the inlet, and repeats the process. Lastly, he chooses a spot half-way between the centre of the pond and the outlet, giving a little food to those still collected round the centre in passing, and acts as before,—the great object to achieve being to collect the bulk of the fish in the centre of the pond, where the water is deepest and the fish have most time to seize the particles as they descend. Girls make far better fish-feeders than men, as they are not so apt to hurry over the work. With fry at this stage starvation is the principal source of loss, and, if fed without collection, many would be missed. They so soon become weak without food, and lose energy, it becomes almost impossible to induce them to collect, while, if sufficient food is spread broadcast over the pond to ensure every fish having a bite, the bottom and sides get so fouled with the surplus food decomposing that fungus will in all probability attack the fry. Decomposing animal matter forms a favourable nidus for the *saprolegnieæ*.

After a pond has been fed in this way for a fortnight, the fish collect very rapidly, and five minutes suffices for feeding each pond. Sixteen ponds can then be fed by one attendant eight times a day, and this is continued until September, when the morning and evening feeding is dropped. By October the fish are fed only four times a day, between 10 A.M. and 3 P.M., and during winter the feeding-time is still further reduced to between 11 A.M. and 2.30 P.M. But the amount of food consumed increases regularly. One hundred thousand ten-month-old trout would consume between two and three horses a week. In March the two-year-olds for the following season are selected, and transplanted to the two-year-old ponds Nos. 9, 13, 14, and 16. The few thousand yearlings remaining for the season's delivery are removed, if possible, into one of the 130-feet plank ponds, so that the whole of the 100-feet ponds can be run dry and cleaned. The plugs and the iron pipes which pass below the 100-feets being removed, any remaining fish are caught in the wells at the foot of the works. If possible, the ponds should remain empty, exposed to the air and the sun, for at least a fortnight, and the fry do better if they remain full for another fortnight.

THE TWO-YEAR-OLDS

require to be carefully selected, as it is very important, in growing large numbers of fish together, to start them as equal in size as possible—and with trout there is always a small proportion of fish of inferior size,—although, I believe, at Howietoun this proportion is much smaller than it would be in Nature.

The feeding of two-year-olds is very simple. Chopped horseflesh is merely scattered by hand out of a pail on the surface of the water. As the two-year-old ponds are from 8 to 12 feet deep, the fish have plenty of time to pick up every particle before it reaches the bottom, and so knowing do they become that the shoal of trout raise a regular wave on the water so soon as their feeder comes in sight. A man is better than a woman for feeding two-year-olds, because it requires considerable strength to scatter the food over a large pond, and if he walks round while he scatters, there is little danger of his feeding too fast.

The quantity of food required is also large. Three pailfuls of chopped horse are given daily to pond 15, which yields from 20,000 to 22,000 each season. The food is measured, not weighed; but each pail holds 14 lbs. It is very important that the pails are shallow and wide, as shown in the cut (Fig. 24), otherwise they are very inconvenient to feed from; and the food will not be thrown nearly so evenly over the surface of the ponds if the feeder has to stoop down for it, while, with a shallow pail, it can be scattered as evenly as seed from a sower's apron.

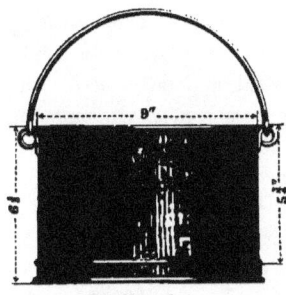

Fig. 24 —scale ¼.

Hardly any fish die between one and two years of age; and as it is very injudicious to overstock a pond, 10 per cent. is an ample margin to allow in stocking with yearlings to produce two-year-olds. It is a very different matter stocking with fry to produce yearlings. Usually, at least double the number of fry must be used. In fact, in the 100-feet ponds, 30,000 fry are frequently required to produce 10,000 yearlings. But this seeming waste is more a matter of economy than necessity, as, if sufficient care and attention is given to the feeding at first, 10,000 yearlings can be produced from 15,000 fry; and in the 20-feet ponds, with mechanical feeding, I have obtained even a better proportion. *Mais le jeu ne vaut pas la chandelle.* A farmer might just as well sow his turnips seed by seed to avoid the trouble of thinning. A larger proportion of the seed might of course be grown into turnips, but at a greatly increased cost of labour and much risk of failure. The egg-producing power at Howietoun is at present in excess of its requirements, but the margin is growing less every year as the ova sales increase, and probably in a few years it will not pay to allow a margin of more than 50 per cent. in stocking the 100-feets with fry. There is not the slightest reason why the necessary loss should be over 10 per cent. It is merely a question of cost.

CHAPTER VI.

DESPATCHING LIVE TROUT.

THE transport of live trout entailed so much expense, and was accompanied with so great risk, that until within the last few years it could hardly be considered a practicable mode of stocking waters. Howietoun has changed all this, and quarter-of-a-pound trout can now be carried 500 miles by rail, and fattened for the market, with considerable profit to the farmer, even although the carriage, in this instance, still equals the first cost of the fish. Trout require careful preparation before they can be safely despatched to any distance, long or short; and when it is considered how few fish survive a journey during which the water in the tanks has been repeatedly changed, to say nothing of the expense of the arrangements required to enable this to be done, the immense importance of preparing trout in such a manner that it will not be necessary to change the water during transit is obvious. Each time the water was changed in the old and now exploded method of transporting trout, three malignant fiends watched over the operation, each ready to seize an opportunity to destroy. The first, and most frequently fatal, can only be detected by a most delicate thermometer. Though trout can live through a great range of temperature, a sudden change, especially if repeated at short intervals, induces what is commonly known as gill fever. The second fury is seldom so prolific of loss as her elder sister; but she never fails to claim some victims whose deaths may be classified under the heading— Injuries due to Handling. The last fiend happily rarely claims her toll, but she makes up for the seeming courtesy by the totality of the loss where her death-dealing waters are used; and when the tanks are replenished with strange water it is often impossible to tell by any test of taste or smell whether they are suitable or very much the reverse.

There is one small stream near Craigend, the Auchenbowie burn, which rises in a bog called the Black Dam, which is not unsuited for growing yearlings; but if travelling tanks are filled with it these trout cannot be conveyed for more than half an hour without great loss; and the fish from the ponds at Craigend are now always transferred to Howietoun in tanks which have been filled with the pure water from the Loch Coulter burn. I am unable to give any reason, but many seasons' experience has proved that burn-water, although unpolluted, may be absolutely fatal to fish transported in tanks filled with it. To enable trout to travel in tanks without change of water, all that is necessary is to prevent the fish themselves contaminating the water, and to so construct the tank that the oxygen extracted by the fish is replaced by the splash of the water. Many very ingenious contrivances have been made: electrical air-pumps, foot bellows, rotatory bellows, false bottoms, and circulating tanks. Some of these answered the purpose well, others very much the reverse; but none of them were sufficiently practicable to enable trout to be transported on a commerical scale; and in nearly every case the inventor ignored the anatomical fact that trout or salmon cannot respire freely if lying against a curve. All that is necessary to demonstrate this is to lay a dead fish in an oval fish-carrier or round wash-tub. If the fish is as long as the radius of the curve one gill-cover will be tightly closed, and the other, though slightly open, will be pressed against the side. It is all very well to say the fish might lie in the middle, but, if the tank is sufficiently stocked, a large number of the trout must lie against the side; and if only a few fish are placed in the carrier, for some reason—probably because they are afraid of knocking their noses—they will not remain in the centre, but will probably take up their position against the side at right angles to the radius. From this it follows that tanks for the conveyance of large trout must be rectangular, although those for carrying yearlings are more conveniently made round, their length bearing so small a proportion to the diameter of the circle that the angle subtended by a chord of equal length is too obtuse to cause more than a slight interference with the action of the gill-covers. For travelling yearlings, a conical tank with a bottom 2 feet in diameter is therefore suitable (Fig. 25).

The weight of the tank is the next consideration. It must be heavy enough to induce porters and carters to handle it delicately. Human nature has a wonderful respect for its own toes, and although a lady's band-box may afford infinite amusement as a catch, a tank weighing 1½ cwt. will always secure respectful attention; while, on the other hand, it is very easily lifted by two men, handles for the purpose being fixed a little above the centre of gravity and a little below the centre of the figure. When these tanks have to be carried where there is no road, or across mountain paths, two poles are inserted in iron lugs fitted between the carrying handles, and the tank forms a sort of sedan-chair. In this way many of the highest lakes in Scotland have been successfully stocked. The oxygen in the water is renewed by placing an inverted cone of zinc in the bottom of the lid, so that the apex just touches the surface of the water. The sides of the tank converge upwards, and the jolting *en route* forces the water into the lid, from which it falls downwards, and becomes converted by the cone of zinc into fine spray. This cone is also used as a receptacle for crushed ice, thus securing cold fresh spray continually falling on the surface of the water in the tank so long as it is in motion. The colder the water is kept, the fewer the respirations per minute of the trout, and the less the quantity of oxygen exhausted from the water. The only remaining difficulty to overcome is to prevent pollution from the fish. If the reader

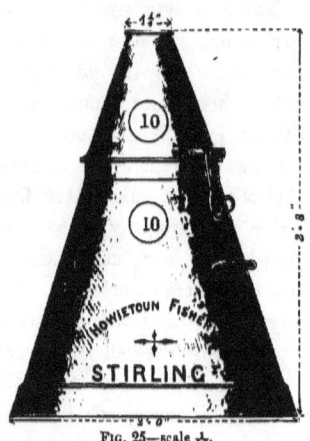

FIG. 25—scale $\frac{1}{17}$.

will only place a few freshly-caught trout in a clean tank, he will probably be surprised to notice how dirty the water becomes after

FIG. 26—scale 1/14.

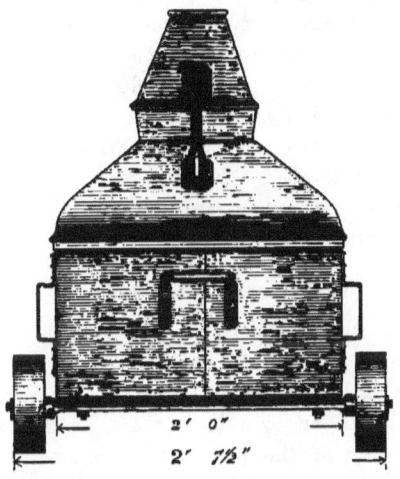

FIG. 27—scale 1/14.

a few hours. If the fish have been kept several days in a stew where there is nothing to eat before they are placed in the tank, the water will remain sweet and clear for many hours. The principal secret to travel fish successfully is to prepare them properly before despatch.

Two-year-old trout do not travel well in the conical tanks used for yearlings; at least not if they are over 7 inches long. They are therefore usually sent in tanks weighing a little over 5 cwt., which are built on a rectangular base, the top being brought in as an ogee curve to direct the water into a wedge of perforated zinc to spray the water, in the same manner as the inverted cone described above. These tanks, being very heavy, are placed on small wheels, so that they can be conveniently moved about railway stations, piers, etc.

The most suitable material for making these tanks is galvanised iron, but as the soldering requires to be done with the aid of spirits of salt, the tanks require to be well steeped before being used. At Howietoun, new tanks are generally ready early in summer, and stand full of water, which is occasionally changed, for three months before being placed in the tank-house. To enable the large tanks for two-year-olds to be easily loaded and unloaded at stations, two pairs of iron lugs are riveted on the sides, in which wooden handles are fitted, thus enabling four men to lift the tank easily. An ordinary lorry carries four large tanks, or ten small ones, and a Scotch farm-cart takes two large tanks, or four small ones. English carts are usually a little smaller than the Scotch, and many will only take one large tank, or three small ones.

PREPARATION OF YEARLINGS.

From one to three days before the despatch of any order of yearlings, one of the ponds, Nos. 17-32, is netted with a bag-net made of coarse peach netting, the lower side of the mouth being sewed on to a light chain, so that it takes the bottom and sides of the pond evenly apart; or the whole pond is drawn, according to the number of fish it contains. It is not found advisable to catch more than 2000 yearlings in one net. If the ponds are frozen, a saw is passed down the sides to make a passage for the ropes, and the net is drawn below the ice. When the net is brought to the end of the pond, and the mouth rolled back, the lower part of the net is then gathered on shore; considerable care is necessary in doing this to prevent any of the fish being lifted out of the water. Men are then stationed at distances of 30 yards between the pond and the despatch-house. When all are in their places, a landing-net is used, and the fish transferred from the net into five-gallon pails. About 200 are placed in each pail, and when two pails are filled the nearest man carries them to the next, and by the time he returns a second pair of pails are ready. We find in practice a man with a landing-net can easily place 200 fish in a pail in the same time that a carrier walks 30 yards, and the transference of 2000 fish in ten pails from the ponds to the despatch-house is a matter of a very few minutes. As the fish arrive in the despatch-house, they are at once emptied into the six preparing-tanks facing the door, and a strong current of water turned on. So soon as the water is clean, a netful is taken out and placed in a pail; a second, fitted with a square perforated zinc window near the top, is placed in the centre of the floor over the grating of the waste-pipe. The fish are then poured from the first pail over the hand of the operator, and any under-sized fish removed. The yearlings are counted while passing over the hand, a good percentage being allowed to cover any possible loss in preparation or transportation. They are then placed in one of the twelve preparing-boxes running at right angles to the door, each box holding the same number, to be sent in a small tank, or half the number to be sent in a large tank—that is, 125 to 175 in the one case, and 200 to 300 in the other. So soon as a preparing-box is filled, its lid is placed on, and the number noted against the order. When all the preparing-boxes in the despatch-house are filled, the old hatching-house at Howietoun is used as a supplementary despatch-house. It holds eleven boxes and a large tank for two-year-olds. Fourteen large tanks and one small one can thus be despatched by one train, containing over 7000 yearling trout. The time occupied in transferring the fish from the preparing-boxes to the travelling tanks on the cart is less than a quarter of an hour.

PREPARING TWO-YEAR-OLD TROUT.

The two-year-old trout for the market are grown in the island pond No. 13, and in ponds 14 and 16. The island pond will rear about 30,000 two-year-old trout, and ponds 14 and 16 10,000 each. These ponds are netted with an ordinary seine-net of small mesh, made of cotton and untanned, it being found they last quite as well in fresh water, and the white colour, by driving the fish forward, as greatly increases the catching capacity of the net in the ponds as it would decrease the same in the sea by scaring the fish. The seine-nets have a light chain substituted for the bottom rope, so that they absolutely sweep the bottom of the pond. As two-year-old fish generally swim in shoals, it is often difficult, especially at the beginning of the season, to avoid catching too many, and it is frequently necessary to allow several thousand to escape before the net is completely drawn. The two-year-olds are then removed with a large landing-net, the bag of which is made of soft peach netting so as not to hurt the fish. They are carried in this net to the despatch-house, and placed at once in the large 20-feet tank, which is covered over with the same soft material to prevent their jumping out. There they remain for several days, according to the distance they are going to be sent, the temperature of the water, and condition of the trout. Twelve hours before despatch they are counted out into the small preparing-boxes, not more than 50 being placed in one box. Prepared in this way, two-year-olds make magnificent travellers, and the loss even of a single fish is very rare.

PREPARING LARGE TROUT.

When it is necessary to forward large trout, the square concrete tank in the despatch-house is filled. Each side of this tank measures 17 feet 3 inches, and the depth of water is generally regulated to 4 feet. Large trout require at least a fortnight's preparation. They are caught with the spawning-bag nets, carefully selected,

F

82   DESPATCHING LIVE TROUT.

Fig. 28.—Despatching-House, Howietoun.

DESPATCHING LIVE TROUT.

and rigorously starved in the concrete tank. The day before despatch the number required are placed in the 20-feet tank for convenience, and when the carts with the travelling tanks are ready to start, the water is run off, and the fish lifted off the bottom. The temperature of the water in the despatch-house should never exceed 40°, or the fish will become dull when placed in the iced travelling tank; nor should the water in the travelling tank be more than 3° below that in the despatch-house at starting. In practice, we find 37° and 34° the most convenient temperatures. The crushed ice in the perforated zinc cone in the lid will cause the water in the travelling tank to fall nearly one degree before reaching the station; and so long as the ice remains in the lid it will remain practically constant. Where the water into which the fish are to be turned out is above 40°, only sufficient ice to last half the journey should be placed in the spray cone, so that on the completion of the journey the water in the tank may approximate to that into which the fish are to be turned.

When the carts arrive at the Fishery, they are loaded in front of the tank-house, the tanks being placed in numerical order, with their numbers placed to the backs of the carts. The travelling tanks are then filled, either by pails at the Loch Coulter burn, or by the stand-pipe on the loading-bank in front of the despatch-house. Should that be connected with unused Loch Coulter water, which, on account of the Fishery not being already completed, is not always convenient, two lorries, with four large tanks each, and a cart, with two large tanks, can be backed against the loading-bank at the despatch-house, while a third lorry can be loaded at the old Howietoun hatching-house. Two hours and a half before the train starts from Stirling Station the work of transferring the fish is commenced. The lids are removed from the preparing-boxes containing the fish to be carried in the travelling tanks in the first lorry; the flannels which heighten the water are stripped off the outlet screens; the numbers on the tanks and on the preparing-boxes are checked with the despatching-house note, a copy of which is given below; the temperature in the travelling tanks ascertained, and ice removed, or snow added, as required. Snow is very easily

DESPATCHING LIVE TROUT.

Fig. 29.

stacked, and keeps well until May, and reduces the temperature of water much more rapidly than ice.

One man is now stationed on the lorry, a second stands at the door of the despatch-house, a third holds a short-handled landing-net, and a fourth gently presses the end of the first preparing-box forward. So soon as the bottom of the box engages the front roller on the stand, it moves through its own weight, and, steadied by the hand, gently tilts up, discharging nearly the whole water through the outlet screen. The box is now quite light and easily reversed, the fish being poured out from one of the top corners into the net, which is handed to the man at the door, who passes it on to the lorry. The next box is treated in the same manner, and, on the second net being passed to the man at the door, the first net is returned ready for the third box. When all the tanks in the first lorry are filled, the numbers of those in the next lorry are checked, and the lids removed from the corresponding preparing-boxes, thus making a mistake in despatch almost impossible.

Two minutes are allowed for each thousand trout travelling in big tanks, and three minutes for each thousand trout travelling in small. As each lorry receives its fish, a man with a mallet fastens the lids by driving home the wooden pins. Three and a half ton weight of fish, in their travelling tanks, are frequently despatched under fifteen minutes from the time the first lid is removed from the preparing-tanks in the despatch-house until the last horse has started from the loading-bank. Such is the advance trout-farming has made in the last few years at Howietoun.

CHAPTER VII.

BREEDERS.

BY far the most important feature introduced by Howietoun is the production of ova from carefully selected breeders. Elsewhere, before Howietoun, a few stock fish might be kept for the sake of their ova,—but this was the exception, not the rule; and on the Continent the opinion was very generally held that the ova from trout confined in tanks was of little value; and as no one attempted to rear a stock of eight- or nine- year-old fish to breed from, and as the conditions under which the very best ova are produced were absolutely unknown, this opinion was at the time well founded. It is here that Howietoun has worked a revolution in fish-culture. With its magnificent supply of water, used in the most economical manner possible, it has demonstrated that a flow of less than 5,000,000 gallons per diem can support in rude health, from fryhood to old age, a sufficient number of spawners to produce annually 20,000,000 ova, measuring 700 gallons, weighing over 3 tons, or, when packed for transport, representing a freight of 50 tons. Compare this with the amount of salmon eggs which can be procured for fish-cultural purposes by netting even our best rivers during the spawning season. The excellent little hatching-house at Dupplin, in the Tay district, can hatch about 350,000 salmon ova. And last season (1885-86) it took five men twenty-two days' netting the best shots in the Tay and Erne before the boxes were filled. For many seasons I have superintended netting the Teith, in the Forth district, to obtain ova to incubate for the Fishery Board, and I never remember as many as 50,000 salmon ova spawned on any one day.

On the western coast of North America, where another member of the salmon family, the *O. quinnat*, or, as it is now called, the

Salmo quinnat, runs up the Sacramento river in great numbers; and in the McCloud river, a tributary of the Sacramento, the eggs are procured by erecting a dam across the river and netting the fish in the pool below, and in this way very large numbers are obtained. But even under these favourable circumstances the cost is very great. Sir Samuel Wilson, after quoting a report, dated April 5th, 1875, addressed to the Hon. Spencer Baird by Mr. Livingston Stone, containing a description of the mode of obtaining salmon eggs in the McLeod river, says: "In the season when this report of Mr. Stone was written (1874), the total number of salmon (*O. quinnat*) eggs taken in this river by him was 5,752,500, at a cost of 7s. per 1000."[1] What the cost of these eggs would have been if properly hatched, instead of imperfectly developed, I leave the reader to judge.

The original stock of breeding-fish at Howietoun was raised from eggs taken at Loch Leven in the autumn of 1874; and in 1875, in addition to a further supply of eggs taken at Loch Leven, a batch of burn-trout (*S. fario*) ova were laid down, the produce of the small trout caught in the burns on Sauchie Muir. As the fish grew older the size of their eggs increased, and the fry from these ova were bigger and stronger each season, till at last it became apparent that the ova of old trout were much the most valuable. A new generation of breeders are now springing up. They have been carefully selected from the eggs of the largest and best trout spawned 1882 and 1884. It is too early yet to ascertain whether their ova will be larger and finer than that of their ancestors when at the same age; but if rapid growth, rude health, and early maturity form any basis for prognostication, it will be so.

In February the best pond of yearlings is selected. No. 9 pond is emptied, cleaned, and prepared for their reception. After it had been refilled for a few days, 5000 are placed in it, and carefully and regularly fed on horse-flesh for one year. The following January they are transferred to one of ponds 10, 11, 12, or 13,

[1] *Salmon at the Antipodes:* Being an Account of the Successful Introduction of Salmon and Trout into Australian Waters, by Sir Samuel Wilson, chap. x.

according to the rotation, in which they remain until they are nine years old, after which they are of little value for breeding, the size of the egg having reached its maximum, and the number having dwindled down to 500 to the pound. Of course I am merely speaking generally, as some fish continue to improve for several seasons after the bulk of their contemporaries have become barren from old age. When trout are in their fourth year they receive one meal of mussels and two of horse-flesh daily. In the fifth year they are fed with more mussels and less horse-flesh. The ova of fish on this diet is a beautiful orange yellow, and very transparent. The next year clams (*pecten*) are substituted for mussels, and the ova acquires a slight pink tinge; after this they are fed entirely on clams, and each succeeding year the ova becomes of a darker pink colour. Fish fed on horse-flesh give the largest number of eggs and of the palest colour. Trout fed on clams yield the smallest number proportionally of eggs, but of the largest size and darkest colour. If the conditions of food be equal, the oldest fish give the largest and darkest eggs, and the fewest proportionally. There are, however, many exceptions to the general rule, for which I am as yet unable to account.

SEGREGATION OF SEXES.

Males of six years old and upwards are very subject to fungus (*Saprolegnia ferax*), and if there is much infection in the pond it is apt to spread to the females. It is therefore advantageous to remove the males after they have been spawned the first time. Females, when alone in a pond, feed more freely, and are almost entirely free from disease. A great saving is also effected in cost of the food. The expense of feeding a pond entirely on clams is not grudged when the inhabitants yield a plenteous and rich egg-harvest; but it does seem wasteful to gorge on costly food a lot of old males, not one-fourth of whom are required for breeding purposes. Moreover, I think I have noticed better behaviour in these gentlemen when living in bachelor quarters. They do not seem to fight so much, and the wounds, which form the usual seat of an autumn appearance of fungus, are chiefly conspicuous by their absence.

S. FONTINALIS AS BREEDERS.

Fontinalis require much more attention when kept for breeding purposes than either *S. levenensis* or *S. fario*. They are greedy feeders, and very susceptible, especially if in gross habit, to changes of temperature. Fungus does not grow so luxuriantly on their skins as on the skins of English salmon or trout, but it grows there all the same, and is none the less fatal because it is composed of shorter and silkier spores. An east wind in spring, when *fontinalis* are often in high condition—for they come into season much earlier than trout in the same water—often causes *fontinalis* to break out in blotches, which speedily become covered with fungus. Dissection discloses considerable inflammation in the lower portion of the gut, extending forwards. If such a thing were known amongst fish, I should be inclined to think it a form of gastric fever. If, on the other hand, *fontinalis* are under-fed, the yield of ova is very much reduced. But with a moderate allowance of food in spring and autumn, they may be fattened in summer and starved in winter without risk; but only where they are confined in water over 8 feet deep. Two-year-old *fontinalis* yield small eggs; there is not much difference between the size of eggs of three- and four-year-old. At four, *fontinalis* appear to be thoroughly mature. Those that have been bred for several generations at Howietoun are easier managed than those from imported ova. They interbreed freely with British char, and the cross is fertile.

SELECTION OF BREEDERS.

From the foregoing it will be seen that artificial cultivation, by careful selection of mature spawners, improves any particular variety of trout within itself; but it is highly probable, by mixing a strain of some other well-chosen variety better and permanent results may be attained, and in time many well-marked artificial crosses will be bred, each true to a type most suited to the class of water it is intended to stock. Nor need this take many generations to accomplish if the guiding rule be borne in mind that the produce of young fish, even of the best-marked lake-trout, throw back to the original type of *fario*, and only the produce of the oldest fish transmit the characteristics of variety.

The foregoing chapters give a general sketch of the work performed at the Howietoun trout farm in the various seasons of the year, and the general results already obtained. I will now describe the gradual growth of the fishery year by year, from its inception in 1873 to the present date.

CHAPTER VIII.

Season 1873-74.

CONSTRUCTION—MIDDLETHIRD.

Some words of Frank Buckland's induced me first to try to hatch out trout eggs. I got a copy of Francis Francis' *Fish-Culture*, and had a box made something similar to the one he describes on page 53 (second edition). This box I shall hereafter refer to as the

FRANCIS BOX.

It is built of elm, and is in good preservation to-day, although it has been more than twelve years in use. The dimensions of the box are shown in the cuts (Figs. 30, 31, and 32). The trough at

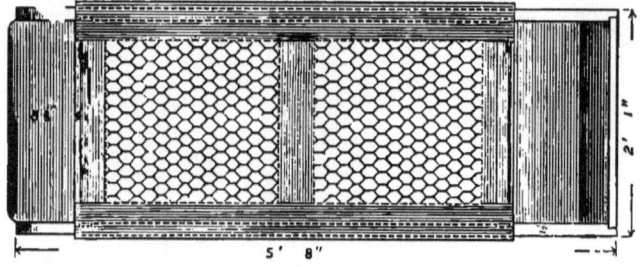

Fig. 30—scale $\frac{1}{12}$.

the upper end receives the water from the stream, and a screen of perforated zinc (not shown in the woodcut) fixed across the opening into the box confines the fish, or defends the eggs,—for the box can be used both as a stew and as a hatching-box,—as the case may be. This zinc screen clogged up very shortly after the box was in use, and I altered its position from across the end of the box to the top of the trough. This was the first step towards inventing the leaf-screen (see page 108). The lid of the box was covered with fine wire-netting to keep out birds, and a square cut was made in the lower end, furnished with a shoot to enable the water to be caught, and used in other boxes if desired.

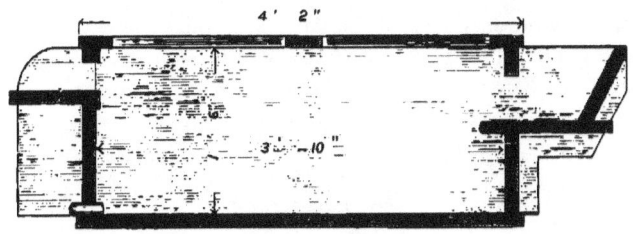

Fig. 31—scale $\tfrac{1}{8}$.

A hole was bored in this end near the bottom, to run off the water when it was wished to clean the box, a plug of wood (Fig. 31)

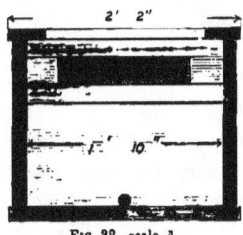

Fig. 32—scale $\tfrac{1}{8}$.

being inserted when the box was in use. The outlet was guarded with perforated zinc (Fig. 32) one number larger than the inlet, so as to ensure its always keeping free. The Francis box did not prove satisfactory as a hatching-box, but it is admirable as a stew, and fish can be fed and kept for weeks in it safely, which is not the case with the ordinary floating stew used at Loch Leven for trout.

SLATE TRAYS.

I got a dozen slate trays made in Leith 20 inches by 5 inches inside measurement. The sides and ends were grooved to receive the bottom, and the sides were further grooved to receive the ends. The tray was held together by four iron rods, two passing through each end as close to the slate as the groove in the sides would admit (Fig. 33). These rods have square bolt-heads on one end, and are tightened by a nut on the other. The grooves are painted

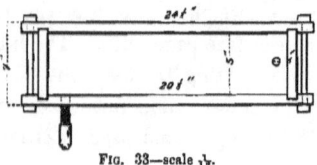

FIG. 33—scale 1/12.

with a mixture of white lead and slate dust, which makes the joints water-tight. A ledge is left on the slate at each end to support the grille (Fig. 34). This is far superior to earthenware sup-

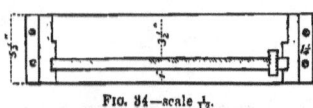

FIG. 34—scale 1/12.

ports, as it leaves no space for dirt. A hole was bored in the bottom at each end alternately, that is to say, six trays have the hole bored at the right-hand end, and six at the left. In the side, near the end opposite the hole in the bottom a second hole is bored, half an inch in diameter, the centre being three-quarters of an inch below the top of the side (Fig. 35), in which a pipe having a male screw is inserted and held water-

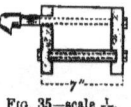

FIG. 35—scale 1/12.

tight by a nut tightened against the slate, the end of the pipe having a flange (not shown in cut) let slightly into the side of the tray. A nozzle to stop any drip running back was next screwed on to the pipe. This completed the tray. When in use a cork closed the hole in the bottom, but only sufficiently to prevent leakage, so that it could be withdrawn at a moment's notice without shaking the tray at all. No grilles were made this season, the eggs being either hatched on the bare slate, or on a thin sprinkling of gravel.

THE NINE-FEET PLANK POND.

I built a small 9-feet plank pond. It consisted of a frame of 2-inch plank, the ends being checked into the sides and the bottom. It was made 2 feet wide inside measurement (Fig. 36), and the bottom was carefully jointed and slip-feathered, the

Fig. 36—scale 1/12.

grooves being thickly painted with red lead. To economise height, the inlet screen was sunk level with the top of the sides, being supported on fillets. This screen was made like a leaf-screen, covered with perforated zinc.

Lids were made with frames of 1¼-inch wood, between which fine wire-netting was stretched (Fig. 37), and one lid was hinged

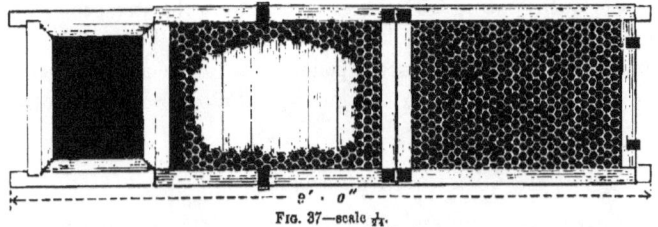
Fig. 37—scale 1/12.

to the other, so that the uppermost could fold back on the lower. This was held in position by two iron angle-pieces, from below which it could be easily slipped forward and removed, but only when the upper lid was folded back.

Two padlocks were used;—fish-breeding being a new thing to the natives, their curiosity had to be restrained by due precautions.

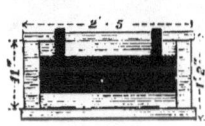
Fig. 38—scale 1/12.

The outlet (Fig. 38) was guarded by No. 7 perforated zinc, and was cut down within 3 inches of the bottom; thus a strong current was produced even when the flow of water was slight, and when the supply was plentiful the depth was easily increased by placing a piece of flannel on the outlet. Fig. 39 is a longitudinal section of the 9-feet plank pond. In it I placed some great lake trout eggs in two of the slate trays. When the fry hatched out they passed freely into the plank pond. The perforated zinc I had fastened on the outlet was quite small enough to retain the fry. The pond was set in the course of the little burn at Middlethird. All flood-water was diverted, and the supply obtained through a leaf-screen, and quite regular. I

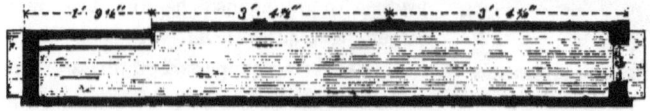

Fig. 39—scale 1/12.

thought everything safe, and was astonished to find the fry in numbers dead against the outlet. They had hatched irregularly, and were what I should now call a bad lot. They could not keep off the outlet, so it was necessary to reduce the strength of the current. I did not like to lessen the supply, and I placed a bank of fine gravel right across the pond. This made matters worse; the fry burrowed through the gravel, and died against the outlet as before. I then invented the

SAFETY-SCREEN.

It answered perfectly, and since then has, in one form or another, been in constant use. The screen is only a rectangular frame of light wood, on which is stretched No. 9 perforated zinc. This size seems large, but is safe, much more so than a smaller size. If any part of the yolk-sac slips through, the fish can draw it back without damage. With small-holed zinc death is always the result of the yolk-sac coming in contact with the zinc, as once the smallest bit is sucked through, the rest follows from the pressure of the current. Fig. 40 is a drawing of the safety-screen now in use in the hatching-house at Milnholme.

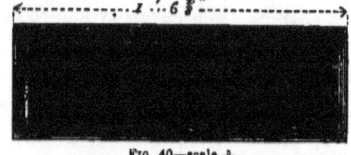

Fig. 40—scale 1/12.

The safety-screen is fixed 13 inches above the outlet by a strip of flannel doubled and passed round so as to jam the screen tightly to the pond. Nothing else will do so well as flannel; the fry seem to hate it, they will not go near it, and never try to escape under the safety-screen. If sand is placed in front of the safety-screen, the fry collect and soon remove most of it; but they leave the flannel alone. Thus the difficulty of a tight joint is overcome; no one who has not tried has any idea of the difficulty of making a joint tight enough to confine young trout. Stone says, "Then woe to the trout-breeder if his troughs are not perfectly tight! for if there is a loose joint in the box, or a nail-hole, or aperture, under or about the screen, where water comes in or out, these little creatures will be sure to find it, and one by one will go through it in thousands, even if the crevice is not much larger than would admit a snow-flake."—(*Domesticated Trout*, p. 144.)

The safety-screen is sufficiently far above the outlet to be unaffected by the suction caused by the water passing over the ledge; and as the frame is only an inch in thickness, the space for the water to flow through is nearly the section of the pond instead of a narrow edge; for example, if the plank pond is 5 feet wide, and the depth of water on the overflow is 1 inch—that is, if the surface of the water in the pond stands 1 inch above the edge of the outlet,—there will be 60 square inches of water in section; now 13 inches back the water stands its own depth above the bottom of the pond, say 13 inches (which is a good workable depth for fry); if we allow 1 inch for the thickness of the frame of the safety-screen, then 5 square feet, or 720 square inches, is in the section of water, or just twelve times as much; and, conversely, the force of the suction will be only one-twelfth.

OVA-EXTRACTOR.

The various modes of removing ova for examination, or dead ova to prevent the contamination of the surrounding eggs, were tried one after another. They are all open to the same objection, viz., that the nearest eggs to the one selected are disturbed to a greater or less extent. Perhaps the most objectionable is the French glass syphon, described by Francis Francis, and of which he furnishes a cut on page 80 of his *Fish-Culture*. It consists of a bent glass tube blown into a bulb at one end, the bulb being finished off like the mouth of a pickle-bottle, and closed by a cork through which a short straight glass tube is inserted, projecting an inch or two beyond outwards, and about half an inch inwards. The diameter of this tube should be three-eighths of an inch. I quote Mr. Francis' own words, explaining the mode of using it: "The thumb is placed on the top of the implement; the nozzle is then plunged into the water, and placed before the ova or small fry it is desired to extract, and the thumb being suddenly withdrawn, the ova is drawn up into the body of the vessel, and can be dropped out at the thumb end if required, or examined in the bowl of the instrument. This is a useful implement if it is wished to examine ova or fry without damage, but it is a clumsy affair to remove dead ova with, as it draws up everything that comes within its influence, and often more than the operator requires." Mr. Francis further writes, as to tweezers of various shapes: "These also are clumsy, and disturb the surrounding ova more than is necessary, and often crush the ova and scatter the contents, which speedily putrefy all over the tray."

He then refers to a fine needle stuck on the end of a stick and used as a spear; but from the toughness of the shell of the ovum it is very slow, and on glass grilles, where the ova lie in rows, would be impracticable. The last implement referred to is one invented by Mr. Francis himself, and, until the invention of the ova-extractor, was by far the best thing out. It is simply a fine-pointed handle to which is attached a piece of brass wire, twisted into a loop, and bent to any convenient angle. Mr. Francis justly praises it as follows: "Softly introduce it between the ova and under the one you wish to withdraw, and fetch it out swiftly but steadily. No disturbance is created, and the method is almost infallible, if quickly and neatly done, while the rapidity which can be exercised after a little practice is astonishing. A dexterous operator can pick the ova up almost as quickly as a fowl can pick up barley."

One dark afternoon in December, while I was ordering some glass tubes to experiment on grilles, my eye fell on a pipette for measuring drops. Why not reverse the principle, and use the suction caused by the air expelled from the bulb to hold an egg against the end of the tube? I went home and measured the eggs carefully; they were all hill-burn trout eggs, and about the same size. I then ordered a pipette to be made about 6 inches long, with a tube just large enough to admit the ovum; but the eggs, though nearly, were not precisely the same size, and one soon stuck in the tube. For five minutes I was occupied with my scarf-pin—for the egg had gone a couple of inches up before it jammed. —but to no purpose; eventually I had to remove the india-rubber and shove it out with a straw. Next day I consulted a very clever glass-blower, and by the aid of a blowpipe we put a constriction in the tube a quarter of an inch from the end, and widened the mouth to a like dimension (Fig. 41). It answered well, and now all my ova-extractors are made with tubes a quarter of an inch in diameter, inside measurement, and a constriction a little less than a quarter of an inch from the end (Fig. 42). The top of the bulb is covered with india-rubber, so that it acts as a vacuum-chamber, and the ovum is firmly held against the constriction at the end of the tube. Old tobacco-pouches make the best covers for the ova-extractors.

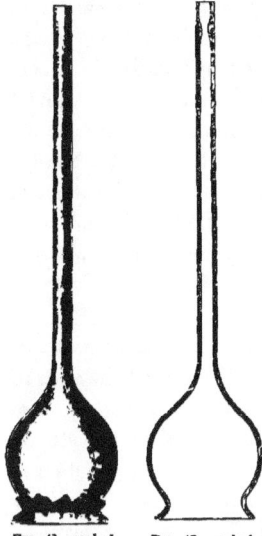

FIG. 41—scale ⅓.   FIG. 42—scale ⅓.

To use the extractor, the glass is grasped in the right hand, the ball of the thumb presses on the india-rubber and expels a small portion of air. The tube is then directed towards the dead ovum—it is not necessary to touch it,—and by gently raising the thumb the egg rises and rests in the cup without disturbing any of the surrounding ova. The quickness some girls acquire is marvellous. In the large hatching-house at Milnholme, sometimes as many as 250,000 eggs have to be gone over for packing in one day, and all the unimpregnated ova picked out; and even where the number is as high as 5 per cent., though this is unusual, two girls can get over the work easily in a morning.

SEASON 1873-74—FISH-CULTURE.

In the autumn of 1873 I collected about thirty small trout from the hill burns on Sauchiemuir, and confined them in the Francis box, which was placed in the stream in Middlethird wood. On October 23d I went to the box in the morning as usual, and I found all the fish dead. The night previous had been very stormy and wet, the stream had risen, and brought down fresh-fallen leaves in thousands. The grating which admitted the water had clogged, and the flow through the box stopping, all the fish were suffocated. Next day I invented the leaf-screen. This was my first experience of fish-culture. A week later I caught a few more trout, and obtained some 3000 ova.

I liberated the kelts, and filled the Francis box with stones and gravel to the level of the overflow. I then buried the eggs in the gravel, and dug them up once a week to see how they were getting on. This killed some, and the sediment from the stream clogged up the interstices between the bits of gravel, and smothered the rest. Why do not eggs laid by trout and salmon in a river die from this cause? The answer is twofold: first, that many of the eggs deposited do actually perish, and this is one of the ways in which drainage affects the supply of fish in the inland waters; and, secondly, that the parts of the river bed chosen by the fish are those where the current to a great extent prevents the deposit of sediment amongst the gravel. Again, in many parts of a river, especially those parts chosen for redds, there are springs of pure or at least filtered water rising through the gravel. These conditions not being present in the Francis box, it is only suitable for hatching ova when it is supplied with very pure water. By the end of December I had very few eggs left, so I wrote to Mr. Parnaby at Keswick, and purchased some great lake trout eggs, which he had imported from Switzerland. The slate trays were ready by the New Year, and, as I had no hatching-house, I placed two trays in the 9-feet plank pond, and laid the eggs on the slate. They were about a month from hatching when they arrived. I had not thought of placing a screen in front of the spouts of the slate trays, and was much surprised one morning to find about half the alevins had passed into the 9-feet pond. This was the more annoying, as I had intended to move the pond further down. However, the stream at Middlethird could not be depended upon much later, and I levelled a part of the bank just above the junction of the Middlethird burn with the stream from the Grey Mare's Tail. Across the latter I made a dam to raise the water, and left the Middlethird burn to take away the waste. I then got as many foresters as possible, and taking the end of the 9-feet pond myself, carried it bodily, with its water and fish,—for there was no way of catching them out of the gravel without hurting them,—out of the wood and through the park for a distance of half a mile. Since that day I have never put gravel into a box with young fry ; it is so easy to pour them out if the bottom of the box is clean, and no danger of harming a single alevin.

I then placed the 9-feet pond on the place I had levelled, and fed the water from the dam through a V-spout, the front of which was protected by fir branches, to prevent leaves or débris stopping the mouth of the spout. The old course of the Grey Mare's Tail stream I left free to take the overflow of the dam, and I thought things were safe. But I was mistaken. Below the dam the Loch Coulter burn passes under a bridge in Stockbridge wood, and immediately above the bridge the Grey Mare's Tail stream, reinforced by the Middlethird burn, joins it. With the first big spate, this bridge dammed the water back to the foot of the dam, and reached the 9-feet pond. At first there did not seem much danger, but by four in the afternoon the flood stood level with the top of the dam, and the 9-feet pond began to float down stream ; the head keeper had come to my assistance, and we both were in the water up to our waists trying to fasten ropes to the pond, when the keeper lost his footing, and in trying to save himself, as he could not swim, upset the 9-feet pond. The lids being of wire-netting, of course most of the Swiss trout escaped, but some were found in the pond when it righted; luckily it had not turned over, and we got it securely tied, and, after the water fell a little, replaced. After this loss I surveyed all the district round

FISH-CULTURE. 101

for miles for a suitable site, and at last fixed on Howietoun, on the Loch Coulter burn, which is regulated by a sluice on the loch, and under perfect control. The water too was of the most suitable character.

The fry had been several months in the 9-feet pond on the Grey Mare's Tail stream before they escaped, and I had fed them on raw rabbits' liver. I found a sprig of water-cress which had rooted in the gravel kept the water sweet; for wherever there is gravel there is dirt, and every little thing that tends to cleanliness is of importance; I laid great store by that plant of water-cress; it grew rapidly, and the fry used to shelter in hundreds below it; but one day I took a friend to see the fry. He had been long in England, and acquired a taste for water-cress, and, before I knew the plant was in danger, he had eaten some, and pulled off most of the rest. Never show fish to visitors, at least without taking extraordinary precautions. One never knows what harm they may unwittingly do: they may move a sluice, or open a valve, or poke a stick through a fine screen, or feed the wrong fish, or frighten the tame ones till they refuse to come to their meals; for trout, to thrive, must be fed regularly and with judgment; in short, the less trout are disturbed the better.

My first experiment in carrying fry was made in May, when I took about a couple of hundred of the Swiss fry to Mayfield, where they were placed in a small pond under half an acre in the garden of the late Provost Russel of Falkirk. The journey was only some 10 miles in a dog-cart, yet I thought it necessary to change the water when half way, not knowing that the water fry are reared in was much safer to travel in. Now-a-days yearlings are sent from Stirling to Cornwall without change of water and without loss.

These fry afterwards grew to average 2 pounds in weight, a wonderful growth in so confined a space for a fish which inhabits deep lakes like Geneva.

A few weeks after the 9-feet pond upset I took the remaining fry, numbering 117, and turned them out in Loch Coulter. Nine years afterwards one of these was taken, or rather knocked on the head, weighing 7 pounds, and measuring $33\frac{1}{4}$ inches. Old age I now know to have been the cause of this extraordinary disparity between length and weight, but two years ago I was hardly sufficiently advanced to be quite sure. He must have been over 16 pounds in his prime. A large proportion of these Swiss fry gave an account of themselves afterwards. Although the loch was swarming with perch when they were turned in, these in four years became comparatively scarce, nor have they ever since been caught in anything like the same numbers as formerly. Prior to 1874 I do not think there ever were any trout in Loch Coulter before I introduced these strangers, at least not for many years. Some time last century the loch was raised and a sluice placed on the outlet for the mills below, most of which are on the Bannock burn, and as the loch is fed by springs there is no place for trout to spawn. A small ditch runs into the west end of the water, but most summers this is completely dry. And even if trout did succeed in depositing a few eggs, they would come to nothing, or if they did nine years out of ten the fry would all be dried up before they were able to take care of themselves: fry seldom do anything in still deep water before August in Scotland. For several years I caught Swiss trout in Goldenhoof dam, which supplies the mills on the Bannock burn; but I found it necessary to run the dam dry for some time to enable me to clean and enlarge it, so as to retain the water I drew from Loch Coulter at night, so that there might be no waste of water-power. Since the dam has been restocked I have cut off the passage of wild fish from below, and have not seen any more there.

Such were the results of my first season's fish-culture.

As yet I had no hatching-house, and the experiments were carried on in the open air, with only such shelter as the trees over the stream afforded. The necessity for shelter was felt, and a hatching-house begun early in the spring of 1874.

CHAPTER IX.

Season 1874-75.

CONSTRUCTION—MIDDLETHIRD HATCHING-HOUSE.

In Sauchie Park there is a little glen running north-east from the large wood, and separating the kennels from Sauchie House; a small stream runs through the centre, rising near the basaltic crags overhanging the Bannock burn, and fed by springs in the limestone that outcrops in parts of the large wood. The water is very clear, of even temperature, and in every way suitable for egg-hatching; but in summer it is uncertain, and in dry seasons it vanishes entirely. It cannot therefore be used for rearing fry.

This seeming defect has since been found to be perfectly immaterial. The water which produces the firmest, darkest, and strongest alevins is far too pure to prove a kindly nurse to young fry.

This burn in Middlethird wood being all that could be desired in winter, I saw no reason why the fry should not be removed in summer, when the water got light. At that date expense also was a great consideration, and it was advisable not to attempt anything the ordinary estate labour could not overtake. The powers of the foresters were limited in the extreme, and the gamekeepers, though very anxious, were hardly up to navvy work.

I drew the ground-plan to suit the site, and designed a shed to suit the capacity of the foresters. The shed answered so well I will hereafter refer to it by the dignified name of hatching-house; and its simple construction renders it a useful model for those who wish to undertake trout or salmon culture on a modest scale. The description will not be without value.

I chose the least uneven part in the bottom of the glen, cut a few trees, and removed the soil down to the rock,—no very difficult matter, as there was merely a few inches on the surface.

The foundation thus obtained was of rotten whinstone, which after two days' quarrying yielded a level site. As the rock in the foundation forbade posts being driven in the usual way, I got a blown-down beech-tree cut up into four planks, two for the sides of the new house, and two for the ends. The planks were 6 inches thick, and from 10 to 14 inches broad. They were laid on the foundation, and bolted together to form a frame on which the the door and corner posts were set up; intermediate posts were placed where necessary, and a wall-plate on the top, on which the roof rested. In the two ends above the wall-plate two windows were fitted, each as large as the angle of the roof would admit; they were provided with shutters to darken the house when I was not working in it. Ventilation was made by leaving the eaves open. (They had afterwards to be protected by wire-netting, as the birds got in and made a mess. I am sorry to say a robin actually was suspected of eating the ova in one of the trays.) The windows were also covered. The house was built entirely of home wood grown on the estate, sawn into 7-inch sarking at the saw-mill at Milnholme, now used in connection with the hatching-house there. The whole house was built clinker, that is, with the boards overlapping a little. The roof was made in the same way as the walls, of sarking overlapping; the couples were given a high pitch. The door was made by the estate carpenter, who also fitted the shutters to the windows; all else was done by the foresters. See plan of the house, showing dimensions (Fig. 64, page 118).

MIDDLETHIRD DAM.

While the hatching-house was being built, with the assistance of the head keeper I made the dam above (Fig. 43). The dam was built in the shape of a horse-shoe, and formed right across the old course of the burn by a row of large whinstones such as dry dikes are generally built of in this part of Scotland. Behind, and with a foot of interval, a second row was formed, and the space between carefully packed with well-puddled clay.

FIG. 43—scale 1/12.

A V-SHAPED SPOUT

was then placed on the first row of stones, and two sluices fitted in the spout,—one in the line of the stream discharging the water on a leaf-screen, the other at a considerable angle to be used for washing the filter-screens or any other purpose. Below is a drawing of the spout (Fig. 44).

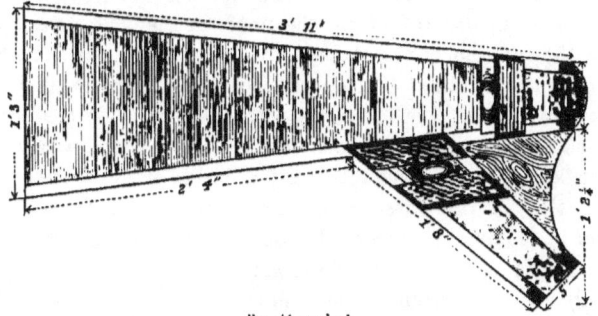

Fig. 44—scale $\frac{1}{12}$.

The dam was then heightened by another course of stones, and clay again placed behind them, the whole being covered with turf

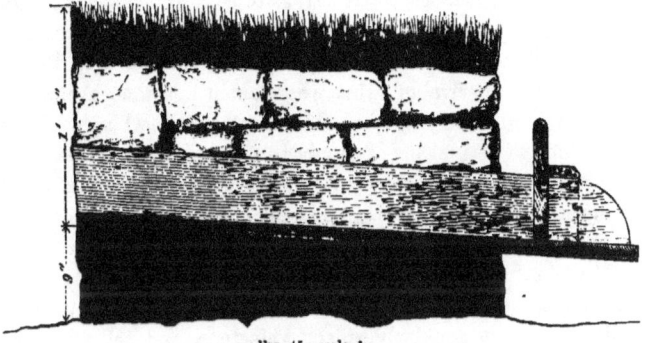

Fig. 45—scale $\frac{1}{12}$.

to protect the clay (Fig. 45). This dam has now been built eleven years, and is still water-tight; it has only once required repair, and that was in the second season, when it was pointed inside below the water-line.

The sluice fitted near the upper end of the dam was at first only intended for cleaning it out, but it was found in extraordinary spates that the spout shot the water over the leaf-screen, and although the conducting spout from the screen was so arranged that no loss ever ensued, it was felt that the possible danger should be obviated. This was done very simply by cutting the sluice-boards, so that, whenever there was sufficient water passing the V-spout on to the leaf-screen, the water in the dam stood level with the top edge of the sluice-board. The sluice was the same width as the mouth of the V-spout, but the clearance behind the sluice was perfect, the fall being perpendicular, while the spout lay at a very slight angle, and, moreover, from its shape, was necessarily less than half this width a few inches in rear, the effect being that, as the water rose, much more than half the flood-water passed over the sluice. The object in the wide mouth of the -spout (Fig. 46) is to take all the water required without raising the level in the dam perceptibly, and thus ensure an even head. The reason of raising the dam at all is to stop gravel and dirt being carried on to the leaf-screen, as well as to gain a convenient height for placing the screen. The mode of regulating dams by overflow sluices is still common in parts of England, and was used by the monks. It is a survival of a time when labour was almost valueless, as, although admirably adapted for waste water, nothing could be more primitive as a means of supply to a water-wheel. It is much as if the supply were obtained by building a beavers' dam to collect the water, and then removing stick by stick to obtain the power. On next page is a drawing of the sluice (Figs. 47, 48).

FIG. 46—scale 1/12.

The next work was to excavate a ditch to take all the flood-water passing the sluice; this proved a hard task, the rock being basalt, or, as it is popularly called, whinstone, and the formation known to quarrymen as "teeth on edge." Of course a working face was impossible, and the "quarrying" consisted in smashing the "teeth" out with a sixty-pound hammer. This took me weeks, and I often look back with amusement at brute force painfully overcoming obstacles in weeks which a little skill would have removed in as many days.

OVERFLOW SLUICE.

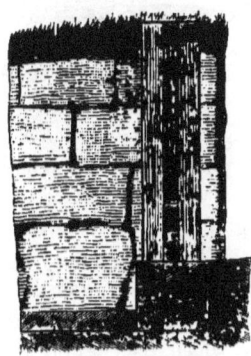

Fig. 47—scale 1/15.

Fig. 48—scale 1/15.

When the course for the waste water was finished, a rustic bridge was formed of wood, and a second below in front of the door of the hatching-house.

A LEAF-SCREEN

was placed 2 inches below the narrow end of the V-spout at an angle of 10 degrees from the horizontal. This is a most valuable

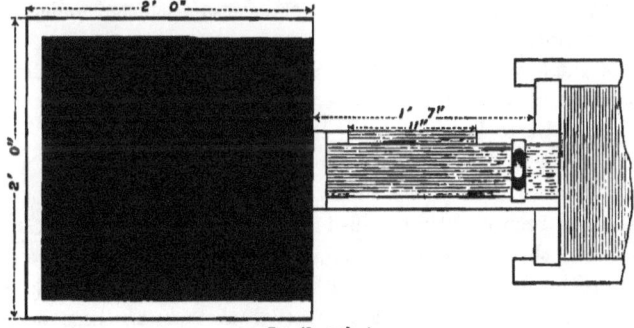

Fig. 49—scale 1/15.

invention. It consists of a frame batten, with a bottom of flooring and a top of perforated zinc stretched on a moveable frame (Fig. 49). A pipe is inserted in the centre of one end of the box (Fig. 50) to carry off the cleaned water, while all leaves and débris are swept off the zinc by the force of the water.

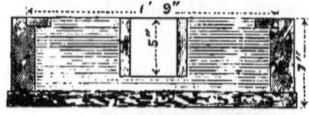

Fig. 50—scale 1/12.

Care must be taken to place it at an angle to the direction of the stream, and the lower edge must be given a slight fall. The principle is, that water passes over the zinc with sufficient force to keep it clean; the swirl formed by the hang of the screen and the angle of its inclination greatly assists this. When the quantity is insufficient to fill the pipe, it all passes through the screen, and the débris, leaves, etc., collect, from the lower edge of the zinc upwards, till they almost cut off the water, which then begins to flow over the top, and soon cleans the screen again. In floods, when much more water is passing the screen than the pipe can take, the surge back from the full pipe clears the surface from any débris held by the suction of the water. The only danger, if the screen be placed in an exposed situation, is cat ice, which might freeze to the zinc; but in practice it is found that although a bridge of ice forms across the screen the water passes freely under. The great principle is to have a little waste always running over, and a perfectly even flow through the pipe is assured. But the screen will also act in the most satisfactory manner under all circumstances.

A small sluice (Fig. 51) is formed behind the box to regulate the flow of water through the pipe. This should be set so as to keep the water level with the lower edge of the screen-box, so that no rise of the stream may increase unduly the supply. The leaf-screen has since been slightly modified to enable it to be placed in the water-course itself, thus avoiding the expense of building a dam. I have now had one at work at Craigend for eight years, and although the zinc has been many times renewed, the screen has never once failed me: it has always taken in the last drop of water in dry weather; it has never once clogged in floods; it has never frozen, though some winters have been severe; and, lastly, it has required no attention except new zinc at most once a year,—no daily inspection, no hourly cleaning, as I have too often known hakes or gratings require in wet weather.

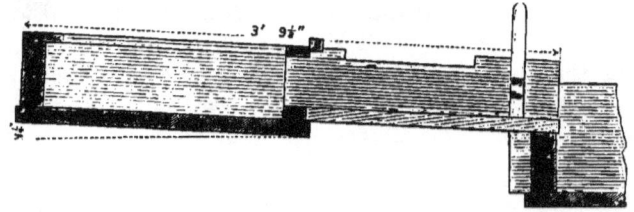

Fig. 52—scale $\frac{1}{12}$.

A short spout from the leaf-screen (Fig. 52) conveys the water to a filter. This spout was cut on one side so as to give an overflow, and covered with perforated zinc No. 9 to guard against any leaves or dirt being washed in off the top of the zinc of the leaf-screen. Both this spout and the end of the leaf-screen are supported over the old bed of the stream, so any débris washed off them is freely carried away. At the lower end of the spout a sluice is fixed to regulate the supply to the filter; this is set against a head of water equal to the depth of the interior of the spout at the cut, so that no more than the maximum supply required can pass. All over this of course flows through the cut in the side of the spout, and the flow into the filter remains constant.

It is unsafe to attempt to regulate water by a sluice until it has been passed through a leaf-screen; in fact, with burn-water it is impossible, as sooner or later the sluice will clog. Water may be passed over an overflow sluice with safety, but it cannot be passed under a sluice under the pressure of a head of water, however small, before it has been screened, without the certainty of its stopping. If this is forgotten the penalty will be loss, perhaps total loss.

MIDDLETHIRD HATCHING-HOUSE.

Water must never be passed through any valve unless the water has first been passed through some screen sufficiently fine to ensure the valve remaining free. This is a first principle of fish-culture, and applies equally to taps and sluices. There is however one form of sluice which is safe with unscreened spring-water. This consists of a set of sluices, all fitting the same groove, and bored with round holes with a brace and cutter-bit, the holes varying in diameter from one just large enough to pass the smallest supply used, to one that will pass the maximum. These holes must all be centred the same height above the lower edge of the sluice, so that the head of water is equal over the centre of the aperture; no difficulty will then be found in regulating the supply through them. This is made plain in the sketch below (Fig. 53).

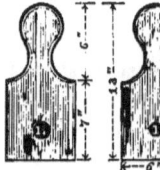

FIG. 53—scale 1/12.

PLANK FILTER.

The filter, slightly modified from the one described by Livingston Stone on page 51 of his *Domesticated Trout*, was built of 2-inch plank (Fig. 54), and the screens fitted in grooves cut slanting in the sides; a 1½-inch hole was bored in front of the lowest

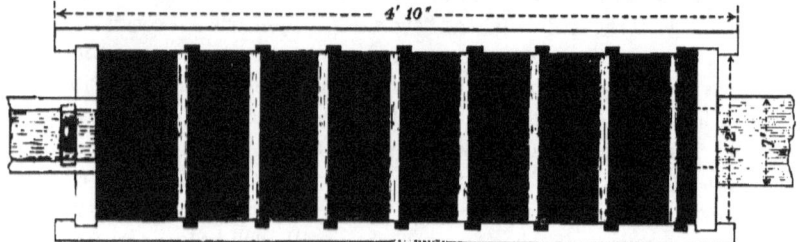

FIG. 54—scale 1/12.

screen, and a wood plug fitted for cleaning (Fig. 56). The filter was charred inside, and painted outside with three coats of red lead; a light lid of lining, also painted, covered the filter, and two straps of flooring, 3 inches wide, nailed inside, kept the screens from rising, which they had a tendency to do when clogged.

This floating of the screens was very troublesome at first. The upper screen, or, more likely, No. 2, would clog, and the water flow over on the next. They are about 1 inch below the top edge of the filter. The screen in front of No. 2 now floats and discharges most of the débris it has collected on to the next. The first seldom rises until No. 3 has clogged, as the weight of the supply falling on it from the spout keeps it to some extent in its place, and also cleaner than the lower ones. The simple expedient of nailing the straps (Fig. 55) on the under side of the lid so as to engage the upper edges of the screens overcame this difficulty, and prolific source of dirt and annoyance,—the weight of the lid (Fig. 56) being sufficient to overcome the tendency to

Fig. 55—scale 1/12.

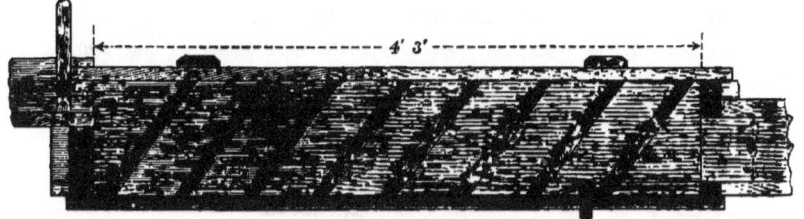

Fig. 56—scale 1/12.

float. The screens were first covered with flannel, as recommended by Stone. I soon found they required more time and attention than I could afford. Fine wire was substituted, sixty-four threads to the inch; then coarser wire, thirty-two threads or thereabouts; afterwards, when a second filter was added—above the hatching-house, but below this one,—the wire was used as coarse as sixteen threads to the inch. The daily cleaning of

MIDDLETHIRD HATCHING-HOUSE.

the screens was very simple. They were merely reversed, and held for a few seconds below the side sluice from the V-spout, and then replaced, care being taken not to move the lowest one oftener than necessary, and always to remove the plug and clean the bottom of the filter first.

Frost never interfered with the working of the filter, but the sheltered position and the comparatively high temperature of the stream to a large extent account for this. I do not think such a filter would be safe in many situations in Scotland; in the south of England, on the contrary, it would be safe, the depth enabling it to stand a long and severe storm.

A dike was next constructed from the lower end of the filter to the hatching-house, and on it a covered spout of flooring was laid, the soil being made up level with the dike on one side, and rising perpendicularly from the old course of the stream. By this means the spout was at once supported and protected from frost. The old course of the stream received all the waste from the filter, and also from the leaf-screen, and passed along the back of the hatching-house, immediately below which it received the used water of the boxes and trays. A new course in front of the house carried the overflow from the dam. This new course required to be carefully built with stone until past the hatching-house, as the soil above the whinstone was very free and sandy. The two courses joined a little below the house, and flowed on in the old course (Fig. 57).

FIG. 57—scale ₁⁄₁₀.

SLATE FILTERS.

The set of slate trays, one of which is described in the last chapter, being ready early in summer, I had two slate filters made to match,—one to use at Middlethird and the other for Craigend hatching-room. The bottom of each was the same size as that of a slate tray, but the ledge was placed on the sides instead of the ends. They were made 9 inches deep inside, and divided by two divisions into two compartments of $7\frac{1}{2}$ inches and one of 3 inches (Fig. 58). Two frames of wood, well charred, were covered with wire-cloth and rested on the ledges 1 inch above the bottom;

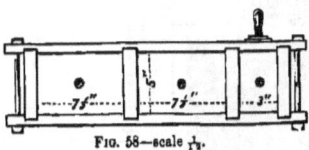

Fig. 58—scale ¹⁄₁₂.

the two compartments were then filled with washed and boiled gravel to within 3 inches of the top. Three holes are bored, one in each compartment, to facilitate cleaning, and a hole near the top in the last division admits the filtered water to the feeding-spout (Fig. 59). The division between the two filtering compartments is stopped 1 inch from the bottom. The action is as follows:—The water is received into the first compartment, either from the cistern, as at Craigend, or from the house-filter, as at Middlethird; in both cases the

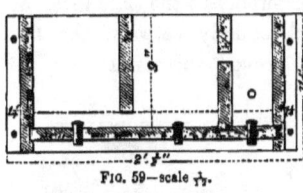

Fig. 59—scale ¹⁄₁₂.

supply is regulated above the slate filter, which must be regarded as an extra purifier merely. The water falls through the gravel, and passes freely into the centre compartment, where it rises through the wire-cloth and gravel, and falls into the small compartment, from which it passes to the trays (Fig. 60). The advantage of this filter is the very large filtering area it possesses compared to the space occupied and the quantity of gravel required. By removing the corks the filter can be cleaned in a minute if necessary. The only objection I found was its liability to freeze at Middlethird, where it was subsequently discarded, and an extra slate tray substituted; but at Middlethird I had placed a

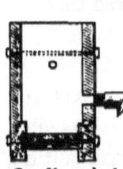

Fig. 60—scale ¹⁄₁₂.

WOOD FILTER

inside the house to receive and divide the water used in hatching (Fig. 61); it held three screens, and the water was dammed back

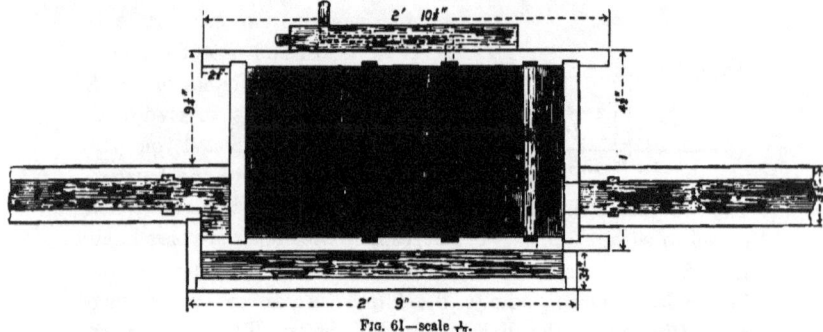

Fig. 61—scale 1/12.

by an overflow-board to secure a full supply to the slate filter, all passing the overflow being divided equally between the two wooden hatching-boxes. This box proved successful; Fig. 62 is a section. The principal advantage is that it never freezes up, as the depth is sufficient to allow the water to pass below any ice likely to form during the night, while, the screens being some distance below the top, when the first one clogs,

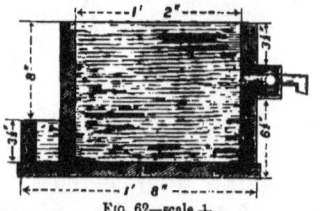

Fig. 62—scale 1/12.

the water merely runs over its edge on to the second, and so on. The importance of this is apparent when it is remembered that the water off for a single hour may mean the loss of the ova or fry in all the trays below. Should taps be used for regulating the supply, an overflow must be fixed, over which a constant run must be kept, else the flow from the taps will not be regular. One of the most important points to attend to in fish-culture, and one of the most difficult to attain, is—perfect control over the supply. Perfect regularity of supply, whether the source from which it is drawn is in flood or low, whether the leaves in October are turning the stream into a vegetable soup, or the frosts of December chill the water till it freezes to the screens in passing through, or the drought has diminished its volume till there is barely sufficient to fill the conducting spout. The principle of safety is the same : it is to be found in the "theory of waste." To make this plain in the case of water-supply (for the theory of waste applies to nearly every process in fish-culture), we have only to remember a chain is no stronger than its weakest link. No more can be done with water in fish-hatching than can be done with the least supply running through the pipes on the driest day of the hatching season. After this quantity has been ascertained, all over may and should be regarded as waste ; the hatching-house tap or sluice should be set to take this, and no more. Above the hatching-house tap (which in the case now under consideration is in the filter-box) an over-

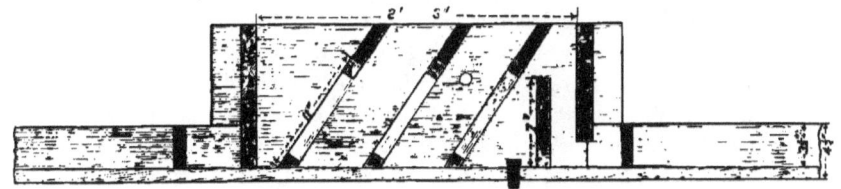

FIG. 63—scale $\tfrac{1}{12}$.

flow must be formed, care being taken to make it as wide as space will allow. So long as a drop of water passes the overflow, so long will the head of water remain constant, and (since the taps or sluices are below the filter-screens, they are always free from obstructions) the flow to the hatching-trays will be absolutely constant. The theory of waste applies most strongly to the intakes of the main supply ; but it may be convenient to consider here the nature of the theory, more especially as to many it will seem opposed to old notions. In Nature, "who never errs," young fish are produced in quantities so great, that, if they all attained the age of even one year, the waters would be overstocked and pollute the riparian land.

Where the conditions are so variable, and the limits between which existence is possible are so narrow, without waste there could be no survival. With large numbers the loss of entire broods often opens a more favourable field for the remainder. So with the regulation of water-supply: so long as some waste flows over, so long the pipes and spouts and sluices distribute an even supply, —so long, and no longer. It is only to hold as waste, water in excess of the permanent supply, an excess which, if used, would assuredly, sooner or later—but most probably very much sooner— land the user in trouble, and probably prove the destruction of the whole season's work. Nor should it be supposed this seeming waste cannot be safely utilised. Outside, much assistance can be got from the surplus. The readiest use to put it to is to pass it over the main screen to the works. If this is done with skill, no attendance will be required on that screen—a matter of no small importance, as those who have care of fish-works soon discover. The *modus operandi* will be shown in its place when the intakes come to be described. Enough has now been said to fix the reader's attention on the theory of waste. When his boxes are overcrowded with fry, let him remember the theory of waste. If it is set at nought, disaster will follow. If he is wise, he will pause before he piles his ova inches deep, in the Canadian fashion, as shown at the London Fisheries Exhibition of 1883.

The first season the incubators in the hatching-house consisted of one set of slate trays and two hatching-boxes of my own design. These were the forerunners of those now so well known at Howietoun; in fact, they differed only in being half the size. The length was almost the same, but they were only 10 inches wide, inside measurement. As, when I come to the description of the Milnholme hatching-houses, it will be necessary to discuss the general principles governing the hatching of trout ova, it will be sufficient here to consider the mechanical construction of the boxes and grilles.

The first object is to convey a sufficient supply of oxygen to each ovum; the second is to arrange so that no sediment may cover the eggs; the third is simplicity for working; and the last, protection from injury. The first object is attained by dis-

Fig. 64 - scale 1/16.
PLAN OF MIDDLETHIRD HATCHING-HOUSE IN 1874-75.

tributing the current so as to flow evenly in the plane of the ova. Danger from sediment renders it advisable to leave some space between the bottom of the tray and the ova, and experience has shown the best results are obtained with not more than an inch of water over the eggs. At least 1¼ inch is required below the ova, so that the current may be increased just before hatching without disturbing the sediment at the bottom; there is always some deposit, even from the clearest spring-water. The width of the box is important. It is much more difficult in practice to ensure an even flow where the width is great than where it is narrow, and the Howietoun hatching-box is now divided by a moveable board; but at Middlethird I did not require to deal with large numbers, at least not at the time of which I am now writing. The width was fixed solely with the view of keeping the current under control, and 10 inches inside measurement was thought suitable. I afterwards found another reason for this width when I made the glass grilles. The hollow tubes of glass are pliant to a degree, and if more than 9 inches long—that is, 8½ between the fastenings—they bend out in the middle, and allow the ova to slip through. The width being determined, I considered whether a slight fall on the box would not be of service; and the first season I fixed the boxes with a fall of a quarter of an inch to the foot. This did not answer, as, when the water was turned off for cleaning the filter, the eggs nearest the top of the box were left dry. I then tried heightening the water in the box, by placing flannel on the outlet. This was worse; the eggs at the lower end of the box were too deep: they got too little oxygen, the current being modified by the depth of the water. I next set the boxes level, and placed cleats across the bottom, which answers perfectly, and are so used in the Howietoun hatching-boxes at present. Having at last achieved an even flow, the eggs are supplied with oxygen by the water, and the gases given off in the process of incubation removed. The amount of gas given off is great, and, if not removed would suffocate the embryo, especially just before hatching. Place a dozen or two eyed ova in a dish, and leave them for a couple of days in a room, the windows of which are kept closed, and although the embryos are still alive, the smell in the room will be overpowering. A small room is the best for this experiment; if the temperature is above 50° F. one night is sufficient.

Another mode of demonstrating the exudance of gases by the ova is to place a single ovum on a plate of glass, or between two glass rods, with only a drop of water, and in a damp atmosphere; and also lay a few eggs on damp live moss, and some on swan's down in the same atmosphere. In a couple of days the embryos in the ova in the drops of water on the glass will be dead, with the white streak so suggestive of suffocation; those on the moss will be as fresh as the moment they were laid out, and those on the swan's down pale, but quite alive. This shows the first were suffocated by the deficiency of oxygen, caused by the gas given off by the ovum being retained by the drop of water, and possibly forming a cloud round the ovum, as at first sight one would suppose that in air (which surrounds the top half of the egg, for the drop need not cover the ovum to drown it) oxygen would have free access and preserve life; but it is not so. Those on the moss do best, because the live moss feeds on or rather absorbs the gas given off by the embryos, leaving the shell free to receive all the oxygen necessary for the growth of the future fish. In the last case, the swan's down acts merely by capillary attraction, and the result is a pale embryo, the gases having only been partially removed, and still to some extent preventing the free absorption of oxygen. In the above experiments the temperature never fell below 45° or rose above 50° F. In a low temperature the life of the embryo is so sluggish that no difference would have been perceptible between the three lots in two days. Had the temperature been high, and the eggs nearly hatched, those on the moss would still have received no injury, as the moss would itself have stimulated into quicker action, unless, indeed, some of the alevins were hatched prematurely; those on the swan's down would become very pale indeed; and those in the drops of water would die in less than twelve hours. These experiments are of the utmost importance in connection with the transportation of salmon and trout ova.

Sediment had much to answer for in the early days of trout-culture; all sorts of disasters were laid to its charge. If there were an undue proportion of deformities, it was due to sediment; if half the eggs were lost during the incubation, it was due to sediment; if the outlet clogged, and the box ran over, it was all the fault of the sediment. Now it is possible that some deformities may be caused by sediment; it is even probable it is so; but the experiments with young breeders have shown that improper selection of the parents is a much more prolific cause, and hybridism sometimes produces an entire batch of malformations. If the ova lie on gravel, and sediment is allowed to collect, it will smother most of the embryos,—but this is supposing an extreme case. The real harm results much more frequently from inconsiderate washing at an early stage. Sediment sometimes may cause an overflow, but only where the outlet screen is too fine, and at certain stages the fry are not slow in taking advantage of the chance of escape.

Two inches of free space between the bottom of the hatching-box and the glass grille is ample provision against sediment; a little on the eggs at first, or up to the end of the first half of the hatching period, does little harm; after that time the eggs may be washed with safety. In a well-arranged establishment there should not be enough to discolour the eggs. But at the time of which I am now writing nearly everything had to be discovered—that was part of the charm in fish-culture,—and sediment was a terrible bugbear, and had to be provided against. Flannel filters, wire screens, and that dirtiest of all abominations, gravel filters, were thought necessary, and the simple settling well was unthought of. Sediment constituted a real danger, the more so on account of the precautions taken against it.

To prevent an overflow, No. 9 zinc was used on all the outlets, and after the fry hatched a safety-screen with No. 8 was fitted so soon as the grilles were taken out. This screen was 1 inch lower than the sides of the box, so, even if it did clog, the fry were to a large extent caught between it and the outlet screen, only a few hanging themselves in the No. 9 zinc in the short time elapsing till the next visit of the attendant.

Simplicity for working is the next thing to be considered. There must be no crevices for dirt to lodge, or young fry to suffocate under; there must be no part of the box out of sight; the whole bottom, when there are fry, and every egg, when there are ova in the box, must be capable of being searched at a glance.

The sides of the box above the ova should allow the removal of dead ova with ease, as, if the sides are too deep, the attendant will disturb other eggs, which, especially for the first month or so, is highly undesirable; if the sides are not high enough when the water is heightened for the fry, they can and will jump out.

The ends of the hatching-boxes should be made to catch all the water from the overflow without projecting unnecessarily into the hatching-house. All the fittings for the grilles should be removeable, and taken out with the grilles; this leaves the bottom of the box clear for the fry. In the first boxes at Middlethird I left the ledge which supports the grilles solid on the side. This entailed too much labour, and wasted too much wood; but I mention it to show how the Howietoun hatching-boxes have originated.

Protection from injury is now an easy matter, but at that time I did not know what to protect against. The first danger that showed itself was mice. These little rodents have a partiality for trout eggs, and made a great mess in the boxes at the beginning. But they left foot-marks one wet morning on the edge of the hatching-box, and the murder—in my eyes it was nothing less —was out. A trap supplied at once the punishment and the evidence of crime. Lids were made and fitted, and the eggs were safe. Light is a danger against which ova require protection. I do not know the reason as yet, but I have compared many millions of trout eggs, some hatched in total darkness, some in a dim light, and some in ordinary daylight; but the sun has always been excluded. The principal effect of light is premature hatching. Small eyes in the embryo are much more frequent where the eggs have been exposed to light, and if these small eyes are frequent in any box, the best thing to do is to throw them away; they are for no use. The proportion of injury due to different degrees of light I intend to treat of further on, when the Milneholme experiments are recorded.

Fungus is another cause of injury. There are two forms,—one generally referred to as byssus, the other as saprolegnia, akin to *S. ferax*, of which so much has been heard in connection with the salmon disease. Byssus is harmless in a well-regulated establishment; it grows slowly (for a fungus); it is easily seen; it never grows at all without a preventible cause, and that cause is one that never ought to exist in any fishery, viz., dead animal matter. Only go over the eggs three times a week and there will be no byssus. The other fungus is a very different thing, the most subtle and Protean of monsters, especially if the water is clear. It may have laid hold on the ova for days unperceived. No amount of attention will save the ova if once they be attacked. Shutting out all light decreases the vitality of the ogre, increasing the current strengthens the embryo in the eggs; but this fungus must be met in an earlier stage,—the boxes must be made disagreeable to him before the eggs are laid down. This is done at this fishery in the way recommended by Mr. Livingston Stone, *Domesticated Trout*, p. 48. He says: "Char the plank. This I consider very important indeed if you use plank, for you cannot be certain without charring it. Do not imagine that you are safe from fungus because your hatching-boxes themselves are well guarded from it. It may grow in the aqueduct and be borne down by the stream, and before winter is over you may find to your dismay that it has fastened its fatal grasp on your eggs; if so, they are ruined. There is no remedy for fungus which will make healthy fish of the eggs attacked."

All the hatching-boxes are charred every season. The process is very simple, and costs less than paint, and much less than asphalt varnish. A hot iron, made heavy for the purpose, and kept square at the edges, is rapidly passed over the inside of the box, and *voilà tout*. Frost is a danger, but protection must be sought in the construction of the hatching-house itself, and not in the hatching-box. The first pair of

HATCHING-BOXES

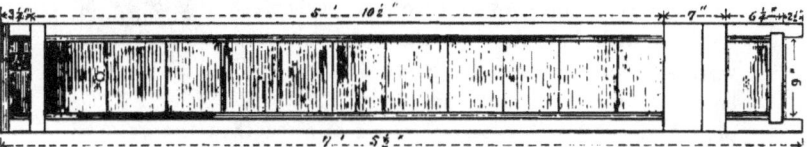

Fig. 65—scale ¼.

embodied these principles very fairly (Fig. 65). Little alteration has been found advisable; and the changes have been principally in the direction of lightness and aëration. The wood chosen was yellow pine; the sides were reduced from 2-inch plank, got by running a cleft of 3 inches. The lower edge was kept its full width, and the reduction stops 1½ inch from it. The width of the plank was 8 inches, so 6½ had to be worked down to the extent of half an inch. This was to give a support for the grilles, and also to leave more hold for the nail fastening the bottom. The bottom was of flooring, tongued and grooved, as is usual with flooring in Scotland. The back of the groove in flooring is always slack, to show a neat joint when laid; the groove therefore had to be re-dressed and deepened, and the tongue or feather squared. This is of more importance than it seems, as flooring is the most convenient size of wood in the market for nearly every purpose of fish-culture, and its last and fitness depend much on the nature of the joint. The flooring after being thus prepared was cut into short lengths, just wider than the hatching-box. The upper end of the hatching-box was of 1¼″ plank; the lower was formed of four pieces of the same—one of the depth of the water in the hatching-box, its upper edge being chamfered slightly to form an overflow. The upper piece was kept a sufficient depth for strength, and two narrow side-pieces, to stretch the zinc on, more than for strength, held the upper and lower pieces together with mortice joinings. The two ends being now complete, two grooves were run in each of

the side-pieces to receive the ends, and the box put together
Fig. 66). The bottom was next nailed on, and the tongues and
grooves well coated with red lead. Each bit of
flooring was cramped up after nailing. This must
be done with judgment, or the wood, swelling
when wet, will force open the joints, and there will
be a drip, with all its mess and misery. The sides
project about 2 inches past the ends to strengthen the grooves,
and also at the lower end to form a receptacle for the used water,
from which it may either be used for the next box or run waste as
the case may be. The last piece of the bottom is also brought out
flush with the end of the sides, and a small piece nailed across the
end, and to the projecting bottom, forming a small trough from
which the water can be disposed in many ways. The ends of the

Fig. 66—scale 1/12.

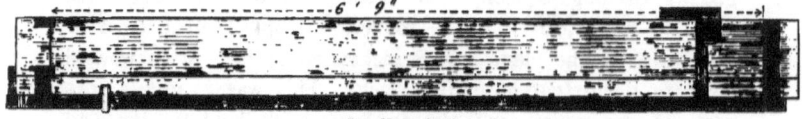

Fig. 67—scale 1/12.

flooring are dressed off, and the inside of the box well charred.
The first charring must be very thoroughly done. The hatching-
box is now ready for painting, and three coats of red lead are
recommended. The last thing is to fit a piece of No. 9 zinc over
the outlet, and the box is ready to be placed in the hatching-
house. Fig. 67 is a section of the hatching-box.

THE GLASS GRILLE

was a long time coming to its present form. At first I thought
the tubes of glass should run with the current; I now know that
eggs get more oxygen when the tubes lie across.

The first grille I made was for the slate trays. It was a light
wooden frame, the tubes running with the length, fastened at the
ends by brass rabbit-snare wire, and in the centre a twist of silver
wire to prevent the tubes spreading; this was tedious to make,
and expensive. The first grille I made for the wooden hatching-

box, the tubes were cut to 8 inches, and placed across the box, as now used, but the fastening was even more troublesome than the last. I spent many hours with a small thumb-drill and a large school slate. I cut a narrow slip off the slate the length I required for the inside of the grille frame, and with a pair of compasses I divided it accurately; and with the thumb-drill I bored holes opposite the end of each tube, and when a pair of these slips were ready, I sewed with fine wire the tubes to the slate. A quarter of the sides of the frame of the grille were cut away, forming a ledge for the slate. Thus the wood covered the wire sewing, and there was no necessity to use silver wire; brass wire would kill any ovum in contact with it. Stone says, in the *Domesticated Trout*, p. 55, "Fourteen trout eggs were placed on a copper screen, in November 1869, at Cold Spring Trout Ponds, and in fifty days they had absorbed so much copper that they were of a dark brown tinge, and hard as peas." Grilles made in this manner were an impossibility for work on more than a merely experimental scale, but had so many advantages that I persevered; and the next improvement was the substitution of perforated zinc for the slate. Two strips were cut off a sheet through contiguous lines of holes, and one was fixed in the check of the frame, and the other into a fillet. The fixing was simple, merely a draught with a sharp bradawl, and the zinc pressed in. It held as long as the wood lasted sound. But the labour of arranging the glass tubes was enormous, and if one—at that time a by no means infrequent chance—got broken, the whole had to be taken out before it could be replaced. One day I was carrying over a broken grille to the carpenter's shop (a distance of nearly two miles from Middlethird), when the idea struck me, Why should not the holes in the zinc remain whole? The apparent answer was, that any size of perforated zinc large enough to admit the glass would keep the tubes so far apart that the eggs could drop through. This was so, but I made one to try. The small ova of the burn-trout passed through with ease, not to say rapidity; the eggs of the Loch Levens behaved better; some, not many, remained on the grille. The problem was solved (Fig. 68). I had only to use a smaller size zinc, and widen the holes, and the grille was perfect. I believe I spent more thought over that mode of fastening the glass tubes into the frame than

Fig. 68—scale ½.

over any other individual part of the works (Fig. 69). Grilles were no longer impossible for the largest piscicultural establishments; they were a commercial success. Fry could now be

Fig. 69—scale ¼.

sold in hundreds of thousands from ova incubated on grilles at less money than those hatched in any other way;—yes; and leave a larger profit! The weight of the grille, dry, should equal that of the water displaced when the grille is soaked. It will then sink and rest on the supports provided; if made any heavier, the wooden frame becomes too weak, and is liable to cast. The weight is only gained in making the wood proportionally lighter than the glass, so that their combined specific gravity is that of water, or a little more. The difference in the vitality of fry is very great; and as most pisciculturists purchase their eggs as near hatching as possible, when they will stand a very strong current, the temptation to use trays on the deep principle is very great, and the advantages of grilles are yet but little understood. This will be treated of more fully hereafter (Fig. 70).

Fig. 70—scale ¼.

The next point in the hatching-boxes was to introduce the water; and here I had several failures. The first idea was to let the water fall on a sheet of perforated zinc (Figs. 71, 72, 73).

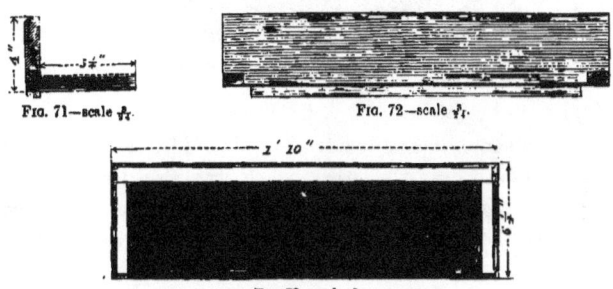

Fig. 71—scale 1/12.   Fig. 72—scale 1/12.

Fig. 73—scale 1/12.

This had answered so well in the leaf-screen, I did not see any objection. But I soon was undeceived. The water on the small sheet behaved abominably. The very excellence of its power of keeping the sheet free slopped half the water on the floor whenever the supply was increased. This in frost meant the floor one sheet of ice at Middlethird.

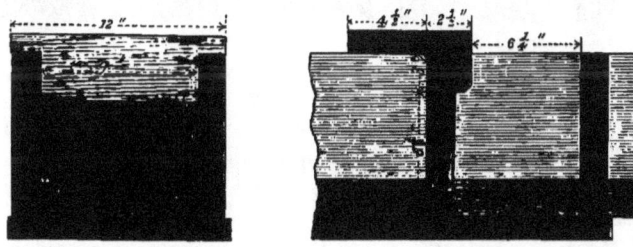

Fig. 74—scale 1/12.   Fig. 75—scale 1/12.

The next move was to let the water fall freely into the end of the hatching-box, and drop a perpendicular screen in front of the top grille (Figs. 74, 75). This was all very well when the eggs were incubating, but after the fry hatched, they amused themselves by getting under this breakwater, and could not be brought back for feeding.

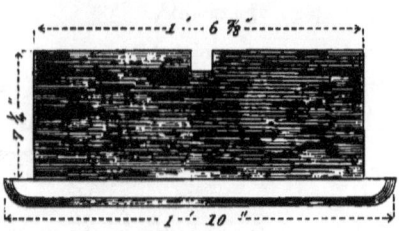

FIG. 76—scale 1/7.

At last a simple board was tried, and found to work (Fig. 76). The water spread over the board, which was placed at an angle, and was thoroughly aërated. It was the cheapest, and there was no mess, as the low edge of the breakwater touched the top end of the hatching-box, and the water passed evenly through the fissure. Sections of this breakwater and the safety-screen are given below (Fig. 77).

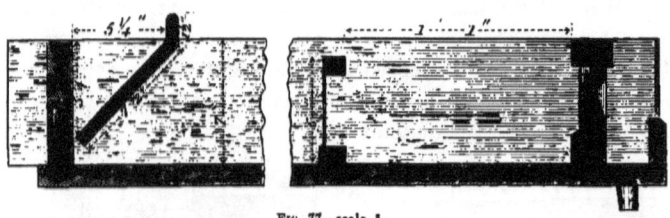

FIG. 77—scale 1/7.

When the fry hatched, a safety-screen was fitted in the boxes, and great trouble was found in making it tight, on account of the ledge left for the support of the grilles. Now, with loose fillets, which are removed, leaving a square corner, there is no difficulty.

The two hatching-boxes and the slate trays were arranged in

I

the upper end of the house, and a close wooden trough, in the shape of the letter E without its centre prong, was connected with the supply outside; and passing under the beech base of the end

THE E-SPOUT.

Fig. 78—scale 1/4.

Fig. 79—scale 1/4.

Fig. 80—scale 1/4.

wall of the house, and under the floor to a little past the centre of the doorway, and then rising to feed a set of rearing-boxes, the object being to leave as much floor-space as possible. A thermometer was inserted in this leg to show the temperature of the water.

A frame was made as a stand for the five rearing-boxes, and a waste-spout was led along the outlet ends; a supply-spout started from the upright of the E-trough, and fed all the rearing-boxes (Fig. 81). This feeding-spout was made much larger than necessary for conveying the water, so that the water might be dead opposite the little sluices that supplied the rearing-boxes; and it was

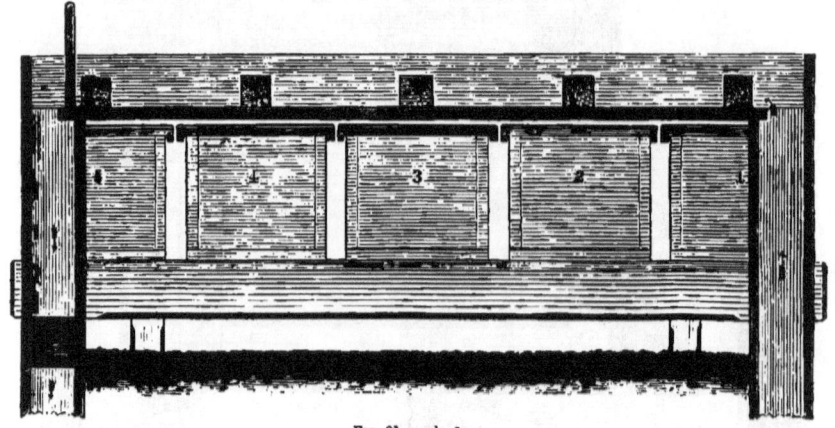

Fig. 81—scale 1/12.

thought that the sluices could be set against a head of say 4 inches of water, and run a constant flow; but in practice it was not so. I therefore filled the grooves of the sluices with a 4-inch piece of wood (Fig. 82), and made them into overflow sluices; the water then either divided equally over all, or was shut off any desired boxes entire by shutting a sluice above the 4-inch piece (Fig. 83). This is a sufficient power of regulation even in the largest works, for it is not possible to feed more than a small number of boxes from one spout, on account of the expense of a very long level. This expense is due not only to the long and expensive foundations required, but to the necessity of increasing

Fig. 82—scale 1/12.

Fig. 83—scale 1/12.

the size of the feeding- or rather distributing- spout out of all proportion to the increase of the quantity of water. If this is not done, the current is so much stronger at the supply end, it sets past the first sluices, and not only vents irregularly, but is always short in quantity.

In the despatching-house it was necessary to have a long distributing-spout, giving an equal supply to twelve boxes. The conditions forbade a very large spout, and the difficulty was overcome by a false bottom, to which I shall again refer. All the spouts at Middlethird were of flooring, charred inside, and painted outside. Fig. 84 is a plan.

Fig. 84—scale 1/12.

THE REARING-BOXES

Fig. 85—scale 1/12.

complete the furnishings of Middlethird hatching-house. They were built of larch an inch thick, the bottoms being of flooring, as in the hatching-boxes (Fig. 85); the outlets were cut to retain 3 inches of water, in case of the supply being stopped through any accident. Nothing was left to chance. The lids were a light frame of wood covered with half-inch wire-netting for three parts of the length, the remainder having No. 9 perforated zinc,

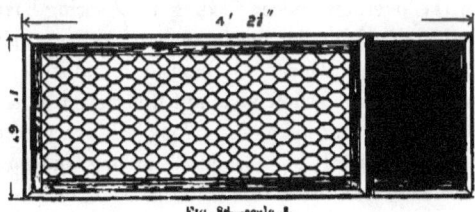

Fig. 86—scale 1/12.

and a splash-bar separating the two. The water fell on the zinc, and became a shower of spray.

This inverts the old myth—the recipient fry became golden, the shower remained soft water. All the rearing-boxes were fitted with safety-screens, and the water was heightened by means of a strip of coarse flannel laid across the outlet. Below is a section of the rearing-box (Fig. 87).

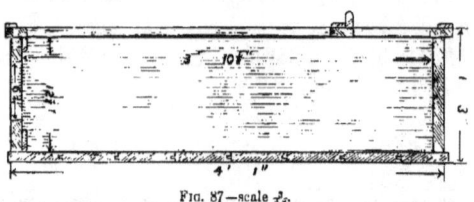

FIG. 87—scale $\frac{1}{12}$.

In arranging the internal fitting I was guided by a desire to be able to show everything off to the best advantage. The whole thing was yet a toy, and the problem was how to walk round it. It was to this end the E-spout was adopted; without it I could not have fed the rearing-boxes, except by a spout across one of the passages. The arrangement will be best understood from the plan. The water from the outside filter was conveyed in a covered spout to the outside of the hatching-house. This spout was carried on a dike to the level of the top of the inside filter. Just outside the water was divided, what was required for the filter passing a sluice which set back against a slight head 1½ inch, if I remember rightly, and all the rest of the water fell into the upper end of the E-shaped spout, through which it passed into the distributing-spout, in the end of which was an overflow, so as to keep the head constant on the overflow sluices feeding the rearing-boxes. The overflow at the end of the distributing-spout was made half an inch higher than the others. This was in practice found sufficient. The water passing the end overflow is an apt illustration of the theory of waste. So long as a drop passes, so long will every other spout, sluice, and tap run exactly as intended,—so long, and no longer.

This overflow waste maintaining the pressure on the tap that fed the slate trays constant, the rest of the water was divided equally between the two boxes at the side.

Drains were laid in the floor, and the waste led through down-fall spouts, so that all used water was concealed; this kept the house tidy. The drain was carried in the centre of the path next the door, and the waste from the downfall of the distributing-spout and from the overflows of the rearing-boxes led into it.

CHAPTER X.

SEASON 1874-75—*continued.*

CONSTRUCTION—CRAIGEND.

I MUST return a little to bring the work at Craigend up to date. In years gone by the house itself had been a distillery, and an old dam, broken and decayed, and planted up with fir-trees, could still be traced in the little ravine running from the lodge to the muir. Still higher, and to the left, on a neighbouring property, lies the Black dam, famed in local story as the guardian of many a cask of whisky. Some time in the beginning of the present century, when the old distillery was about to be subjected to a more than formal visit by the Excise, it was thought unadvisable to give a too cordial reception to the officers of the Crown, and so successfully were they delayed, that when, some three weeks afterwards, a company of soldiers arrived to reinforce them, and prudence forbade any further discourtesy to the representatives of the law, not a single gallon of spirit was found. Whether the whisky had been poured down the large conduits which pass below the house, and at first drained the ponds at Craigend, in a mysterious manner, or whether the casks had actually been conveyed at night to the Black dam and sunk in its mossy bottom, no one ever knew. The making of whisky without due attention to the formalities prescribed by Parliament is not unknown at the present day in the vicinity of Stirling. Only two years ago a respectable farmer with great skill constructed a still under the floor of his barn, and led the flue into the chimney of the steading steam-engine. For long he converted the cheapest feeding sugar into fiery spirit; but in an evil hour, prompted by greed, he sent the town bellman round to advertise his wares. After a short interval the law was expounded to him; but I believe the fine was afterwards modified on the ground that it would be hard on his landlord, to whom he had taken the precaution of being sufficiently back-rented.[1]

The Black dam fed the old distillery dam at Craigend, but it too, at the present date, has fallen into decay, and is no longer any resource.

My first care was to clear out the trees from the Craigend dam; then I scraped away the soil from the old damhead. I found that it would cost more to repair than it was worth, so I built a new wall, 2 feet in front, of heavy dressed stone in cement, taking the stone from Catcraig Quarry, and filled in between the old face with milled clay. This was the most expensive bit of work (for its size) I ever did, and the most unsatisfactory. The old damhead was riddled with mole-holes, and it was years before the dam was tight. While the masons were engaged on the wall, I cleared out the old bottom down to the clay (about 1 foot below its original level), and cut a new course for the stream in flood, round the dam,—a difficult piece of engineering. It is never advisable in new work to alter the old course of water. The safest plan is that adopted at Howietoun, where the ponds are made on one side of the stream, which is left as a waste and flood-water course. But in patching old work it is sometimes impossible to do otherwise; and at Craigend a great deal

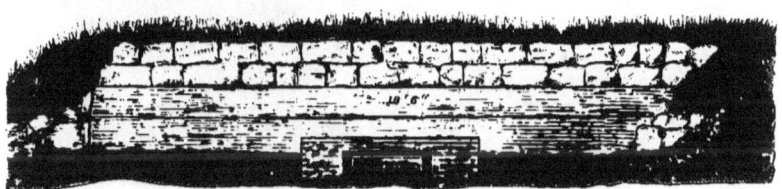

FIG. 88—scale $\frac{1}{12}$.

of labour was expended on the new course of the burn. In winter the water occasionally came down from the muir in heavy spate, and a very large channel (always dry in summer) was neces-

[1] *Stirling Journal*, Friday, April 6, 1883.

CRAIGEND.   137

sary. Only once it failed, and flooded the dam, with the usual sequence,—the escape of most of the fish. The supply was led into the dam through a bulk-head in the side of the old course above the junction of the new cut (Fig. 88). A screen was fixed, not unlike the ordinary leaf-screen, but so designed that no dirty water should pass through (Fig. 89). The principle is simple, merely making use

Fig. 89—scale 1/12.

of the suction, which is generally so troublesome in ordinary intakes. It was accomplished as follows: the screen was laid level with the bottom of the stream (Fig. 90); the side of the screen nearest the

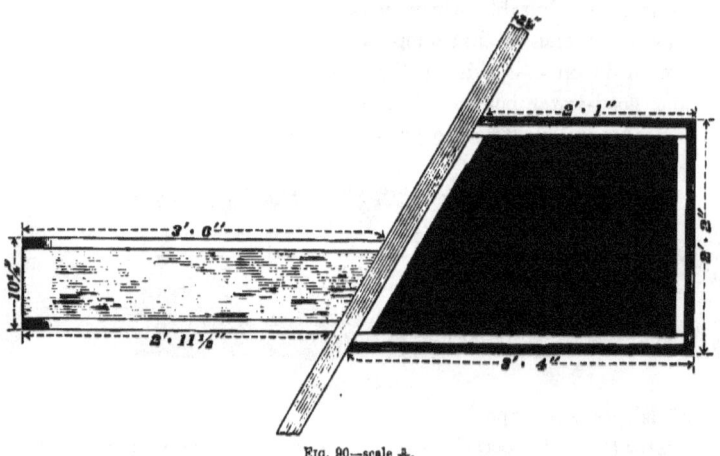

Fig. 90—scale 1/12.

dam was cut at an angle, and the sides of the burn were revetted so as to slightly turn the water (Fig. 91). A box below the screen collected the water, and a pipe from the box passed through the

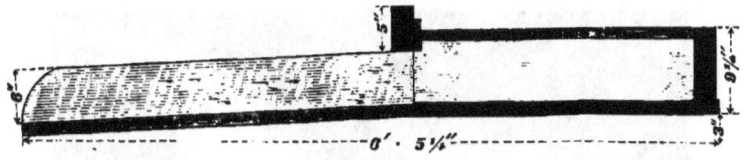

Fig. 91—scale 1/12.

bulk-head and conveyed the supply to the short feeder of the dam (Fig. 92).

Fig. 92—scale 1/12.

When the stream was light, the water passed through, and the screen cleaned itself, as in the leaf-screen, the angle of the bulk-head being sufficient to clear the screen; but when the stream rose in spate, the angle of the revetment, and the narrowed sides of the burn at the head of the new cut (which had been constructed so as to confine a small spate, and offer little increased resistance to a large one), deepen the water at the bulk-head so as to increase the suction on the screen, and cause it to hold all débris, thus completely stopping the supply to the dam. When the water cleared, the débris gradually washed off, and when the stream fell to its usual size, the screen cleaned itself comfortably. This mode of taking water from a stream is very suitable for obtaining a supply for small water-works where economy is an object, as it not only acts efficiently, but can be erected at a very small cost, requires little or no attention, and thoroughly prevents the entrance of silt into the reservoir below, thus saving the expense and inconvenience of frequent cleanings. The fall required is so slight that it can be used in situations where the ordinary methods would entail considerable works. A plan of the screen, the bulk-head, and the commencement of the new cut, showing the narrowed portion, is given below (Fig. 93).

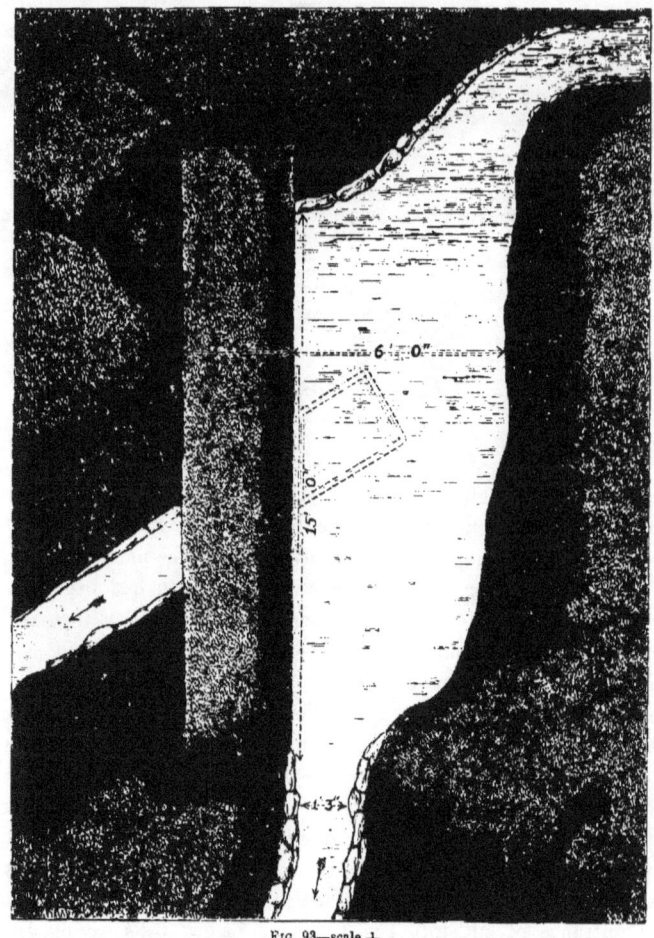

FIG. 93—scale $\frac{1}{16}$.

The sluice of the dam was my next difficulty; it had not only to retain the water, but the fish I purposed to keep in it. I wished to be able at any time to run the dam dry without losing the fish. I also required to feed a row of rearing-boxes outside the dam. I trusted the inlet screen to moderate the water in spate, and as it worked up to my expectations, I had no trouble in providing against floods. The sluice at the hatching-house at Middlethird seemed a suitable model, and I copied it to some extent (Fig. 94). I fixed two uprights in the stone-work of the sluice of 3-inch plank, and cut a check in each to receive the sluice-boards. These were also of 3-inch plank, but only 4 inches broad; the tops and bottoms were bevelled considerably, except the lowest one of all, which was only bevelled on the top edge. A beech sole was laid between the uprights, and level with the bottom of

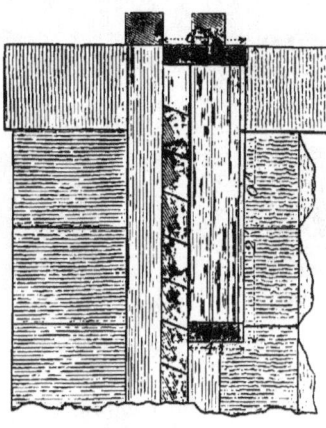

FIG. 94—scale 1/12.

the dam. A small cup-shaped depression was then scooped out to hold a little water for the fish left in when the dam was run down, and the lowest sluice-board dropped into the check. The next sluice-board was then dropped with the sharp edge of the bevel downwards. This fitted the bevel on the top side of the lowest board, and the pressure of the water acting horizontally, while the weight of the superimposed sluice-boards, acting vertically, kept it absolutely water-tight. After the first month, when the plank had swollen, the top board was bevelled on both edges like the others, so the water had a sharp edge to fall over. The height of the sluice to the top board was about 6 feet. There was some difficulty in concreting round the beech sole-plate, and a 2-inch lead pipe was laid below, passing from the bottom of the dam under to the back of the sluice. After the concrete had set, this pipe was closed by stunning together with a hammer. This is a simple and effectual plan. Fig. 95 is a plan of the sluice.

The dam was only used for mature trout, and half-inch wire-netting is sufficient to confine them. If the screen is deep enough

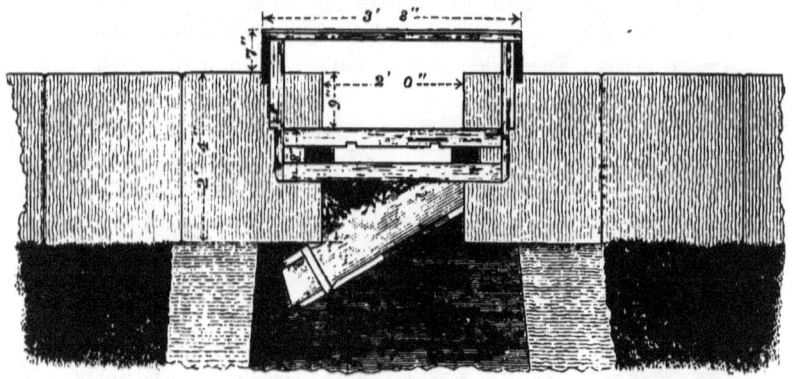

Fig. 95—scale 1/12.

in the water, ice and leaves do not interfere with its working. All outlets of ponds in wild situations should be guarded on this principle. If a smaller size of opening is required to confine the fish, as in the case of yearlings or two-year-olds, it should be placed 6 inches in rear of the half-inch wire-netting; the latter keeps all leaves, etc., off the finer screen. Often a large mass collects on the wire at least a foot in depth; the screen, therefore, should

Fig. 96—scale 1/12.

be 2 feet deep. This always leaves a sufficient space clear for the water to pass, and if there is a fine screen behind, the 6 inches is ample for the water to rise between before passing the zinc (Fig. 96). All screens less than half-inch should be of zinc in trout-culture. Of course, in rearing sparlings (*Osmerus eperlanus*), smaller screens still are necessary, and fine copper wire must be procured. Where the wire-screen has only to confine mature trout, it must be closed underneath; where there is also a zinc screen, it should be left open. The reason frost is powerless against this screen is, the depth of it is insufficient to be below any ice forming on the surface. In Scotland 18 inches is the most I ever knew. The water between the screen and the overflow does not freeze, the current being too strong. Below is a sketch of the screen (Figs. 97, 98).

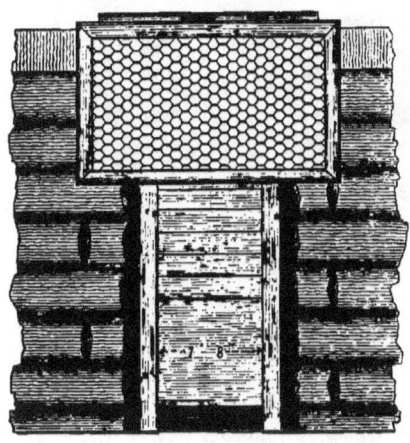
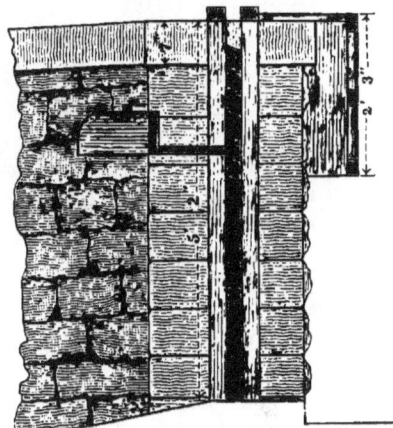

FIG. 97—scale 1/12.   FIG. 98—scale 1/12.

The overflow of the dam-sluice was utilised for a set of rearing-boxes thus: A spout was fixed along the masonry of the section of the dam cut by the overflow from the sluice; a tray was fitted to the back of the sluice and caught below, delivering it into the pipe or spout feeding the rearing-boxes. On next page is a diagram of the tray (Figs. 99, 100).

Before we leave the dam it may be useful to trace a summer spate, and the action of the various works throughout.

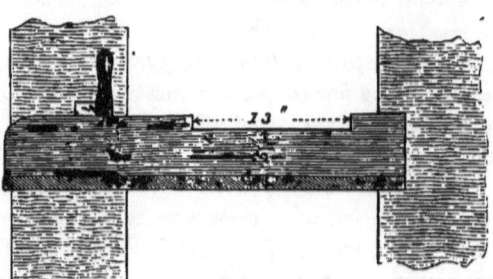

Fig. 99—scale $\frac{1}{12}$.

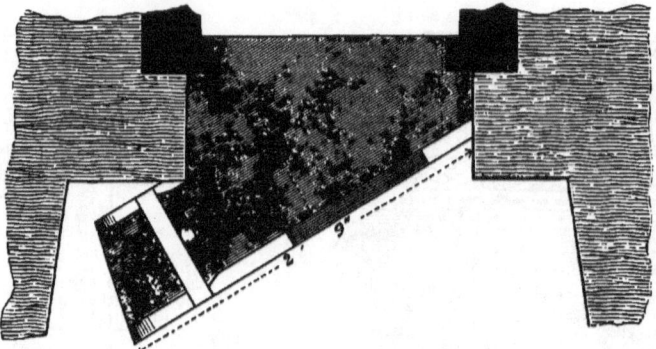

Fig. 100—scale $\frac{1}{12}$.

When the rain first begins to run off the hill after a dry spell, all the sheep-drains through which it finds its way to the burn are full of dust and débris of vegetation, and often in an hour the stream comes down as thick as, and much the colour of, pea-soup, long before there is more than a few inches' rise. When the discoloured water first meets the leaf-screen, it falls through, leaving the débris on the screen. In a short time the screen clogs; and if the burn has not risen much, as the water clears, the screen cleans itself by the eddy formed by the angle of the bulk-head. If, on the contrary, the rain continues, the stream rises rapidly in the narrow neck, and dams back over the stream, completely stopping the eddy, and very much increasing the suction of the screen, so as to prevent the now-increased force of the current sweeping off the débris, and so allowing any dirty water to pass into the dam. As the spate increases it becomes fouler, but the dam is safe; the only effect is to fill the overflow. Now, this being led round the dam, and the soil on the top being gravel, some water filters through, cleansed by the filtration, and a sufficient supply passes the overflow to feed the rearing-boxes below. As the spate falls the water clears, and on more débris coming down, the friction of the current soon cleans the inlet screen, and all goes smoothly (Fig. 101).

In autumn, when the leaves fall, and in spring, when the trees bud, the wind frequently covers the surface of the dam,

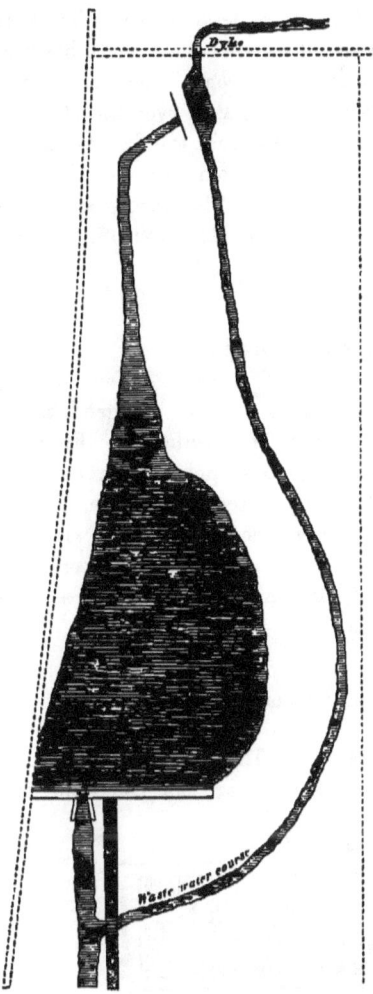

Fig. 101—scale 1/16.

CRAIGEND HATCHING-ROOM.   145

and buds or leaves are borne down against the outlet screen. The wire-netting collects these at the surface, and the suction of the sluice causes them to pile up several inches above the water. The weight sinks the first-formed débris at least to twice the depth below water it is piled above; but after a certain depth has been reached the rest of the flotage collects in front. The screen, being of a size determined by the amount of flow over the sluice, is sufficiently deep to offer an ample surface for the free passage of the water, and all is safe. At Craigend dam once a week is now found often enough to clean this screen. The rearing-boxes were removed years ago when the house in the Howietoun Fishery was built.

CRAIGEND HATCHING-ROOM.

The house at Middlethird was so far from Craigend that I altered the gun-room so as to fit it for experiments. From the dam there was a supplementary water-supply, which could be connected with the house (filtered) water at pleasure. This I turned on to the house pipe, and outside the gun-room window I tapped the pipe and led a branch under the gun-room floor. The branch ended in a Y-upright, on which two rubber hose were attached; one of these I led to a

SMALL SLATE CISTERN,

the other to a tap on opposite wall. The cistern was built on a slate slab, grooved to receive the sides; and bored for two

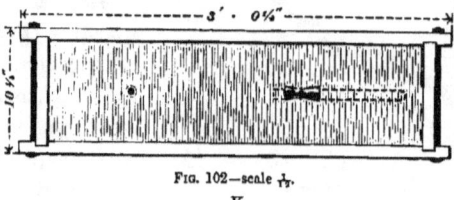

Fig. 102—scale 1/12.

pipes, one a waste stand-pipe, and the other an india-rubber supply-pipe, for the slate-trays (Fig. 103). These pipes were interchangeable, so that the supply could be given either to a right- or left-handed tray. The mouth of the india-rubber pipe was supported by a cork, so as to take only the top water, and allow the slate cistern to act as a settling-tank (Fig. 104). Taps were fixed on both pipes below the bottom of the cistern. Below the cistern I placed a stand supporting a set of six slate trays (Fig. 112), and a slate filter similar to the one figured on page 114.

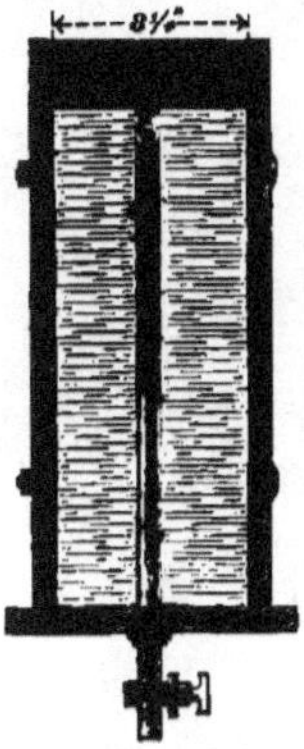

These trays I fitted with grilles, made also of slate, as in so small grilles wood frames are apt to float. The glass rods ran longitudinally. The flexion of the tubes was overcome by silver wire laced across

FIG. 103—scale 1/12.

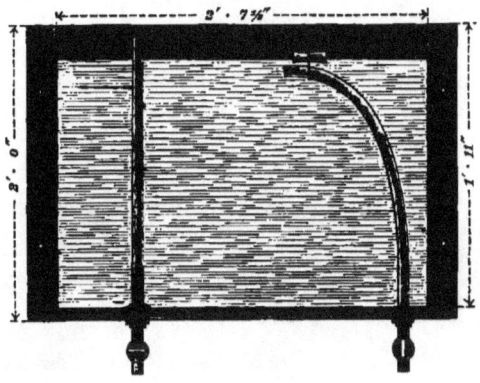

FIG. 104—scale 1/12.

the centre. For experimental work these grilles offer certain advantages, as they enable small quantities of eggs to be segregated, and several experiments in contiguous troughs are sufficiently close together to be compared at a glance. The slate and glass grille is also very easily handled, and can be removed for observation without disturbing any of the ova. They also ensure absolute security from fungus. Figs. 105, 106, 107, show a plan and sections of the slate and glass grille.

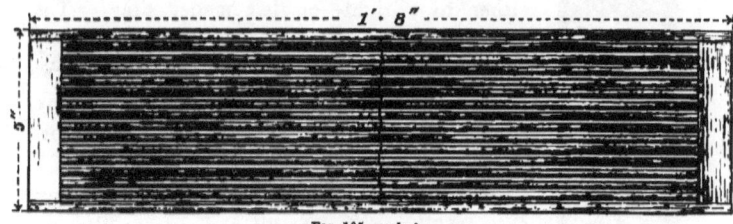

Fig. 105—scale ¼.

Fig. 106—scale ¼.

Fig. 107—scale ¼.

A slate trough was placed against the wall for fry or yearling fish, the supply obtained from the tap. The outlet screen was No. 8 perforated zinc fixed in a groove in the slate. Figs. 108 to 111 show a plan and sections of the slate trough.

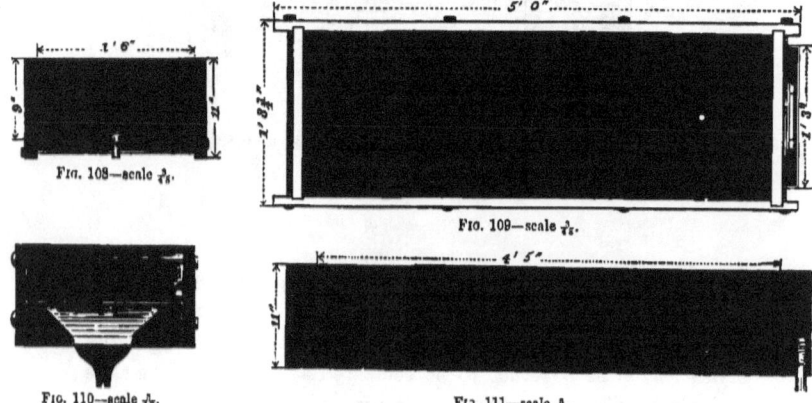

Fig. 108—scale 1/18. Fig. 109—scale 1/18.

Fig. 110—scale 1/18. Fig. 111—scale 1/18.

My experimental apparatus was now complete, and the waste was skilfully led through the floor. I flattered myself all was right. The slate trays were water-tight, so was the slate trough, and I never dreamed of any trouble with the water. I was

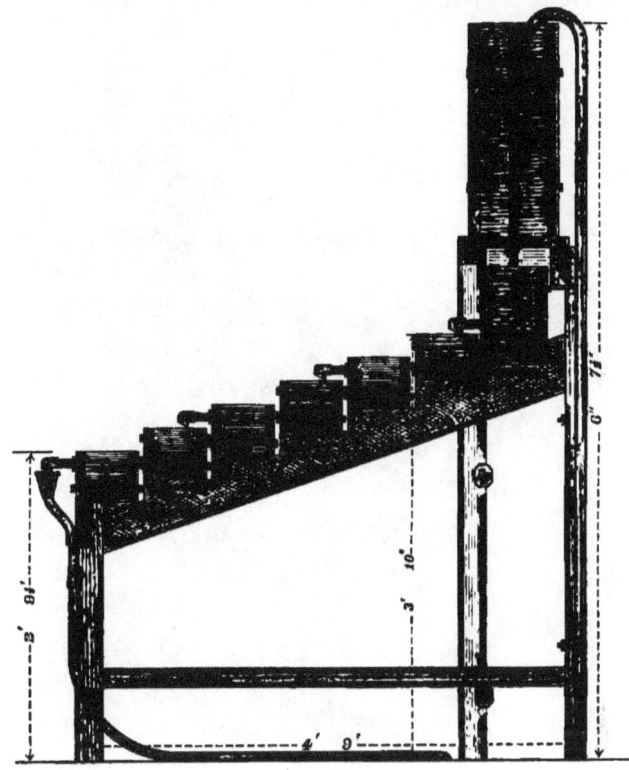

Fig. 112—scale $\tfrac{1}{15}$.

wrong; the slate trays and trough condensed so much moisture from the atmosphere that they dripped continually. This, of course, was worse on cold nights. The house was warmed with hot air, and the water was often little above freezing-point. I (being a married man) had to pay some attention to the *lares et penates*. They stood it for one short season; the amateur gun-room establishment was a thing of the past! Below is a plan of the gun-room in 1875 (Fig. 113).

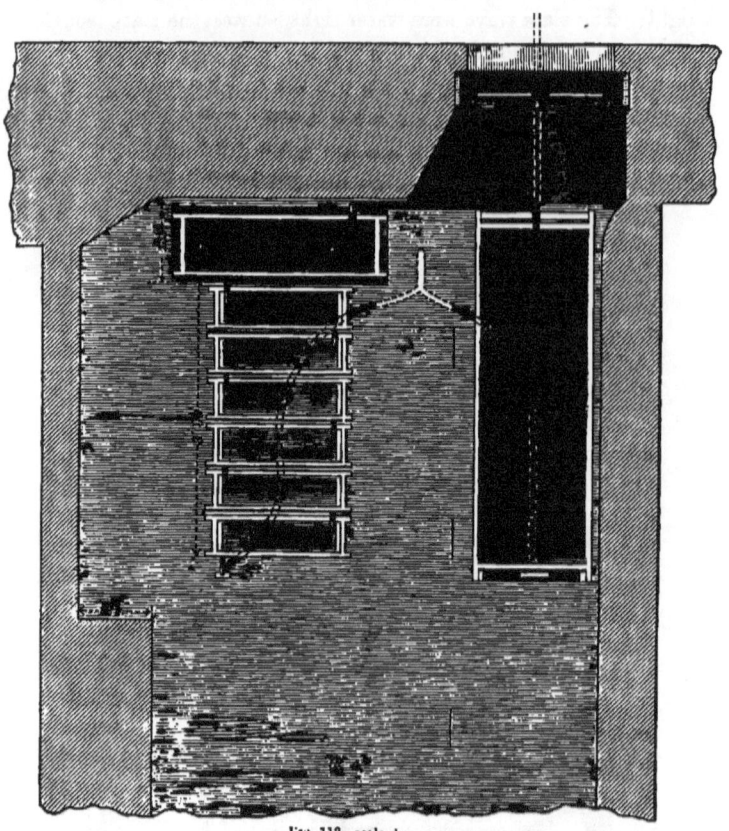

Fig. 113—scale 1/8.

CHAPTER XI.

SEASON 1874-75—*continued.*

CONSTRUCTION—HOWIETOUN PLANK PONDS.

IN the beginning of March I designed the plank ponds, and on the 18th the wood arrived. On the 25th the carpenter commenced building the first plank pond, and from that day the work at Howietoun commenced.

I had long coveted the stream in the Howietoun. It had the two best qualifications for fish-culture: it never rose beyond a few inches in flood, and that small rise was under control; and it never ran quite dry, even on July mornings before the loch was drawn. In 1800 I find the Sauchie mill (whose water the Howietoun Fishery now uses, the mill being discontinued) was joined by a mill-lead to the Loch Coulter burn. A bog marked "Peatfoord" probably received the burn in old times. This bog drains both ways, to the Auchenbowie burn to the east, and to the Sauchie burn on the north-west. From the levels, as they now exist, all the flow would seem to have passed Sauchie, and only in heavy spates could the water have gone eastward. Early in the present century my grand-uncle made a new road from the Whins of Milton to Loch Coulter, and the lead at that time seems to have been altered, at least the bridge under the road is several yards south of the old course on the map of 1800. The lead is now led on the east side of the old road from Milneholme, close to the fence, and parallel to the road. Any flood must overflow the lead, and find its way through the fields to the north of Sauchie mill, and through the old mill-race into the Sauchie burn below the Howie town. The Howie town itself was a township of old crofts, whose names can still be traced in the small fields shown

on that map. This accounts for the great depth and richness of
the soil. The grazing rent of the part in which the ponds are
situated was in 1875 over 90s. per imperial acre. This is an
important consideration, since the magnificent results which have
been obtained would never have been produced in ponds constructed in barren soil. The land that carries the heaviest cattle
will also rear the most and the best trout. I do not say that cold
Highland lakes should not be cultivated,—far from it; but I do
say that no breeding establishment should be attempted except
in the most favourable situations. The principal point in breeding is to grow the best breed, and nothing else; there must be
no chance of making a mistake with the milters. It would
surprise most people to hear how easily even the best men make
mistakes with milters. The smaller ones are always the readiest
when a push comes. With spawners it is different: the eggs can
be recognised at a glance, or at worst by examining the micropile
with the microscope, so mistakes are not made with them. It
is more than probable some of the consignments of salmon ova
to the antipodes were a mixture. In this case the *S. brachypoma*
eggs would get the best of it, as they stand much coarser handling
than *S. salar*.

The location of the ponds is of the first importance. The
direction of the prevailing wind must be studied, and the ponds
placed at right angles to its direction. This was not understood
at Howietoun for ten years; in fact, the importance of wind was
not dreamed of. All the ponds constructed before 1881 run
nearly north, and the two winds which blow strongest, and to
which the Fishery is most exposed, are the east and the south-
west. It was thought that the south-west, the prevailing wind in
winter, might wash the earthbanks of the ponds if it blew down
them, so the ponds were laid off at first slightly west of north and
east of south. The Craigend ponds were constructed in an old
sunk fence, which happened to run due north and south; so it is
only in the last few years any ponds have been constructed which
caught the wind in their length. So far as I have noted, the
south-west wind does little harm, but the east wind in spring,

when the fry have just been turned out, is very apt, after two or three days' hard blow, to cause fungus on the fry in the ponds exposed to it, while at Craigend, where the ponds run across the wind, fungus is unknown. Even at Howietoun, in the ponds parallel to the two (Nos. 22 and 23) that catch the wind, very little fungus is ever seen, the high bank of the island pond (No. 13) sheltering them to some extent.

The east wind seems to affect fish in some as yet unknown manner. I have noticed *fontinalis*, especially in spring, and when well fed, sicken after a few days of east wind, and often become fungussy, even when in deep ponds running north and south.

Fontinalis are very delicate fish in some waters. They do not stand rapid changes of temperature, and this is the more remarkable as they can stand a great range of temperature without apparent difficulty. No doubt, like all other char, they prefer deep lakes, or rivers running out of deep lakes, or streams much shaded by trees, where the changes of temperature are gradual. If this is so, we need look no further for their rapid disappearance before civilisation in America, and that nation, wise in fish-culture, will soon fill their streams with trout already accustomed through centuries to the interference of man,—not trout imported from the forest streams of Norway or the mountain lakes of Switzerland, but good, honest British trout, who a hundred generations ago made acquaintance with mill-weirs and sunny streams. Civilisation must breed its trout as it has its cattle, or civilisation will have no trout. Where would *Bos primigenius* find a representative in England had cattle not been domesticated through thousands of generations? Trout are not yet so highly specialised as cattle, and may in a few generations be moulded to the requirements of man. Here is a great future, yet so present that every wise pisciculturist will consider it before he selects his locality for his ponds. In considering the location of ponds, the side of a slope should be selected, the more gradual the better, so that the old drainage level is not interfered with. At Howietoun the old course of the burn is cut across by the lowest ponds (Nos. 13 and 14), but their banks are sufficiently high to prevent any danger,—No. 13

being 20 feet above the old bed, and the other (No. 14) being 12 feet. The ground lends itself to this formation, and the largest flood would spread itself harmlessly. As a general rule, the ponds should be constructed well above the nearest point of the water-course, and, as it is absolutely necessary to be able to completely drain the ponds or any single pond at a moment's notice, height above the water-course enables this to be done conveniently and cheaply. Shelter is also a consideration; and, as trees are impossible on account of the leaves, which foul the water to an extent sufficient to reduce very largely the number of trout that can be kept in it, shelter must therefore be sought in position rather than artificially, and a valley not too deep, a valley over which the wind is lifted by higher ground, and not one up or down which it sweeps, should be selected.

The Howietoun offers all these advantages, and the site chosen for the plank pond was selected to give the greatest extent to the future fishery, and to command the whole water-supply, and yet leave ample clearance for flood-water, and so that every pond should have an ample fall to the old course for drainage, and by the shortest line. To accomplish this the stream was tapped about 50 yards above the site fixed for the plank pond, and the

FIG. 114—scale $\frac{1}{17}$.

water led through a pipe into a leaf-screen. A square hole was cut in the field, and the sides built with stone hammer-dressed. In this

154.   SEASON 1874-75.

well the leaf-screen was placed, and the overflow and waste from the screen was led through a short drain back to the stream. A common red 6-inch tile, which was replaced a few months after by a 10-inch, as shown in cut, led from the leaf-screen to the plank pond; but the duct to the screen was a 10-inch pipe, the surplus water passing over the screen and down the waste.

FIG. 115—scale 1/12.

This screen differs from the usual leaf-screens. It was necessary to waste as little level as possible, and to return the waste water to the burn, above flood level. The 10-inch pipe to the plank ponds was led away from a sluice-box, and the centre of the bottom of the screen-box was sunk to give the extra depth. The sluice was raised by a screw, thus securing great nicety in the quantity of water passed. The sluice was always set so as to dam the water against the screen, and secure a certain overflow, as the stream often carried gravel on to the screen, and it was necessary to keep

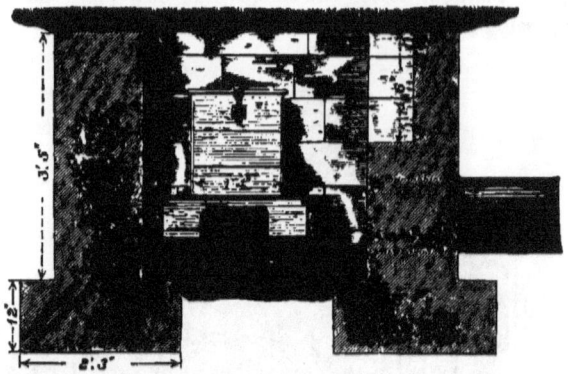

FIG. 116—scale 1/12.

a good flow over it to clear it; now all water is taken from a damhead, and gravel is no longer a source of trouble.

THE PLANK POND

was built to succeed the rearing-box, and it has supplanted it entirely. To-day the rearing-boxes exist, nay, they are numerous, under a different name, but they are no longer used as rearing-boxes. They have been found most useful in preparing trout for long journeys, yearling fish especially; but fry no longer require them. When the great fact was realised that eggs should be hatched where the alevins are to spend the first two or three months of their existence, be it in redds or hatching-troughs, rearing-boxes, as rearing-boxes, became a thing of the past. Now that two-year-olds are the fashionable size for stocking, plank ponds as rearing-ponds bid fair to follow. Plank ponds are the best suited for the preparation of two-year-olds; but in 1875 I knew nothing of the art (for it is a very great art indeed) of transporting live trout. In 1875 our work was to rear the fry, and with a very humble spirit we approached it: from the hatching-trough to the rearing-box, and from the rearing-box to the plank pond, and from the plank pond to the 100-feet earth pond, and in after years to larger and larger ponds. The plank pond was built throughout of 2-inch plank; no nails were used except in the bottom, and there only for convenience in construction. The principle relied on was to treat the plank as if it had been slate. It was seen that wood always decayed first at the nails, so the

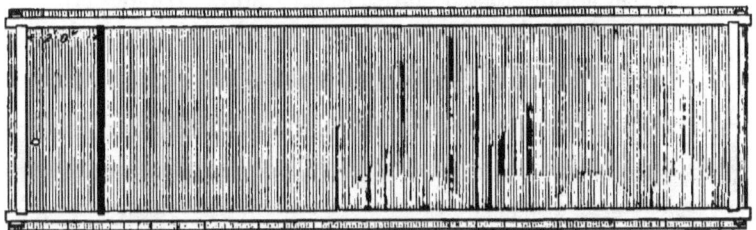

FIG. 117—scale ¹⁄₁₆.

sides were bolted together in this wise: if two planks (which is usual) were required for a side, a groove was ploughed in each plank, and a slip-feather inserted, well bedded in red-lead. The upper end of the pond was formed in the same way as the sides,

FIG. 118—scale ¹⁄₁₆.

and the outlet end was made of one plank, of the depth of the overflow, and two short uprights to carry the top bar mortised into it. The sides were checked to receive the ends, and held together temporarily. The pond was next inverted to receive the bottom, the planks for which were all jointed and grooved for slip-feathers. As each plank was fitted, a check was drawn and cut out for the sides; it was then cramped up with a powerful cramp, and held in place by strong spikes. The pond was kept square by angle-pieces, at least the first-made ponds were; those made afterwards were, like everything else in the Fishery, made on a template. After the bottom was fitted, a runner of oak was laid along each side, and bored for the bolts; the bolt-holes were

HOWIETOUN PLANK PONDS.

charred with a red-hot iron rod; this prevents the wood rotting from contact with the iron. The bolts were driven through from the upper side, and the nuts screwed tight against the oak-runners, and the ends held firmly in their place by four long bolts, passing through four pieces of oak, laid on the sides, just outside the ends. The oak distributed the strain, and the ends were held so as to keep absolutely water-tight. The inside of the pond was next charred, the charring-irons being rectangular blocks of iron weighing 28 lbs. These are heated at a moveable forge, and once a day they are dressed and squared at the smithy. The weight of these irons holds them closely to the wood, and no air reaches the surface. The result is that the wood is charred without being burned. Fig. 119 is a section of the 20-feet plank pond.

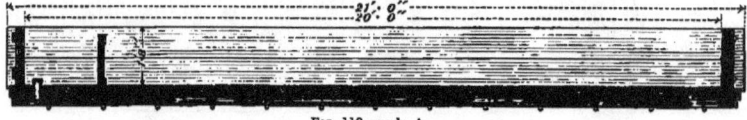

FIG. 119—scale $\frac{1}{15}$.

Charring has many advantages over painting; it is cheaper, lasts longer, preserves the wood better, offers no *solum* to fungus, and perhaps—the most important of all—it is easily cleaned: a hard brush passed once over it is sufficient. All the plank ponds are now furnished with safety-screens. The screens are fitted in shallow checks, cut in the sides a little more than a foot above the outlet. The screen facilitates the cleaning of the ponds, as a plug in the bottom, close to the outlet, can be drawn without any danger of the fish escaping (Fig. 120). In practice, nearly all the dirt rests between the safety-screen and the outlet. If the pond is suffi-

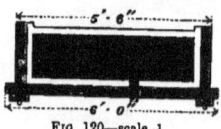

FIG. 120—scale $\frac{1}{15}$.

ciently stocked, and if the current is strong enough, the fish work all fœcal matter, and the refuse of their food, and any sediment brought down by the water, through the safety-screen into the still water below the outlet. Here all dirt rests, and, if stirred up after the plug is drawn, is quickly carried through the plug-hole. There is an art in balancing the current and the quantity of fish so as to ensure the plank bottom keeping always clean. If much mud comes down with the water, some assistance must be given; but with ordinarily clean water no labour is required.

The best mode of bringing the water into a plank pond is undoubtedly by an aqueduct passing the end at a sufficient height to allow two small spouts to feed the pond directly over the end; but at Howietoun, at the time when the first plank pond was designed, the height could only be obtained at a greatly increased cost. The first plank pond, therefore, had its inlet end cut down a few inches, and the water was brought in through a trough run past the end at about the same level as the top of the pond. A cut in the side of the trough, nearly as long as the end of the pond, led the water over a distributing-board, and to a screen of wire-cloth (No. 16), fitted into the cut in the end and sides of the pond. This screen was only 4 inches above the surface of the water. It however was sufficient to spray the water into a fine rain, thus aërating it thoroughly. A plank was fitted across the low end of the cut, to strengthen the pond, and also for the lids to close against. As the pond was in the open air, some sort of protection against birds was necessary. This was obtained by lids, consisting of a frame of wood as light as possible, covered over with wire-netting, half-inch mesh. And to give shade for the fish when they wished it, the upmost lid was made entirely of wood, light lining being used. This lid was hinged to the cross plank above referred to, and a small piece fitted, closing the plank to the inlet screen.

On April 24th (1875) I find the following note:—" There are now 6400 pure Loch Leven trouts in the plank pond: 2400 being from rearing-box 1, and 4000 from rearing-box 2. I find them more difficult to feed than when in the rearing-boxes."

The plank pond was gravelled on the bottom for the first few weeks, but I soon found disadvantages. Gravel held the dirt, got foul, hid enemies, and made itself a general nuisance. The next note of importance relating to the plank pond is May 15th:—" I now find the fish in the plank pond easier to feed than those in the rearing-boxes. About 20 have died in the plank pond since the 24th of April, and these chiefly from choking or the attacks of two caddis worms, which I destroyed when I took the gravel out."

The fry in the plank pond were fed on rabbits' liver and the yolks of hard-boiled eggs. On this they throve amazingly. On the 16th May (Sunday) some were fully an inch and a half long. The question of commissariat became serious; the rabbits' livers would go bad so easily, and the flies seemed to think that rabbits' liver was specially provided to nurse their brood. Something had to be done, and at once. The gamekeepers brought the livers three times a week, and once a collie dog had stolen them, to the starvation of the dear fry. I made a box; and, to keep the livers sweet, I made two sides of perforated zinc. I thought they would be safe. I was wrong. The same collie, or a friend more knowing, tore off the zinc, and again the fry would have suffered; but this I could not stand a second time. I offered to look at the ventilation of the larder. My offer was guilelessly accepted. I have no doubt my opinion on the subject was most valuable; and never understood why the absence of the fillet of beef (which should have been the principal part of the dinner) should have robbed me of my wife's thanks; but the fry looked fat and well next morning. I next designed a moveable larder, to hang up out of the reach of harm. It was a frame of wood, covered on four sides and on the bottom with perforated zinc. The top was of zinc (sheet), arched, to throw off the rain. Two hooks passed through the top, by which it is suspended. By this means the weight of the meat is carried directly by the point of suspension, and no stress comes upon the frame,—a very important point where lightness, or even neatness, is a consideration. The whole of one side opens as a door, and any blood drops through the bottom. These larders have proved so useful, and keep the livers so fresh, I have used them in every outlying pond; and I shortly afterwards built a game larder on the same principle, out of which I this year eat grouse in March, and pheasants in the end of April. The principle is darkness combined with a strong draught. The darkness must be produced by the situation chosen, as, near and to the north of, a high wall (with the small larders under a tree). The perforated zinc will secure the draught if in an exposed situation; top of a hill for instance, or hung to a tree. Only hardwood trees are suitable; firs are too close, as a rule, although an old silver, which has lost some of its lowest branches, and is in fact very bare beneath, does duty at Craigend for the larder for the fish in the two 100-feet ponds (Figs. 121, 122).

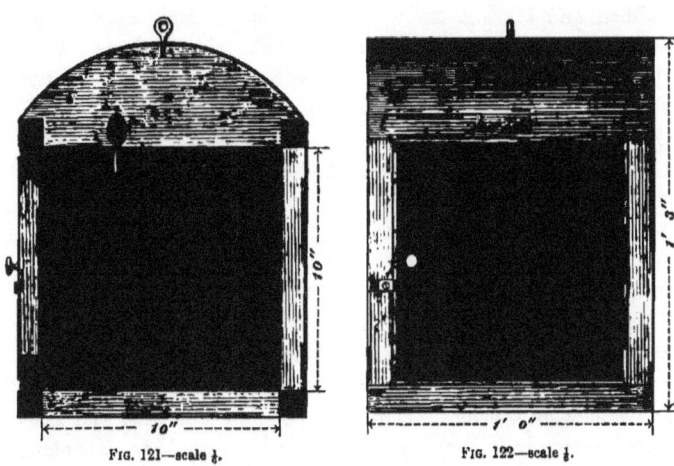

Fig. 121—scale ⅛.   Fig. 122—scale ⅛.

Two ponds had been dug at Craigend in front of the house, but they were only experimental. I had had no experience of earth ponds, and I afterwards deepened and widened these so as to make them almost new ponds. I think it will not be necessary to describe them under this (1874-75) season's work.

On June 6th (Sunday) I fed six rabbits' livers and half a sheep's liver to the fry in the plank pond. They ate it all, and appeared still starving,—not bad for 6400 fry in the month of June! In buying sheep's liver in the country, it is necessary to buy the whole pluck, and the following is entered on June 7th for my future guidance:—"When sheep's is used, the lights should be cut off, the heart should be boiled and cut up for the old trout in Craigend dam; the liver should be used raw for the springlings. Moreover, 15,000 fry during this month (June) will eat one sheep's liver per diem. With regard to rabbits' livers, they triturate better through the perforated zinc if they have first been plunged for a few seconds into boiling water. In short, with sheep's pluck, cut off the lights, boil the heart, leave the liver raw. Plunge the rabbits' livers." On June 13th (Sunday) I ordered a new plank pond; and on the 24th it was commenced; on the 8th of July it was finished, and I began laying a 10-inch spigot and faucet glazed pipe from the leaf-screen in place of the old 6-inch red tile. To do this I took the water off the old pond from 10 A.M. till 2.30 P.M. The fish showed great symptoms of distress, but only 14 died. On the 10th the fish were much fresher; no more had died. On the 12th I moved them into the new plank pond, which had a stronger water-supply, I having led an 8-inch pipe from the new 10-inch into the new pond, and only a 6-inch pipe into the old,—the reason being that the old plank pond was originally only 16 inches deep. It was deepened by planting on a plank the autumn following. The water was at first led into the two plank ponds by spouts from the pipes laid on the ends, and the water fell in a considerable stream, instead of spreading over the inlet screen, and falling as a shower. On the 14th July I noticed the Loch Leven springlings jumping at the inlet screen of the new plank pond, and I have no doubt the jumping accounted for the frayed dorsal fins, more especially as most of the Swiss trout had the dorsal fins frayed last season when they were in the 9-foot plank pond, the inlet screen in which was only 4 inches above the surface of the water. None of the fish in the rearing-boxes were affected. I noticed the fish take advantage of the back-boil of the fall, the current of which is probably nearly equal in velocity and opposite in direction to the falling water.

CHAPTER XII.

SEASON 1874-75—*continued.*

EXPERIMENTAL WORK.

List of Experiments.

Experiment 1.—Loch Leven eggs milted by a burn-trout male. Milt bottled six hours before using.
Experiment 2.—Loch Leven eggs milted by a burn-trout male, same as No. 1, only males transported alive.
Experiment 3.—Loch Leven eggs milted by a burn-trout male, same as above, only the male was immature, and quantity of milt small.
Experiment 4.—Burn-trout eggs milted by a Loch Leven male. Milt bottled twenty hours before using.
Experiment 5.—Loch Leven eggs milted by a burn-trout male. Eggs bottled for twenty hours before using.
Experiment 6.—Loch Leven eggs milted by a Loch Leven male, pure; eggs with red liquid.
Experiment 7.—Sea-trout eggs milted by a burn-trout male. Male very small.
Experiment 8.—Loch Leven eggs milted by a sea-trout male.
Experiment 9.—Sea-trout eggs milted by a Loch Leven male.
Experiment 10.—Burn-trout eggs milted by a burn-trout male. Ova cut out of dead female.
Experiment 11.—Burn-trout eggs milted by a sea-trout male.

OCTOBER 1874 was the month when the first ova were laid down in the hatching-house at Middlethird. The burns on Sauchie could not supply a quarter of the spawners required to fill the trays and boxes. I had written to Sir Graham Montgomery, asking permission to obtain spawn from Loch Leven, the *quid pro quo* being that I should return one-half as fry. This Sir Graham agreed to; and on October 23d I went to Kinross by the morning train, and found 8 females and about a dozen males waiting for me; but only 4 of the females ripe. I noted the unripe fish had no mark on their noses. All the ripe ones had, showing they had been caught on the spawning-beds and not in the lake. After the second or third glass of whisky (a medicine in which most people at Kinross had at that date much faith), the truth came out : rather than disappoint me, they said, they had put a divot in one of the smaller tributaries of the loch (a divot is a cut turf) and lifted out some spawning trout of their very redds, the poachers! Some of the eggs I spawned into a dish, and then milted, and others I spawned into the dishes, after having first milted the males into them. I also tried the following experiments. It will be convenient to follow out the experiments separately as far as recorded in my notes.

Experiment 1.

Before leaving Sauchie I milted a small burn-trout into a test-tube; this was at 9 A.M. At 1.20 P.M. I used the milt on some eggs from a Loch Leven trout; I placed 143 eggs in some sphagnum moss, and laid them down in a slate tray at 11 P.M. same evening.

Experiment 2.

I had also taken with me from Sauchie 3 male burn-trout alive; these I milted on some Loch Leven eggs taken dry at 1.30 P.M., and packed in moss and laid down at Sauchie at 11 P.M. Total, 200.

Experiment 3.

I took a small male, which I had brought from home with the others, and milted him on a few Loch Leven eggs; the quantity of milt was very small, and the male did not weigh two ounces, the object being to see how little milt would be sufficient. This experiment also I packed in moss. Total, 160.

Experiment 4.

On the following day I took some milt I had bottled at Loch Leven, and, stripping a burn-trout which I had not fully stripped on the 21st, milted the ova; the milt had been twenty hours in the small bottle. Total, 15 ova.

Experiment 5.

I took 50 Loch Leven eggs, which I had carried in a carefully dried and tightly corked tube, and milted with plenty of milt from two burn-trout (Sauchie fish). The eggs were taken at 1.35 P.M. the preceding day, October 23d, and milted at 10.20 A.M., October 24th. Most of the eggs stuck to the bottom of the spawning-pan, and behaved in every way like freshly stripped eggs. At 10 P.M. the same evening one egg died, but was supposed to be one that had been dropped on the grass before milting, and most likely injured by being picked up by the fingers. Total, 50 ova.

These five I may treat of together, as they were placed on a glass grille, divided into five compartments, in the top slate tray. They eyed nicely on November 22d; the temperature of the water is not recorded, but it was above 46° F. The embryotic line was first visible on November 9th, and up to November 15th none of the eggs had turned white. On the 30th December the weather was very cold, and all the slate trays were frozen, but Experiments 1, 2, and 3, being in the top tray nearest the water-supply, did not suffer, the ice only forming on the surface. With the exception of half of Experiment 3, which took several days longer, they hatched on January 25th, three days later than the eggs taken the same day, but laid down in the wooden boxes.

Experiment 4 seems to have come to grief; at least I can find no further entry in my note-book. Experiment 5, after hatching, was mixed with Experiments 1, 2, and 3. On March 21st a few of the pure sea-trout fry, then just hatching in the top slate tray, had been carried by the current against the screen, and their yolk-sacs had been sucked through. The hybrids between the burn-trout and the Loch Leven trout, Experiments 1, 2, 3, and 5, commenced feeding in a cannibalistic manner on the débris of the suicides carried into the second slate tray, to which they had been transferred. On April 19th my wife visited the hatching-house and fed Experiments 1, 2, 3, and 5 with liver; their stomachs were much distended, always a good sign. On May 5th, the water having begun to fail at Middlethird, I removed Experiments 1, 2, 3, and 5 to Craigend, where I was living, and had a duplicate set of slate trays; and the next morning I placed a rearing-box for them below Craigend dam. This is the last reference to them in the note-book. The results they established are, that Loch Leven and burn can be crossed, and that the fry produced are as strong and healthy as the purebred fry; this was the object of the set. Experiment 3 points to the possibility of a very young male causing the embryo to hatch later than usual. This is the key to imperfect impregnation. It is also shown that there was no perceptible difference between the Loch Leven eggs milted by a small burn-trout (Experiments 1, 2, and 3) and burn-trout eggs milted with Loch Leven milt (Experiment 4), up to the clear development of the embryotic line. This does not take us very far, but it is interesting as the beginning of a series of experiments which have already spread over twelve years. There is another result, not contemplated at the time, and the importance of which was not realised until afterwards, when I read in Stone the account of M. Vrassky's experiments. Milt was capable of impregnating ova if kept in a carefully dried and well-corked tube; and ova were capable of receiving impregnation, if spawned into a dry bottle, many hours after having been taken. The dry process of impregnation follows as a necessary corollary. This dry process I had always used, not knowing I was singular, in this country at least, in using it. I had commenced with my first spawner, and, having found it answer, never thought any more about it.

On November 5th I went to Kinross, to obtain Loch Leven trout ova, and tried the following experiment:—

Experiment 6.

A spawner of about 1 lb. weight yielded her eggs with a copious flow of red liquid (possibly the fish had been injured in netting). The eggs flowed easily, and were to all appearance ripe; one, but only one, egg was covered with a bloodshot membrane, showing the fish was newly ripened. I was anxious to ascertain whether such ova were capable of being impregnated. I took the ova in a spawning-dish, and milted with a free-running male, and as soon as the eggs had ceased to adhere to the dish, I rinsed them thoroughly and packed in sphagnum moss. Total, 880 ova.

The end was melancholy in the extreme. The eggs were placed in the lowest slate tray at Middlethird. On November 15th they are noted in the book as "going on well," but the tray froze solid on December 30th. On January 3d the trays were thawed out, but those eggs in the bottom slate tray, which had been frozen completely solid, were entirely lost. These were Experiment 6, which up to this date had done very well, the eye being developed, and not a single bad egg having been picked out. This experiment proved that the ova is not affected by the juices in the body of a trout, however copious, as it is by water, for I have frequently found that a short immersion in water before impregnation renders the ova barren.

Experiment 7.

The next experiment was commenced on November 26th. When I netted the burn in front of Touch House for sea-trout, I took 10 : 5 males and 5 females. The first fish was a male, nearly spent; I returned him at once to the water. The next was a female, and I spawned her, milting with a small burn-trout male. These I placed in the third slate tray at Middlethird. Total, 253.

One egg hatched on March 20th, and 5 more on the 21st. On the 27th they had all hatched out, but most of the yolk-sacs were round, and the embryos generally puny. They were 121 days in incubating, a very long time, even considering the frozen slate tray in the beginning of the year. On the evening of the 20th March I made the following note, and subsequent experience has shown I was very near the mark :—" Experiment 7 shows no symptom of any more hatching, but having been in a lower tray, the water may have been a fraction colder; however, I am inclined to think that the true explanation is[1] in the milt being taken from a very small burn-trout (therefore probably a young one). For the first six weeks these eggs were in the same tray as Experiment 9, and latterly the temperature of the air has nearly approached that of

[1] Imperfect impregnation.

the water, so I do not think the difference of two-fifths of a degree, which would be equivalent to one day for half the period of incubation, is possible for two consecutive trays. The average temperature of the last 113 days has been 39°·787."

This experiment was removed to Craigend House on the 5th of May, and to a temporary rearing-place at Milnholme next day; two days afterwards it was mixed with Experiment 11. This experiment showed that sea-trout eggs could be easily crossed with burn-trout milt, and would hatch even under unfavourable circumstances.

Experiment 8.

The idea of crossing Loch Leven and sea-trout occurred to me on 23d November, when I wrote to Mr. Burns Begg, Sir Graham Montgomery's agent at Kinross, asking to get me a male and female Loch Leven trout on the 27th November. Mr. Burns Begg arrived at Sauchie at 4 P.M., with a large tub containing a pair of splendid Loch Leven trout, about 3 lbs. weight each, which had been carried from Kinross without change of water. The snow was deep, and drifted in places; and soon after we left the house at Sauchie, the keepers, carrying the tub across the fields to Middlethird, stumbled, and upset the fish into the deep snow. The excitement was immense, the men almost in tears at the disaster; fortunately it was not freezing, and the trout were conveyed the rest of the way in snow slush. They soon recovered in one of the rearing-boxes in the hatching-house; and I stripped the female, and milted the eggs with a male sea-trout which I had brought over from Touch some days previously. Total, 1296 ova.

Experiment 9.

I then spawned a sea-trout female, and milted the eggs with the male Loch Leven, the converse of the preceding experiment. Total, 912 ova.

These two experiments commenced to hatch on March 19th, and on the following day I went over in the afternoon, and found about 900 of the eggs in Experiment 8 in the act of hatching. It was a most curious sight: in about half an hour the water was white with cast-off shells, and the bottom a dark salmon colour from the yolk-sacs of the alevins. I poured off the shells, and left clean quarters for the young strangers, who were extremely lively, and in whom I hoped one day to see united the flavour of their Loch Leven mother and the sport of their sea-trout sire. They had been laid down 113 days. In Experiment 9 the eggs took a day and a half longer to hatch, only half being hatched on Sunday the 21st, after being down 114 days.

On April 29th I carried the fry (Experiment 9) to the temporary rearing-place at Milnholme, and on May 5th I brought over the fry (Experiment 8). The water had by this time entirely stopped in Middlethird hatching-house. On the 29th May I removed the fry (Experiment 8) to Howietoun, and placed them in the old 9-feet plank pond. On July 12th I removed the fry (Experiment 9) from Milnholme, and placed them in the old 9-feet plank pond, having fixed the screen across the pond. Next day I removed this screen, as I then considered the experiment sufficient, and I wished to give them more range.

The experience I have since gained shows me I concluded the experiments by mixing just when results might be expected to commence. It is only by carefully comparing two lots like these that any opinion can be formed of which parent is nearest the common ancestor. Experiments in hybridism are now one of the most prominent features of Howietoun, and I much regret an experiment which promised (as I now know) so much should not have been continued further.

Mr. Burns Begg left next morning, and I spawned a pair of sea-trout, and liberated all the sea-trout kelts from the rearing-boxes in the hatching-house at Middlethird into the overflow from the hatching-house. It was fun to see them scuttle down stream as fast as a man could walk. One unspawned milter I retained, and took over to Craigend. I placed it in the Francis Francis box. Its after history and untimely end will be shortly recounted.

Experiment 10.

On November 28th I dissected two female burn-trout: one was quite a fortnight from spawning, the other fully ripe, but in consequence of some derangement of the organs I had been unable to spawn her. I rinsed the eggs quickly, and milted them with burn-trout milt. I kept them by themselves in the fish-room at Craigend, and they eyed nicely; but as I was short of room, I mixed them eventually with the rest of the burn-trout eggs taken on the same day. These hatched on March 19th. Total, 127 ova.

Experiment 11.

To complete the set of crosses, on the 4th December I spawned a small burn-trout, and milted the eggs with the sea-trout male. Total, 149 ova.

This was the converse of Experiment 7. The eggs hatched in 107 days; but as they were in the slate trays in the gun-room at Craigend, I have no note of the temperature, and therefore cannot compare them with Experiment 7. The hybrids seem all to have been placed together in the octagon pond at Craigend, and on the 3d December 1876 I find there were only 180 alive, and two years afterwards, viz., on 31st December 1878, the entry in the statement of stock is—20-feet octagon pond: hybrids 9, three-year-old.

So ended my first experiments. Much they left obscure; they did not fulfil the object with which they were undertaken; but I now find valuable guides in my present work. I now know that crossing alone is not sufficient to produce the finest trout, but that the age and condition of the breeders is so important that it overshadows to some extent everything else.

CHAPTER XIII.

SEASON 1874-75—*continued.*

FISH-CULTURE.

THE experiments of this season I have described. I will now touch on the actual fish-culture. My original stock were derived from two sources only, for I never reared any of the Swiss trout hatched in 1873-74 into breeders: the hill burns at Sauchie supplied the *fario*, while the *levenensis* were obtained from Loch Leven itself.

I had only a few Swiss trout and a very few Sauchie burn trout at the beginning of the year 1874. Of the Swiss trout 120 were placed in Loch Coulter in summer, and for seven years little was heard of them; the burn-trout, or rather the few that survived, were placed in Craigend dam.

The Loch Leven trout were all spawned at the loch (except one spawner brought to Sauchie, whose eggs were used in Experiment 8). The burn-trout were caught, and kept till ripe, and then spawned, the kelts being placed in Craigend dam. The sea-trout were guddled in the Touch burn. This burn is so small, it was impossible to net it with any nets I had, but fortunately some old man on the place liked sea-trout, and had made himself acquainted with all their haunts. These were principally in the founds of a stone wall, where the burn was banked to form a terrace in front of Touch House, the understanding being, I was to return half the sea-trout fry and half the Loch Leven fry. I returned half the sea-trout fry, and placed the remainder in one of the reservoirs on the Touch burn that supply the town of Stirling with water. The sea-trout hybrids I retained.

On the 21st I find the following note:—" October 21.—Sorted 56 spawning trout: 29 males, 27 females. Spawned 2 females:

96 eggs from the one, and 207 from the other. Total, 305 ova. Placed the ova in the bottom slate tray in the hatching-house; none of the other females seem within a week of spawning." On October 23d I examined the ova, and found the disc risen to the top, and circular.

On the 27th October I netted the hill burns and got 20 fish, mostly on the eve of spawning. On the 28th I visited the hatching-house in the evening, and found some one had nearly closed the sluice in the aqueduct, leaving the slate trays supplied lightly, and the side wooden boxes so bare that, from the hang they then had, the eggs near the upper end of the boxes were uncovered. Some inquisitive and uninvited guest was the cause.

The fish I had collected in the burns were all in the elm box I had first made from Francis Francis's diagram, which with the gravel removed forms a capital stew, and had been lately placed in the Craigend burn. On the 30th October I noticed that they did not consume the worms on which they were fed, this being the third night of a white frost. On October 31st I found 2 dead,—symptoms similar to those in the case of one that died on October 29th, viz., the hinder part of the body much swollen, very hard, and nearly cylindrical, the hardness extending forward to the front ray of the dorsal; anus much inflamed and bloodshot. I dissected them. One proved to be a kelt, a very small quantity of milt remaining in the sacs. The other had not yet milted. The sacs were full, the milt being about the consistency of butter, the flesh round the anus swollen and hard, the scales much rubbed off the back, colour light, and no appearance of fungus. I then examined all the fish in the box, and found 7 males slightly affected with similar symptoms; they were all kelts. I put them into Craigend dam. I have no doubt the symptoms were sexual. On the 4th November I again netted the hill burns, and caught 32 fish (no kelts), at least two-thirds of them baggets. Next day I again went to Loch Leven, and found 14 spawners and two dozen males; only 2 spawners proved unripe. These I at once returned to the lake, and from the 12 I took about 12,000 eggs, milting with 14 males. I returned the kelts to the lake immediately after spawning. Only one seemed the least sick, at which I rejoiced exceedingly, for there was a widespread prejudice that spawning artificially caused the death of the victims.

On the 7th December 1874 I found one of the Swiss yearlings, which I then had in the slate trough in the gun-room at Craigend, lying on its side, and panting. I held it up to the light, and found its stomach to contain eight ova (on which I had been feeding them), and which it could not digest. I put it into lukewarm water; it was sick; and by 10 P.M. all right. Only a yearling, barely 8 inches long, over-eating itself on ova ! What harm they must do to the spawning-beds !

On the 9th December I noticed the track of an otter at Craigend dam, and set four traps for it, but did not catch it. The fish in the slated trough tried constantly to jump out. I put some earth into the trough to try and make them feel more at home.

On the 12th December one of the fish injured itself by jumping against the cover of the slate trough. It was a Swiss trout, hatched in February 1873,—that is, just ten months old. Its length was 4·25 inches; depth, 0·8 inch; weight, 0·42 oz.;—not bad for house work. I went to Clifton Hall to spend Christmas with my father on 22d December. The weather was cold, so much so that I ran through to Sauchie on the 26th (a distance of forty miles) to see if all was safe. I found everything working well; the temperature of the air in the hatching-house at Middlethird only 28° F. I returned to Clifton Hall the same night; but the frost strengthened, and on the 30th I returned to Craigend; and, going at once over to Middlethird, I found the slate trays frozen. The two lowest were the hardest frozen. I lit a fire on the floor, and cleared the spouts of ice to increase the flow. The two wooden boxes gave me no trouble; slate, being a much better conductor, is very unsafe when exposed to frost. After a time it freezes from the bottom, which is hopeless. Early next morning I went over to the hatching-house. Things were worse. I lit a fire; it was no good. I rummaged the outhouses at Sauchie; I found an old stove in an unused coach-house. The estate blacksmith was summoned, and the carpenter, along with the head-keeper. We four dragged the lumbering, old-fashioned stove over, and set it up on the floor at Middlethird. The carpenter cut a round hole in the end of the house for the chimney; the keeper carried coals over in his game-bag—for the snow made all roads impassable for horses,—and the blacksmith fitted the stove-pipe; then we lit the fire. Smoke, that darkened the house, was the most visible result; but after lengthening the chimney, we at last got the temperature up to 30° F. This was about 8 P.M. I got the water to run nicely through the slate trays over the ice, and as the temperature of the stream in the aqueduct was 36° F., I hoped the worst had passed. But I did not care to leave much to chance. I had my barrack bedstead carried over, and some rugs, in case I was required all night. After dinner I returned, and found the stove burning well. I stayed and saw the new year in, then made up the fire, and, as everything was improving, I walked back to Craigend about 1 A.M.

On the 1st January I visited the hatching-house three times, and found matters improving. In spite of the stove, the temperature of the air in the house was only 32° F. It was not until the 3d of January that the slate trays thawed out entirely. Then I counted up my losses, and found Experiment 6, which was in the lowest tray, a total loss; but as the question at issue was one of impregnation, and as up to that date they had done well, the eye having developed, and not a single bad egg having been picked, I was satisfied. There was also a partial loss in three other trays. By the 9th January all the rearing-boxes were in their place at Middlethird, the first lot of Loch Leven eggs being only a week from hatching. As a matter of fact, they did hatch on the 23d, having well commenced on the 22d. The percentage of impregnations was fully 99 per cent. The alevins were very lively, and dark coloured, the yolk-sacs a deep orange, running far back, and pointed. The water had risen to 42° F., although the air in the hatching-house was only 35° F. The note in my book on January 23d is : "Hatch nearly completed. The alevins very lively; some few get against the screens, and the yolk-sac gradually goes through the perforation of the zinc. The shells in box Z almost clogged the screen entirely. The grilles on which the eggs were hatching have had to be removed on account of the alevins getting inside the hollows of the glass tubes. *Nota bene:* Take out the grilles another time as soon as the first egg hatches."

This was the cause of the ova being laid down to hatch, perhaps one of the most important discoveries in trout-hatching.

Now, when a box is due, the grilles are picked and washed, the box is cleaned out, the safety-screen is fitted, the ova—or rather so many of them as are considered a sufficient stocking—are washed off the grilles on to the charred bottom of the box, and in half an hour or an hour the whole are hatched, except, perhaps, 1 per cent. One of the best arguments to use to the public (who will not understand nice differences in the vitality of the fry) in favour of grilles, is, that no space is required specially for hatching. The grilles enable you to hatch your ova in the boxes necessary for rearing fry, and not only the ova you require for fry, but twice the quantity, so that one-half may be laid down in redds or sold to help—very substantially help—expenses. There is no permanent market for the fry from ova incubated in trays several layers deep. The public may be satisfied at first, but so soon as they hear some neighbour has done better a day of reckoning comes.

On 24th January, Sunday, I fitted up a temporary sluice of paper and zinc on the outlet of rearing-box 1 to deaden the current. From this sprang the idea of deepening the water in all the boxes up to a 20-ft. plank with a strip of flannel, which was next day substituted for the flimsy paper.

By the 1st February the difficulty of feeding my (as then considered) large family stared me in the face. By this time I had procured a copy of Stone's *Domesticated Trout*, and there I read, on page 153, " It would be a great improvement in the way of feeding young fry, if you could prepare some self-acting contrivance which would feed out the required amount of food gradually and continually all day, as, for instance, a closed box of fine wire-netting, partly filled with food, and placed under a fall in such a way that the water would force out the food little by little all day." I read and re-read the passage. I saw what was required was fresh food to be always in reach of the fry. Food when wet soon bleaches, and then the fish will not touch it; neither do the fry care to pick any motionless particle off the bottom. The solution which occurred to me was to enclose finely grated liver in a tube, and cover the end of the tube with coarse wire net, a piston at the other end slowly forcing the meat through the net. So I made a small water-wheel, with buckets set on its circumference, and the axle bored to receive the thread of a male screw. This screw was cut on a shaft or piston-rod, a part of whose length was square in section, and ran in a guide. Water dropped into one bucket at a time, and, as it filled, the wheel turned a small part of a revolution, forcing the piston forward. The supply of water was reduced to fill the bucket two or three times per minute, and each time the bucket filled and emptied, a small portion of food was forced through the netting and fell into the rearing-box or pond.

For experimental work this device is useful. It works much better with dry food than with liver, but it is absolutely valueless for work on a large scale. Whether any other than hand-feeding is advisable where the number of fry is so great as to occupy the whole time of one person is a moot point. But there will always be experiments and odd lots out of the ordinary routine, and with these mechanical feeding may be a convenience. There are other and better plans, which will be described in their place. The best and simplest is to form the food into thread resembling maccaroni; the movements of the fry and the swirl of the current keep these artificial worms always *en évidence*. There is no waste; the food never gets time to blanch, and the surface exposed to the water is small.

I still hoped to find a mechanical feeder, one that was handy and cheap, so that it could be used in all the rearing-boxes. My next plan was to place the food in a glass jar, fitted with a neck in the centre of the side. In this I placed a cork, through which a bent tube passed nearly to the bottom of the jar; the top of the jar was covered, and a straight tube passed through the cover, ending in a funnel. Water dropped slowly into the funnel, fed by a syphon from the hatching-house aqueduct. The food was kept in motion by the funnel tube, and the amount of disturbance was regulated by the height of the funnel. By raising or lowering this any desired movement could be given to the food, which was carried up the bent tube and fed evenly to the fry. The great objection to the feeding jar is the waste it causes; if left to feed out all the food of a charge, the *fushion* is all gone off the latter half. This is its worst fault; as it is easily cleaned, one can see in a moment if any dirt has accumulated; and it does its work well. Of course it is only suitable where the water-supply is high enough above the box.

The next day I ordered a delicate thermometer from Kemp's in Edinburgh, reading from 30° to 50° F., and half an inch to a degree. This enabled me to read tenths without going too near the glass and raising the quicksilver by the heat of my body, a very necessary precaution where minute differences are to be noted and compared.

On the 3d February the first of my own eggs hatched, that is, the ova taken from the burn-trout caught at Sauchie. The temperature of the water was 42° F. The descendants—or rather some of them—of these Sauchie fry are now sporting in New Zealand.

The winter was a very severe one. The average temperature of the water in the hatching-house at Middlethird for the 113 days preceding the 20th March 1875 was 39°·787 F. The sea-trout which hatched that day were 114 days in incubation.

On April 7th I brought 1000 alevins, *S. levenensis*, from the hatching-house at Middlethird, and placed them in rearing-box 6 at Craigend, and next morning I started at 7.30 A.M., carrying them in a 2-gallon tin, to Thormanean, Mr. Horn's seat, near Milnathort. I inspected Mr. Horn's pond and streams, and liberated the fry at 11.30 A.M., they having been four hours on the journey without change or aëration of the water. There were no deaths, nor did a single fry seem sickly. The alevins were turned out immediately before coming on the feed. I saw a very few (not more than half a dozen) natural fry in a spring-hole; they were slightly larger than the artificially reared ones; but although large swarms of fry are frequently seen by the 1st of April in the burn above

Mr. Horn's pond, on account of the severity of last winter not one was visible.

On the 22d April I returned the second lot of *S. levenensis* fry, 3737 in all, from rearing-box 2, a few being added from rearing-box 1. They were placed in the Gairney, and carried in a new tank, which did its work well, with about 10 gallons of water, which was not changed on the journey. The fry were five hours in the tank, and there was not a single death. Figs. 123, 124 are drawings of the tank.

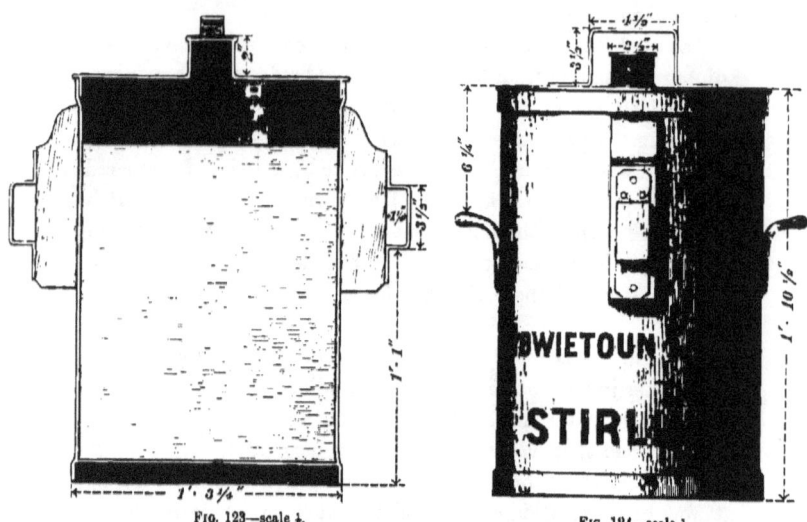

FIG. 123—scale ¼.   FIG. 124—scale ¼.

On the 12th May I returned the last lot of *S. levenensis* fry to Loch Leven, 1200 in all. They were hatched on the 23d January, and were put into the Gairney, about three miles above the loch. The first year's stocking of Loch Leven thus amounted to only 5937 fry. In the pamphlet on Stocking, I stated the number at 9000, but I was wrong; the mistake probably arose from between 3000 and 4000 eggs having been left with Mr. Burns Begg at Kinross on the 5th November 1874, while the total number spawned (12,000) was entered on my notes.

On the 24th April there were 6400 pure *S. levenensis* in the plank pond, 2400 being from rearing-box 1, and 4000 from rearing-box 3. The *S. levenensis* eggs used in experiment numbered 2734, and the Loch Leven eggs laid down were only 15,513, a loss of only 442 eggs and fry up to the middle of May, out of the 12,779 pure-bred *S. levenensis* ova. The eggs and fry were all counted one by one in those days, as I was anxious to ascertain the best mode of treatment. Personally I have never seen this work surpassed. The perfection of the impregnation is due to the fact that the ova were milted in small quantities; and the success in rearing the fry I attribute to their never having, either in the egg or fish, been overcrowded. The record of the burn-trout this season is not so clear in the note-book. They seem to have been crowded out to a great extent, and it was not till the following season I began to rear burn-trout for breeds. This brings the work of the first winter to a close. And it is from this beginning that I, unaided by Government and laughed at by my relations, have reared the largest and most successful fish-farm the world has seen. Many in this country seem to take a delight in crying out that England is behind the rest of the civilised nations in fish-culture; but it is not so—she is in the culture of the *Salmonidæ* immensely before them. We have no market for coarse fish, thanks to the bountiful supply on our coasts; if we had, private enterprise would do all that was required. Enterprise is not hampered with the theories of crotchet-mongers, nor does it appraise scientists by their readiness and skill in bowing to a popular cry. In fish-culture, in the wider sense, no country has done so much or acted so early for the fisheries as England. The late Trawling Commission was fish-culture of the most important order. Many people think fish-culture merely consists in hatching fish eggs; others, a little further advanced, realise the insufficiency of this idea, but believe that if the fry hatched be reared for a few months, all that can be possibly included under fish-culture is accomplished.

Fish-culture is the only means of increasing our food fishes, and whatever under man's direction tends to increase the number or size of our food fishes is fish-culture. Thus the Fishery Board for Scotland, which is now empowered to carry out experiments on the effects, destructive or otherwise, of different modes of fishing, is a Government fish-cultural department of the first importance. It is far more extensive in its powers and more practical in its work than any department of Fisheries in any other country in the world.

TABLE OF OVA, SEASON 1874-75.

1874.	S. fario.	S. trutta.	S. levenensis.	Total.	Remarks.
Oct. 21.	305	...	...	305	
23.	...	...	5,480	5,480	508, Experiments 1, 2, and 3.
24.	15	...	50	65	65, Experiments 4 and 5.
31.	950	...	...	950	
Nov. 1.	187	...	...	187	
2.	90	...	...	90	
4.	135	...	...	135	
5.	...	...	8,687	8,687	880, Experiment 6.
6.	1,229	...	...	1,229	
10.	1,190	...	...	1,190	
15.	118	...	...	118	
19.	418	...	...	418	
20.	560	...	...	560	
25.	...	872	...	872	252, Experiment 7.
27.	...	912	1,296	2,208	2208, Experiments 8 and 9.
28.	840	1,368	...	2,308	127, Experiment 10.
Dec. 4.	403	...	...	403	149, Experiment 11.
Totals,	6,540	3,152	15,513	25,205	

Above is the return of eggs spawned in the autumn of 1874. Of *S. fario*, 6540 ova were taken; of sea-trout, 3152 ova; of Loch Leven trout, 15,513 ova; making a total of 25,205 ova, of which 4189 ova were used experimentally, 3182 being hybridised.

CHAPTER XIV.

Season 1875-76.

CONSTRUCTION—MIDDLETHIRD.

MIDDLETHIRD hatching-house was too limited in hatching capacity for next season's work; so, after much thought, I determined to clear out the rearing-boxes, and fit the house up solely for hatching; but as sediment was still a danger, and as a filter in the house would, under the proposed arrangement, take up much space, I cut the supply aqueduct a few feet above the house and placed a second filter, fitted with finer wire screens, immediately above the house. I then made

A DISTRIBUTING-SPOUT

the length of the house, and fed it from the outside filter. This

Fig. 125—scale 1/12.

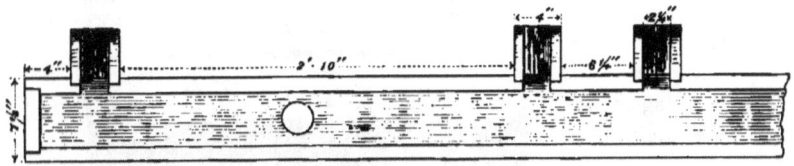

Fig. 126—scale 1/12.

spout was placed perfectly level, and small spouts fed the hatching-boxes. The distributing-spout was built of flooring, 1⅛ inch thick; it was charred inside and painted outside; the small

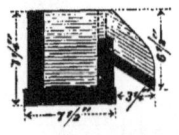

Fig. 127—scale 1/12.

spouts to feed the hatching-trays were planted on, and holes were cut in the side of the distributing-spout for the water; all these holes were carefully levelled by measure-

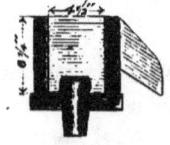

Fig. 128—scale 1/12.

ment from the top, after the distributing-spout had been tested with water.

The spout had a hole 2½ inches diameter cut at the end farthest from the supply, to facilitate cleaning. Fig. 129 is a diagram of the spout.

A batten was bolted on to the standards of the side opposite

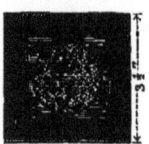

Fig. 129—scale ¼.

the door, and carefully levelled on its top edge, to support the ends of the hatching-boxes; the drain near the door was re-cut, and carried the whole length of the

Fig. 130—scale 1/12.

house; the sides were formed of flooring (Fig. 130); a beech plank was laid as a cover, and twelve holes bored to receive the waste water from the boxes. Round these holes a square cut was sunk, and twelve small uprights fixed. These uprights were made of flooring in four pieces, charred inside to protect the wood, and formed a down-fall spout for the waste water from the trays.

They also formed the supports for the hatching-boxes, which rested on the batten at the top end and on the down-fall spout at the lower. Fig. 131 is a diagram of the down-fall spouts.

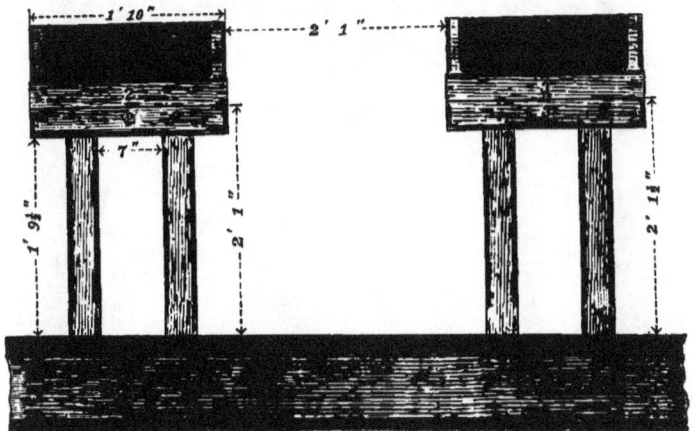

Fig. 131—scale 1/12.

The two old wooden boxes of last season were placed at the two ends of the house and numbered 1 and 6; they were partly carried on brackets, as the single down-fall spout was thought insecure. Four new boxes were made similar, only about double the width, with a moveable division in the centre to support the grilles. This division was held in its place by cleats jammed in between it and the sides. These cleats also kept the water back to a sufficient extent to make an even top flow, so that the eggs got all the current and the still water on the bottom held all the sediment. Lids were fitted to all the boxes; they were made as light as possible. Inlet screens of zinc were used this season; they are shown in Figs. 71, 72, and 73, page 128.

The house was provided with five duplex lamps,—one hung over each path, so as to drip clear of the boxes if there was any leakage. This enabled us to work in the long winter evenings if necessary, and also to warm the house in frost; but oil occasionally did get on the boxes, and, sinking into the wood, it gave trouble for many a day. I am now quite sure that artificial heating should never be resorted to, and that the only plan advisable is to build the

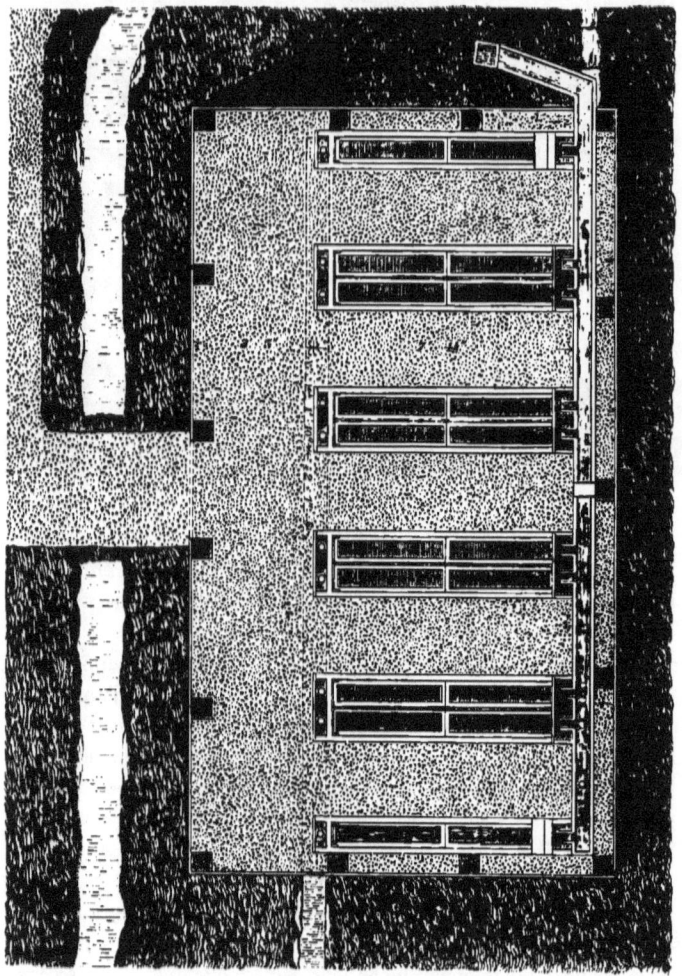

Fig. 132—scale 1/70.
PLAN OF MIDDLETHIRD HATCHING-HOUSE IN 1875-76.

184   SEASON 1875-76.

hatching-house so that it is impervious to frost, and to use water that never falls below 40° F.

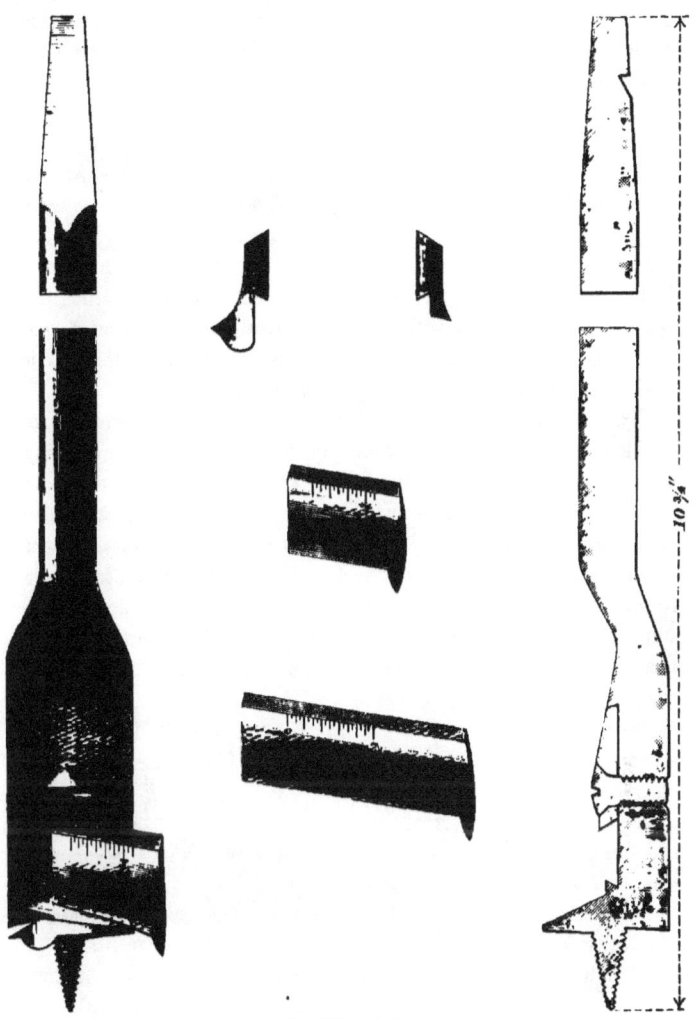

FIG. 133—scale ¼.

In all future distributing-spouts the cuts were replaced by circular holes bored with a cutting-bit, with an adjustable cutter, to cut from 1- to 3- inch holes. This bit is, I understand, an American invention, and is so useful in practical fish-culture that to facilitate others obtaining it I sketch it. Fig. 133 is a sketch of the moveable centre-bit.

CRAIGEND.

The work here was chiefly in the digging and construction of ponds in front of the house. These ponds were merely dug out of the ground. The upper one was finished by the 7th December 1875. No drain was cut to run it dry, and when it had to be emptied it was necessary to pump the water out. The water was taken from the overflow of Craigend dam, and a red-clay pipe led from the leaf-screen in the wood under the public road, and through under the approach to the house.

The leaf-screen was a modification of the one at Middlethird, but as it had to be laid in the bottom of the stream—there being no dam, and it being very dangerous to make one, as the stream often rose 5 or 6 feet in a few hours, and in summer occasionally failed entirely,—the little dribble that ran for the three dry months would have been seriously reduced if any attempt had been made to gain a head by damming. So the screen had to be modified to suit, and the experience I had gained from the inlet to the dam at Craigend came in useful. There the water closed the screen whenever it rose; here the problem was to keep the screen clear in all waters: and it was solved by placing the screen at an angle to the stream, so as to create an eddy when the stream rose. This was done successfully, the situation being chosen at the foot of a rocky fall.

FIG. 134—scale 1/12.

The leaf-screen discharged into a sluice-box, so that the flow to the ponds could be regulated to some extent, although the pressure produced by a rise of water was never at Craigend perfectly compensated. But as the ponds were under constant supervision, no loss has yet occurred through floods, although very considerable trouble and anxiety has often arisen. The sluice-box was furnished with a screw-sluice, and could be set to any opening very exactly. Below is a plan and section of the leaf-screen and box (Figs. 135, 136).

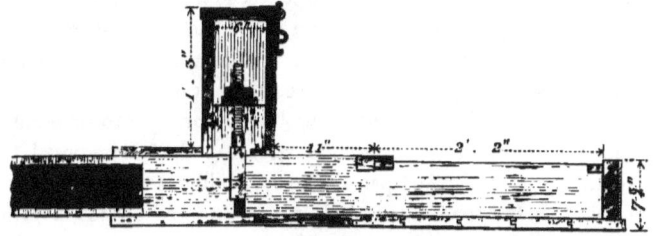

Fig. 135—scale 1/15.

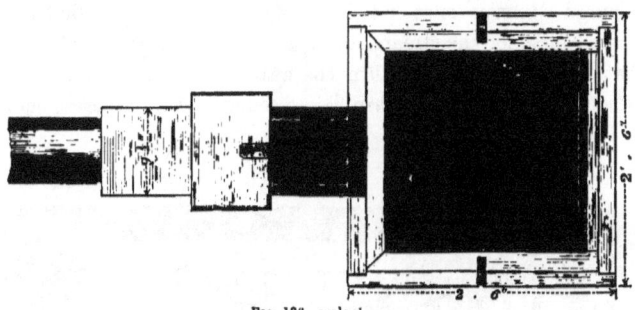

Fig. 136—scale 1/15.

The upper pond at Craigend was originally made about 100 feet long and 16 feet wide, the lower one the same width, but not quite so long; the depth of each was only 4 feet. As these ponds have since been very considerably altered, it is not necessary to describe them more fully here. They will be again referred to under the date of their improvement and completion.

HOWIETOUN

received the most attention. On the 7th December the ice was making much trouble, and half the Loch Leven springlings (hatched January and February 1875) were removed to the upper (100-feet) pond at Craigend. On the 14th the rest of the fish at Howietoun had been removed to Craigend, and the work at Howietoun begun in earnest. The leaf-screen was quite insufficient to pass the water required for the proposed improvements, so I determined to take the whole stream, and at once designed a sluice capable of doing so. This was no easy matter. Hitherto I had had to deal either with tiny burns, or to take only a small quantity of water from a stream. Now I proposed to take 1,000,000 cubic feet per diem, or $6\frac{1}{4}$ millions gallons! And not only this, but to take the whole stream on two hundred days of the year, and leave only an insignificant overflow, except in the largest spates. The sluice I designed has done this, and has only required attention once or twice a day, even in frost. I first cut a waste course for the stream, and made use of a slight wooden dam that had been erected to turn the water on to the intake for the discarded leaf-screen. I then laid a foundation of concrete across

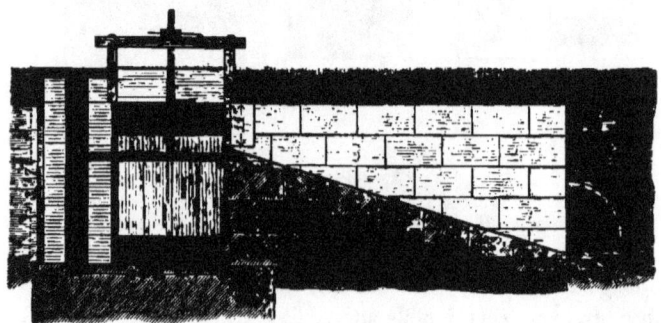

FIG. 137—scale $\frac{1}{12}$.

the course of the stream, and on this two blocks of stone weighing a little more than a ton each (Fig. 137). This formed the floor of the water-trap. I built a dam, behind and partly on these blocks, in the usual way with ashlar and concrete, having first cleared the rock for a foundation. The top of this dam tailed at an angle to the bottom of the old course, and was faced with courses set in Portland cement. A second dam of wood flooring was formed by slipping the boards into a groove, in two posts fitted into a wood sole in front of the water-trap. A bridge was formed by two planks, 2 inches apart, and holding the top of the upright posts in position. Between these two planks the boards of the wood dam slid so that they could be removed in a second or renewed. The wood dam is a few inches higher than the stone one, and the space between is roofed in by a strong frame covered with perforated zinc (No. 15). (Fig. 138.)

FIG. 133—scale 1/12.

A well was built of ashlar to one side of the dam and divided into two compartments by a low wall. From each compartment a spigot and faucet glazed pipe led the supply to the ponds,—a

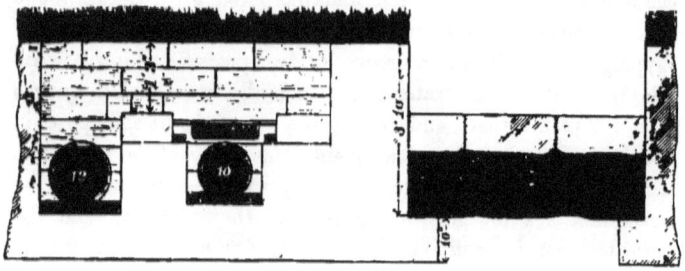

Fig. 139—scale $\frac{1}{12}$.

10-inch to the small ponds, and a 12-inch to the new extension (Fig. 139). A box, built of plank, and bolted together after the fashion of a plank pond, passes from the water-trap along the end of one compartment. A sluice of 2-inch plank (overflow) regulates

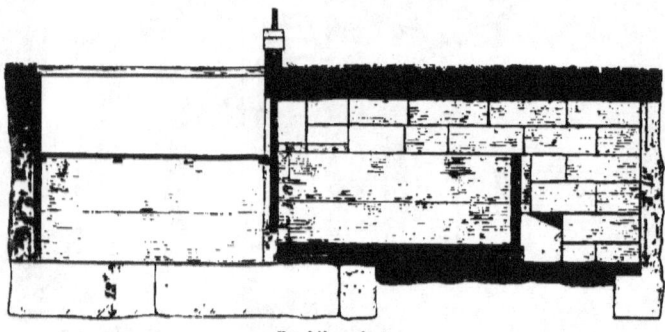

Fig. 140—scale $\frac{1}{12}$.

the supply to the other compartment, from which the 12-inch pipe leads to the ponds; and an opening is cut in the side of the plank box to discharge on to a screen of zinc covering the compartment, from which the 10-inch pipe leads to the 20-feet ponds (Fig. 140). An opening was left in the well immediately over the mouth of the 10-inch pipe, and flush with the zinc screen. This opening discharged into a waste channel, which returned the surplus to the foot of the apron of the dam.

A screw sluice closed the plank delivery-box from the water-trap. This sluice had iron ties on its screw-nut, so that it could

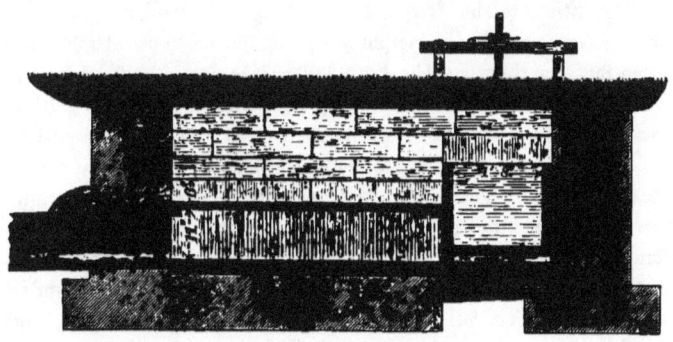

FIG. 141—scale 1/12.

be padlocked after being set (Fig. 141). The screw itself was of thorn, a wood very suitable for the purpose, as it is easily cut with the ordinary French screw-cutter, takes a clean edge on the worm, and lasts for ten or fifteen years, even where unprotected. The worm, on a stick 1½ inch thick and 2 feet long, can be cut without a lathe in less than ten minutes. So easy and so useful are these French screw-cutters, I would advise one to be marked in the inventory of implements in every fish-cultural establishment. Figs. 137-141 are diagrams of the intake works to the Howietoun Fishery.

When the dam and well were completed I filled in the temporary channel, and built an overflow at the point where it had left the stream. This overflow was faced with whinstone blocks, and a beech overflow-board was laid parallel to the stream, and of sufficient length to ensure that no flood ever rose more than 6 inches on its edge. As a matter of fact, up to the present date, no flood has yet risen more than 3 inches on its edge. As the ground fell, the mouth of the overflow was gradually contracted to a neck, so as to save ground, and the course was led into the old course of the stream some yards below the dam. The whole of the overflow course below the whinstone blocks was turfed, as the water rose over it only at intervals, and experience has shown that turf is by far the best and cheapest under those circumstances.

The intake to the Howietoun Fishery acts well, and requires little attention. The principle is equally suited to pass 10,000,000 cubic feet per diem, as the 1,000,000 which is its daily task. It offers no resistance to fish passing up or down stream if a little waste is passed over it. In fact, it is in itself a very perfect fish-pass; no young samlets can get through into the water abstracted from the stream. All the conditions the most sanguine member of an English Board of Conservators could suggest are complied with. No canal company or mill-owner can object, as no water is wasted, and but little trouble, time, or wages expended on cleaning. The fall required for clearance is very slight, and the first cost is not excessive. In no other way can anything like the same quantity of water be passed through a hake or grating of the same area, if the bars are not more than an inch apart; and even with horizontal bars an inch is far too wide, unless the stream is always free from leaves and débris, which no stream is. The zinc (No. 15) should last more than one year; but, even if the sheets had to be renewed every spring, no great hardship ensues; and in winter, when the smolts are not moving much, oak slats could be substituted for the zinc with safety, economy, and advantage, as, with wood, all danger of even a very temporary stoppage through ice is absent.

The intake acts as follows:—The stream is heightened by the wood dam to the height of its top, and rises above it, according to the state of the stream, till in flood it reaches the level of the overflow. Above this it rises very slowly until the maximum is reached. This must never be so high as to flood into the well. The zinc cover to the water-trap passes only screened water, so that no débris larger than the perforation of the zinc can pass to the ponds. All leaves and dirt, if the whole stream is taken, rest on the zinc, and, as they collect, the part free for the passage of the water becomes smaller and smaller; the stream therefore rises on the top of the wood dam, and the weight of the water pushes the débris over the zinc on to the apron of the dam; thus the intake cleans itself. From this it is evident that the height of the overflow is important, for if it is too near the level of the dam, the water could not rise sufficiently to clean the intake. If, on the other hand, it is too high, the stream in flood would flow into the well and mix with the screened water, not only increasing its quantity, but also loading it with dirt, to clog all the screens in the works. It is when the whole water of the stream is not required that the intake is seen to its greatest advantage. So long as a drop passes the zinc cover and over the apron of the dam, the zinc keeps clean, and the quantity passed by the sluice is practically constant. When the whole stream is taken, the sluice must be set so as to hold the water in the water-trap as high as the low edge of the dam, or there would be too much suction through the zinc to allow of easy clearance when the water rose. This is the secret of the success of this intake. Although any quantity (within wide limits) can be passed, the suction does not increase *as a holding force* proportionally to the quantity passed, while, after any water flows over the apron, all increase only tends to clean the zinc more perfectly. In winter, in Scotland, the zinc screen is removed, as the stream falls much in frost, and the zinc is apt to freeze temporarily if there is an insufficiency of water, although, when covered with water, it behaves very well. The hake of wooden slat which is substituted acts well, but would allow yearling fish to pass. This is not of much consequence, as fish move so little in winter, especially small fish, which seem to be very susceptible to cold. The water, having passed the sluice into the delivery-box, is divided by the overflow sluice at the end already described. The sluice is set to send the water back on the cut discharging on the 10-inch pipe compartment, and all not required by the 10-inch or its waste passes over into the 12-inch pipe's compartment, and through it to the ponds. The compartment of the 10-inch is covered by a sheet of small-sized perforated zinc (No. 9 is used). All the débris that has passed the intake screen is shot on to this zinc. A little overflow is always allowed for in setting the sluices, and this washes everything—dirt, and any occasional fry, eels, etc. —into the bottom of the apron of the dam, thus preserving the segregation of the fry in the 20-feet ponds (Fig. 142). In the larger ponds any strangers are instantly devoured, and if not, they would be discovered with ease and certainty at the next inspection.

The intake was completed, and the water let through the new sluice on 3d April 1876.

In the meantime I had increased the 20-feet plank ponds to four, three

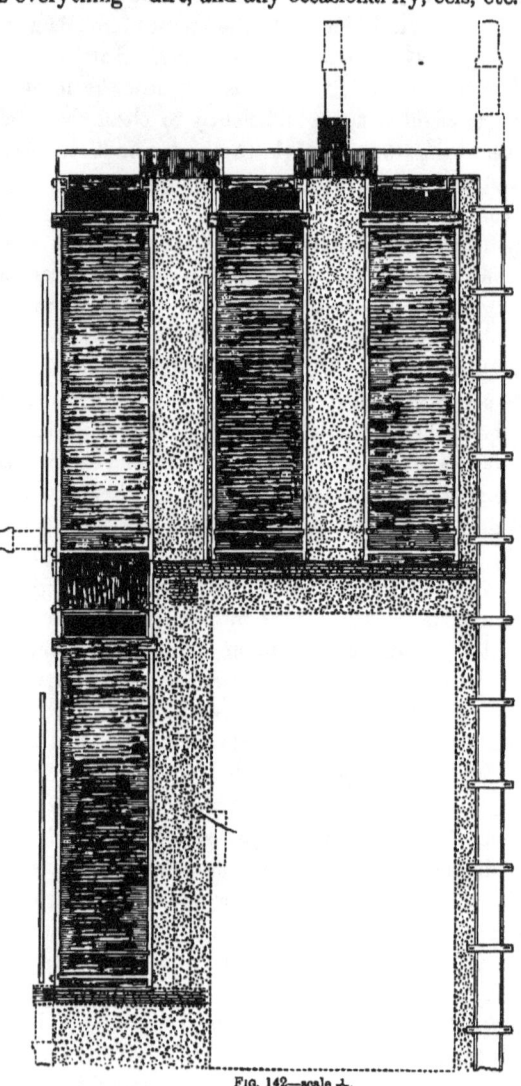

Fig. 142—scale $\frac{1}{14}$.

being fed by a trough, and the fourth was fed from No. 3. The trough was built of flooring, and was set level across the ends of the three 20-feets. The oldest 20-feet was deepened by planting a plank on its sides to make it the same depth as the rest. The trough received the 10-inch pipe, and three cuts were made corresponding to the ends of the three ponds (Figs. 143, 144). These cuts were each provided with a shoot to distribute the water evenly on the inlets of the ponds. A hole was bored in the bottom, and fitted with a plug, to clean the trough. The other end of the pond was provided with a sluice to discharge into a long aqueduct leading from the end of the 12-inch pipe. The water could thus all be turned into the large ponds when the 20-feet were not in use.

A trap-box passed under the ends of the three 20-feets to catch the waste water, and a drain also led to the burn, so that the dirty water, when cleaning, could be directly discharged. A board fitted at the end of each pond directed the water into the drain, or into the catch-box,

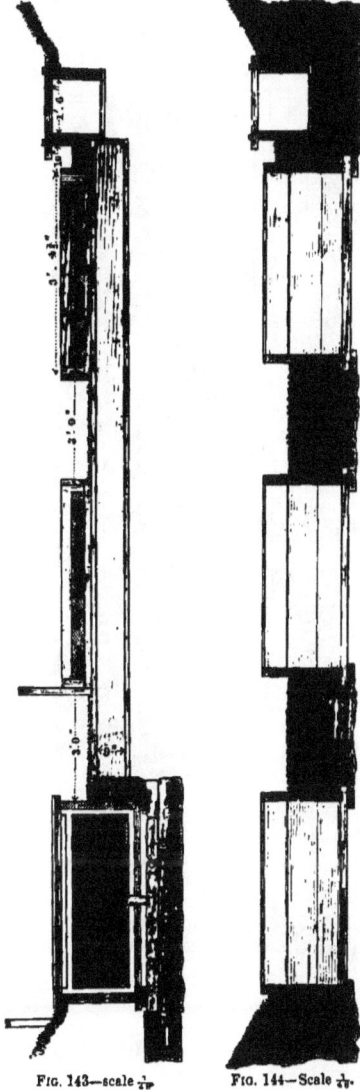

Fig. 143—scale $\frac{1}{12}$.   Fig. 144—Scale $\frac{1}{12}$.

as desired. The plugs of the ponds were placed close to the end, and immediately behind the safety-screens; these plugs are

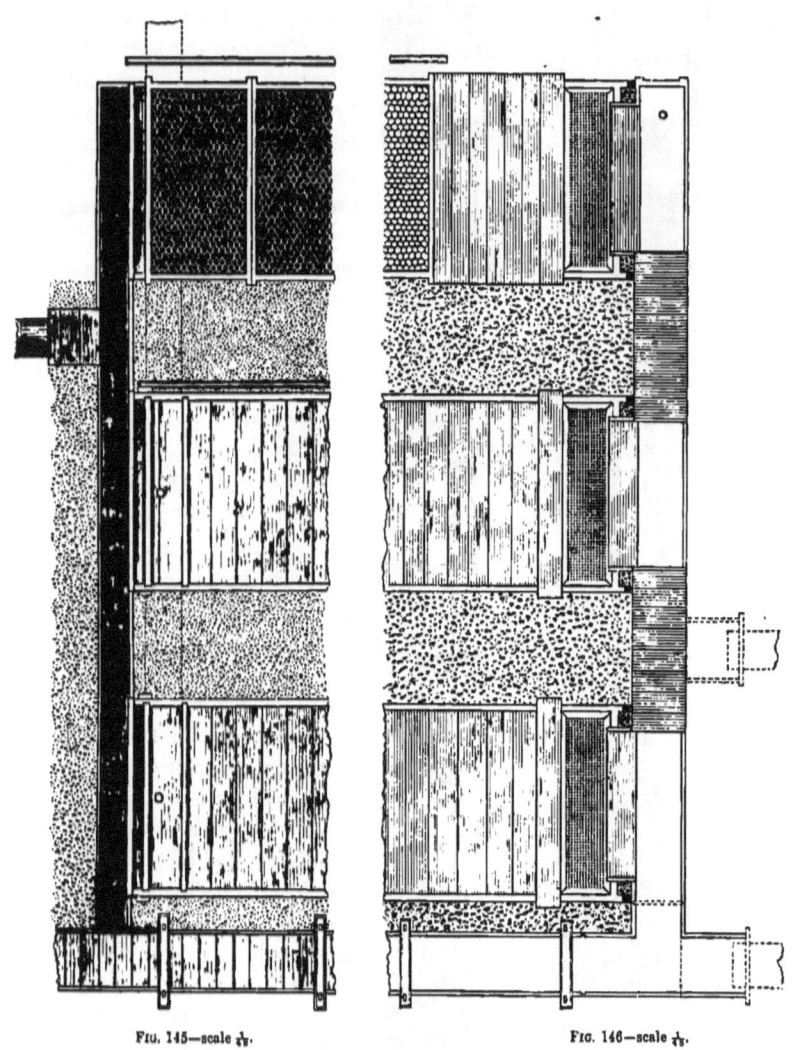

Fig. 145—scale 1/12.   Fig. 146—scale 1/12.

directly over the drain. The safety-screens retained all the fish in the pond, so that the plugs could be drawn at any time, and the ponds cleaned, or, if disease showed itself, any single pond could be isolated by turning the directing-board, and discharging the water into the drain (Figs. 145, 146). The water was led from the catch-box past the fourth 20-feet pond, and onwards, to be

FIG. 147—scale 1/12.

used again as part of the supply to the lower ponds (Fig. 147). A catch-box was also placed at the end of the fourth 20-feet, and a 10-inch pipe received the water from both boxes. Figs. 148, 149 are a diagram of the 20-feets in position, showing the arrangement of catch-box, drains, and distributing-trough.

The next work at Howietoun was the 60-feet pond. It was dug below the fourth 20-feet, and is 60 feet long, 15 feet wide, and 4 feet 10 inches deep. The pond was formed by laying battens as sleepers on the bottom, and nailing battens as uprights. These in their turn were secured by tying back with pieces of home wood to beech-trees cut in half and buried in the bank as anchors. The danger in ponds built in this way is of the sides collapsing when the water is suddenly withdrawn, as it is once a year for cleaning and re-charring. Anchoring is sufficient, but by far the best plan is to build such ponds in sets of three or four, and tie the uprights of one to the next, and so on. A drain was laid to the burn, and iron and sanitary pipes used,—iron under the pond and sanitary outside it. The battens on the bottom were then covered with flooring, of which the tongues and grooves had all been carefully re-dressed. The flooring was laid precisely in the same way as an ordinary floor is in Scotland, driven with a heavy hammer and drawn with nails. This makes an almost perfectly water-tight job, and stands well if there are not many stone-fly

HOWIETOUN.

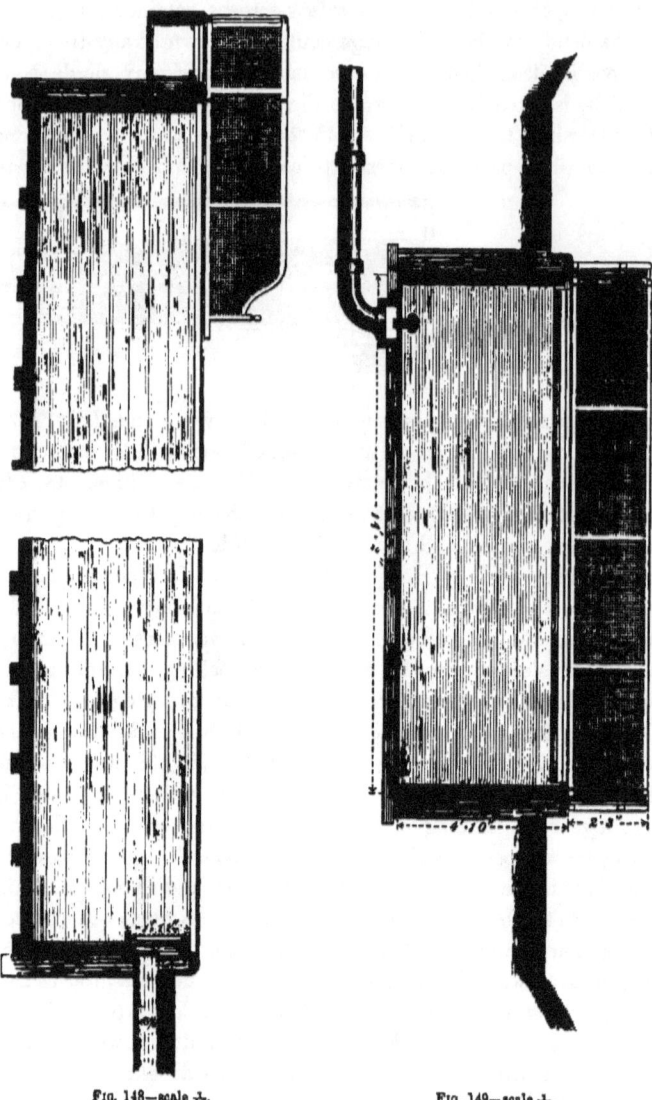

FIG. 148—scale 1/18.   FIG. 149—scale 1/18.

larvæ in the water. These small demons eat into the grooves, and

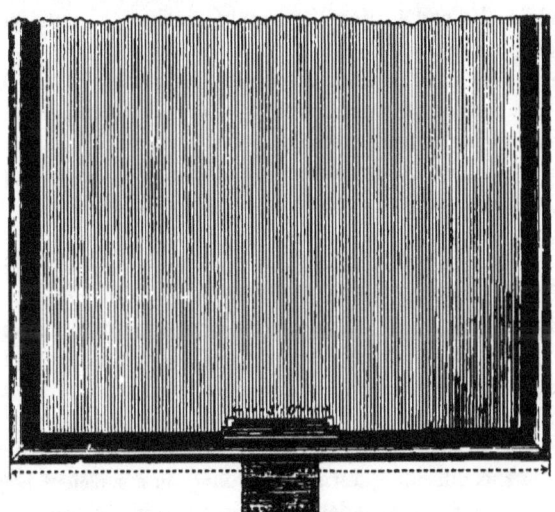

FIG. 150—scale $\tfrac{1}{17}$.

cause great trouble. The sides are next covered with flooring in the same manner at the bottom, and a plug-hole bored over the drain. The outlet of the pond is made by leaving two uprights a little farther apart than usual, and a rectangular wooden spout of convenient size is fitted between them. The flooring is brought tight against this, so as to form a tight joint. In the 60-feet pond no inlet was left, the water being brought in over the top end (Fig. 150). A cope of 3-inch plank was fitted all round the pond, the edges being aitched off, and the upper side of the plank rounded so as to throw off the rain. The whole inside woodwork was charred thoroughly, and the outside, above the ground-level, painted; the cope stood nearly 1 foot above the ground, and a board was nailed on to the standards to finish to the ground.

The water was brought in a trough along the end of the pond. One end of the trough was connected with the supply by a pressure joint, so that the water passed under the path and rose through the zinc screens forming the lids of the trough, and fell into the pond over the end in a single sheet. A hole was bored at the end of the trough in the bottom to clean it, and a moveable sluice was provided for the end joining the supply, so that the water could be cut off when necessary.

The 60-feet pond afterwards served as a model for the 130-feets. The method of construction has several advantages. 1*st*, The great saving of space, besides being perpendicular, and only between 7 and 8 inches in thickness, and the sides being perpendicular, some portion of the bottom is always in shade; the disadvantages are, from the necessarily great depth all over the bottom of the pond they cannot be used for *levenensis* or *fario* fry, although *fontinalis* and char will thrive in those ponds almost from the yolk-sac stage. Again, they cannot be used for large trout, as, from the depth of water at the sides, the fish can spring to a height of 2 or 3 feet, thus making them most difficult to retain in the pond.

Nor will the heightening of the sides materially assist in the solution of this difficult question : by fixing on a sufficient height of boarding, the fish may indeed be maintained in the pond, while a large number will get their physiognomy distorted, and their lower jaw dislocated by frequent contact with the guard.

The fish were afterwards found apt to jump over the trough, on the screens of which they often lay in great numbers. I therefore fixed a frame of zinc round the inlet of the pond; this has answered well. The outlet was guarded by a screen designed to pass the water freely in frost, and it has acted thoroughly with one foot of ice on the pond. The frame is made of batten, and a groove is cut for the screen. The frame is merely planted on the end of the pond, so as to cover the outlet, and, being much deeper, it reaches considerably below the bottom of the outlet; and the water has always a clear space to pass the screen below the ice, and the current it makes passing up the end of the pond to the outlet is sufficient to prevent the ice forming. Fig. 150 is a plan of the pond.

The thin sheet of water falling into this pond the whole length of the end has been found an excellent plan, and I can keep a much larger stock of fish in this pond than in any other pond I have yet built proportionately to its size; and not only a larger stock, but I can with safety keep trout of eight years of age, and up to 6 lbs. weight. It seems, therefore, that, with perfect aëration of the water, a much less depth will suffice; but it is plain that in most cases it is cheaper to make ponds deep than to give this amount of aëration; and if the supply ever becomes light, the fish in the deeper ponds are in hot weather safer than those in the shallower.

A 12-inch pipe brought the water from the intake to a trough at the head, and to one side of the 20-feets. The trough feeding the 20-feets was joined at right angles to this aqueduct, so that the water from the 10-inch could be added to that from the 12-inch if required. This aqueduct was closed at its lower end, and a 10-inch pipe fitted taking water past the 60-feet pond. A T-piece was built, into which the trough feeding the 60-feet was led, and a board in the end was cut to supply the 10-inch, but so as to give the 60-feet the first of the water, the 10-inch only getting the surplus. Of course, as the supply to the aqueduct was a 12-inch, the 10-inch was nearly full after the 60-feet had a sufficient supply.

A pipe (10-inch) was also led from the troughs, catching the water which had passed through the 20-feets along the other side of the 60-feet, and this water was afterwards collected and redistributed to the next series of ponds (the 130-feets).

This finishes the work of construction belonging to season 1875-76, the 60-feet pond being filled for the first time on 24th June 1876.

SEASON 1875-76.—EXPERIMENTAL WORK.

The experimental work of this season was chiefly with a view to ascertain the percentage of incubation accomplished in each period of twenty-four hours by an ovum in water of varying temperature. I calculated by a table based on Stone's dictum that at 40° F. a trout egg takes 100 days to hatch. Subsequent experience has shown that there is a slight difference in the time occupied in hatching by the eggs of various species of *Salmonidæ*; and that hybridism, the age of the parents—especially the age of the male,—causes a prolongation of the period, or the reverse. Happily for the results, only two classes of eggs were dealt with, viz. *S. levenensis* and *S. fario*. The former were all spawned at the lake from obviously mature parents, and the results from these eggs may be depended upon. The *S. fario* eggs were obtained from small hill-burn trout, and these probably varied much in age. They were, however, all apparently sexually mature.

I kept a careful record of the temperatures of the air and water; and from the corrected average temperature of the latter the percentage of incubation of the twenty-four hours was calculated. Unfortunately, I have not kept the original readings in decimals of a degree, which were marked in my rough note-book. In the clean note-book I have only entered the nearest degree, so it is impossible to check the calculations; they were made and entered from day to day, and I believe them to be accurate. They were originally worked to four places of decimals, although only two places were entered in the clean copy. The importance of this table lies in the wide range of temperature that occurred in the winter 1875-76 at Middlethird, in which hatching-house the record was taken. The ova was laid down on twelve different days.

TABLE OF TEMPERATURES AND OF INCUBATION.

Date.	Air.	Water.	Percentage.	Percentage.	Remarks.
1875	Deg.	Deg.			
Oct. 29	46	47	1·53	1·53	*S. fario* ova, 1160.
30	45	46	1·44	2·97	(Spawned Oct. 28.)
31	46	46	1·49	4·46	
Nov. 1	46	47	1·56	6·02	*S. levenensis* ova, 7600.
2	46	47	1·61	7·63	
3	52	48	1·66	9·29	
4	51	48	1·72	11·01	*S. fario* ova, 4905.
5	53	48	1·75	12·76	
6	49	48	1·69	14·45	*S. levenensis* ova, 6325.
7	42	47	1·51	15·96	
8	38	45	1·36	17·32	*S. fario* ova, 2370.
9	37	45	1·35	18·67	
10	36	45	1·31	19·98	
11	34	43	1·20	21·18	
12	33	42	1·14	22·32	*S. levenensis* ova, 13,580.
13	37	43	1·21	23·53	*S. fario* ova, 7560.
14	42	44	1·30	24·83	
15	39	44	1·26	26·09	
16	44	45	1·33	27·42	
17	44	46	1·45	28·87	*S. levenensis* ova, 7560.
18	48	46	1·47	30·34	*S. fario* ova, 1350.
19	42	45	1·36	31·70	
20	38	44	1·29	32·99	
21	42	44	1·31	34·30	
22	40	44	1·25	35·55	
23	38	43	1·19	36·74	
24	37	43	1·18	37·92	
25	38	43	1·17	39·09	*S. fario* ova, 1540.
26	37	43	1·16	40·25	*S. levenensis* ova, 6525.
27	36	42	1·13	41·48	
28	37	42	1·15	42·63	
29	40	43	1·18	43·81	
30	37	42	1·12	44·93	
Dec. 1	36	42	1·09	46·02	
2	36	42	1·08	47·10	
3	35	41	1·06	48·16	
4	34	41	1·03	49·19	*S. levenensis* ova, 19,780.
5	33	40	1·01	50·20	
6	33	40	1·00	51·20	
7	29	37	·87	52·07	
8	31	38	·92	52·99	
9	35	40	·99	53·98	
10	38	41	1·05	55·03	
11	44	43	1·14	56·17	
12	43	43	1·16	57·33	
13	44	43	1·17	58·50	
14	40	42	1·12	59·62	
15	38	42	1·11	60·73	

Date.	Air.	Water.	Percentage.	Percentage.	Remarks.
1875.	Deg.	Deg.			
Dec. 16	39	42	1·12	61·85	
17	40	42	1·13	62·98	
18	44	43	1·19	64·17	
19	40	42	1·14	65·31	
20	47	43	1·22	66·53	
21	46	43	1·21	67·74	
22	45	43	1·19	68·93	
23	43	43	1·16	70·09	
24	47	43	1·21	71·30	
25	42	44	1·23	72·53	
26	46	44	1·27	73·80	
27	45	44	1·26	75·06	
28	44	44	1·27	76·33	
29	46	44	1·28	77·61	
30	46	45	1·30	78·91	
31	47	45	1·33	80·24	
1876.					
Jan. 1	40	45	1·31	81·55	
2	36	43	1·19	82·74	
3	42	44	1·21	83·95	
4	47	45	1·30	85·25	
5	46	45	1·29	86·54	
6	42	45	1·30	87·84	
7	38	44	1·28	89·12	
8	36	43	1·19	90·31	
9	28	41	1·04	91·35	
10	34	41	1·03	92·38	
11	33	40	1·02	93·40	
12	37	41	1·04	94·44	
13	26	40	·98	95·42	
14	32	40	1·00	96·42	
15	37	40	1·02	97·44	
16	41	41	1·04	98·48	
17	41	41	1·07	99·55	
18	45	42	1·12	100·67	
19	47	43	1·20	101·87	
20	39	42	1·08	102·95	
21	33	40	·99	103·94	
22	35	40	1·00	104·94	Ova spawned Nov. 1.
23	47	42	1·12	106·06	Hatched Jan. 23.
24	48	42	1·12	107·18	
25	47	43	1·21	108·39	
26	47	43	1·20	109·59	
27	47	43	1·20	110·79	
28	46	43	1·19	111·98	
29	45	43	1·18	113·16	
30	44	43	1·17	114·33	
31	45	43	1·20	115·53	
Feb. 1	47	44	1·25	116·78	
2	41	42	1·14	117·92	
3	39	42	1·12	119·04	

SEASON 1875-76.

Date.	Air.	Water.	Percentage.	Percentage.	Remarks.
1876.	Deg.	Deg.			
Feb. 4	38	41	1·08	120·12	
5	37	41	1·06	121·18	
6	36	41	1·03	122·21	Ova spawned Nov. 12.
7	37	41	1·05	123·26	Hatched Feb. 6.
8	36	41	1·03	124·29	
9	36	40	1·02	125·31	
10	33	39	·97	126·28	
11	33	39	·94	127·22	Ova spawned Nov. 17.
12	32	38	·91	128·13	Hatched Feb. 12.
13	35	39	·96	129·09	
14	33	38	·90	129·99	
15	35	39	·93	130·92	
16	41	40	1·00	131·92	
17	43	41	1·05	132·97	
18	41	41	1·03	134·00	
19	39	40	1·01	135·01	
20	35	40	·99	136·00	
21	37	40	1·01	137·01	
22	45	42	1·09	138·10	
23	40	40	1·01	139·11	
24	38	40	·99	140·10	
25	36	39	·94	141·04	
26	36	39	·96	142·00	
27	37	40	1·00	143·00	
28	36	40	·99	143·99	
29	37	40	1·00	144·99	
Mar. 1	39	40	1·01	146·00	Ova spawned Nov. 26.
2	41	41	1·04	147·04	Hatched Mar. 1.
3	48	42	1·12	148·16	
4	42	41	1·06	149·22	
5	42	41	1·09	150·31	
6	41	41	1·06	151·37	
7	36	40	1·02	152·39	Latest ova hatched.
8	39	41	1·06		
9	38	40	·99		
10	38	40	1·01		
11	39	41	1·05		
12	38	41	1·04		
13	36	40	1·01		
14	34	40	·99	All ova hatched.	
15	35	39	·98		
16	34	39	·97		
17	34	39	·96		
18	31	38	·90		
19	34	39	·93		
20	34	39	·93		
21	35	39	·94		
22	40	40	1·00		
23	43	41	1·05		
24	44	41	1·07		
25	45	42	1·11		

EXPERIMENTAL WORK.

Date.	Air.	Water.	Percentage.	Percentage.	Remarks.
1876.	Deg.	Deg.			
Mar. 26	39	41	1·06		
27	38	40	1·00		
28	38	40	·99	All ova hatched.	
29	38	39	·96		
30	39	40	1·01		
31	40	40	1·02		

The temperatures of the air were read from a thermometer in the centre of the hatching-house, generally about noon; the temperatures of the water were read from a thermometer, whose bulb was immersed in the distributing-spout, and the temperature was consequently that of the water before it reached the ova. The percentage of incubation was calculated from the temperature of the water, read in fifths of a degree (the nearest whole degree only being entered in the book afterwards), and a further correction was made generally from two other observations, so that the percentage of incubation is really calculated from a very approximate mean of the temperature of the preceding twenty-four hours. The next column is the addition of the percentage of all the preceding percentages, so that, by subtracting the total opposite the day on which any particular batch of ova was laid down, its accomplished percentage of the period of incubation is at once apparent. I think it is best to generalise solely from the ova of the *S. levenensis*, for this reason,—all the spawners were netted in the lake at the mouth of the South Queich, and were all mature fish of 1 lb. and over, while the burn trout were small and very much mixed.

Spawned.	*S. levenensis* Ova.	Eyed.	Per cent.	Hatched.	Per cent.
1875.					
Nov. 1	7,600	Dec. 11	50·15	January 23	100·06
,, 6	6,325	,, 19	50·86		
,, 12	13,580	,, 25	50·21	February 6	99·89
,, 17	7,560	,, 31	51·37	,, 12	99·76
,, 26	6,525	Jan. 7	48·87	March 1	106·75
Dec. 4	19,780	,, 17	50·36	,, 6	102·18

The table on page 205 shows the days the *S. levenensis* were spawned, and on which each batch eyed and hatched, and the calculated total percentages of incubation at each stage.

The lot taken on November 6th were sold for the benefit of the Loch Leven Angling Association, so the date of their hatching is unknown. The lot entered on November 26th were brought to the hatching-house at Middlethird on that day from Kinross, and must have been spawned the day previous, and lain all night in a warm cottage ; this will account for the apparently early period at which they eyed. These eggs were the longest in hatching of any this season, and this may also be due to their being kept overnight without change of water.

The only deduction at present to be made from this table is, that it forms a useful and ready way to compare ova taken at different times and laid down in the same hatching-house. It also points to the percentage of incubation accomplished in any period of twenty-four hours, at any given temperature, being the same whether the ovum is in its early or late stages. It ought to have been mentioned that the lot taken on November 26th was placed in the last box in the house, and the water in February, when the quantity was small, may have fallen below the calculated average, and so the discrepancy not be so great as appears.

I add the table, calculated to fifths, from -40° F. to 48° F.

TABLE OF PERCENTAGES OF INCUBATION (PER DIEM).

Deg.		Deg.		Deg.	
40·0	1·000	43·0	1·176	46·0	1·428
·2	1·010	·2	1·190	·2	1·449
·4	1·020	·4	1·204	·4	1·464
·6	1·030	·6	1·219	·6	1·492
·8	1·041	·8	1·234	·8	1·500
41·0	1·052	44·0	1·250	47.0	1·538
·2	1·063	·2	1·265	·2	1·562
·4	1·075	·4	1·281	·4	1·587
·6	1·086	·6	1·298	·6	1·612
·8	1·098	·8	1·315	·8	1·639
42·0	1·111	45·0	1·333	48·0	1·666
·2	1·123	·2	1·351	·2	1·694
·4	1·135	·4	1·369	·4	1.734
·6	1·149	·6	1·388	·6	1·754
·8	1·162	·8	1·408	·8	1·786

This table is almost perfectly accurate for Loch Leven trout ova. For salmon ova, the figures are about ·04285 too great. This is in practice easily corrected by subtracting four-fifths of a degree before using the table. Thus, for salmon ova, the value of the percentage of incubation for twenty-four hours, with the water at 46° F., would be 1·351, not 1·428, and so on. Similarly, if the time of incubation of any variety or species be known, the table will show, at any stage the period of which has been determined, whether the embryo is in advance or retard of its normal, and this no matter how varying the temperature. In this way experiments all over the world can be compared, and results deduced with great accuracy.

SEASON 1875-76.—FISH-CULTURE.

The fish-cultural work this season consisted in spawning burn-trout and Loch Leven trout; no hybrids were made.

On October 20th I examined the trout *S. fario* in Craigend dam; none of them seemed to be within a week of spawning. I ran the dam dry, and bailed out the last drop of water, and got out all the trout, including the big Loch Leven female "Queichy," so called from her having been caught in the North Queich, near Milnathort. This was the spawner brought last year from Kinross, whose eggs were impregnated by the milt of a sea trout (Exp. 8). The male Loch Leven trout had unfortunately fallen a prey to an otter; at least it was found on the bank of the dam with a piece eaten out, and shortly afterwards the track of an otter was seen in the burn leading from the dam. I placed the trout first in the Francis Box; but although there was a good flow of water, I found they were too crowded; and as the long pond (now called the upper 100-feet) had not yet been used for fish, I turned them into it, where they rapidly improved. The question of the retention of spawning fish is of the utmost importance. At Howietoun it is solved by the construction of the ponds, and where the stock-fish are bred from generation to generation this is the true solution; but in salmon-culture the fish must in many cases be retained for days or weeks before spawning. On the Tay, and also on the Tweed, there is not much difficulty in getting from 250,000 to 500,000 salmon ova in a season, but in the Forth and other rivers only a few thousand can be depended upon, and the cost is very heavy. I have known a season's work in collecting salmon ova average over 30s. per 1000, and it rarely, except on the Tay, falls as low as 10s.

Now, if our salmon rivers are to be stocked, if our salmon rivers are to be as productive, in the future as they have been in the past, ova must be obtained by the million. And this can only be done by retaining the fish till ripe. It seems absurd to have to repeat what to me appear self-evident truisms, but it is necessary; there are so many who, from the difficulty they find in casting off old notions, are continually dinning fallacies into the public, without the slightest attempt at proof,—men who ought to know better, men who have had ample opportunity for ascertaining the truth, and men who, on the foundation of their having had such opportunity, carry a great though fictitious weight with the public. The public has neither the time nor the inclination to compare their statements with the authentic reports, and the old errors still pass as current coin. It is amusing to note that the universal tendency of these men is to ignore the old maxim, *Ex nihilo nihil fit.* Only listen to them, and no expense is required in the treatment of the ova; if you will only intrust them with sufficient public money, the rivers are again to teem with fish! It may be so, but if the hatching and rearing can be done for next to nothing, why should public money be required at all? In Great Britain nearly all the inland fisheries are private property. I do not say that no assistance should be given by Government. On the contrary, I think that all the assistance necessary should be given; but I hold that this consists chiefly in collecting and publishing all the reports of work elsewhere. If this was done, private enterprise would do the rest. This is a work which might be intrusted to the Inspector of Fisheries for England. It cannot be done by private enterprise, as the reports require much weeding; our consuls should be instructed to inquire into the results of the various plants of fish recorded. This is the crucial point. The reports generally very fully *anticipate* the results, but rarely refer back to them. It is the duty of the Government to educate and to regulate; it is the part of private enterprise to produce. At present the law of the land operates prejudicially to salmon-culture. The purchase and retention of salmon for breeding purposes should be legalised; District Boards should have the power of netting for spawning fish, and of retaining those caught, and of working any cruive or other engine in their district for this purpose,—of course under proper restrictions. And one of these restrictions should be that the ova so obtained are properly developed, and the fry liberated, to the satisfaction of the Inspector of Fisheries in England, or the Fishery Board for Scotland; otherwise, salmon-culture would be followed here by the same destruction of the fishery and waste of money which has attended it in Canada. Compare the Tay in the latter days of the Stormontfield ponds with the Tay this season, when the new and properly constructed house at Dupplin, on its tributary the Earn, has told for the first time (1885).

But this is not the whole gain. With retaining-ponds the spawners can be selected, and all the advantages of an improved breed obtained. Rivers will, to a great extent, be early or late, at the option of the District Board. Often it is impossible to change a late river into an early one, or *vice versa*, but an early river can be improved by adding a number of late fish, and a late river very much improved by adding a very large number of early fish. This can only be accomplished by means of retaining-ponds to enable us to select the breeders most fitted to our purpose.

The retaining-ponds require the following considerations to be attended to: they must have water-carriage from the place the fish are caught; they should be capable of being drained dry from the centre of the bottom; they should be shallow at the inlet and the outlet ends; they should have a large supply of water, at least 1,000,000 gallons per diem, to each pond; they should be 10 feet deep in the centre; they must have banks 2 feet high on each slope to an angle of 45°, and turfed, to prevent injury to the fish from jumping. There should be at least three of these ponds,—the lowest one for males, the next for ripe females, and the highest for later females. The same supply of water can be led through each with safety if the fish are in this order; in any other the loss from fungus will be heavy. The males do not fight if kept separate from the females. The lowest mill on the river will usually point to the best location for retaining-ponds, and power to purchase should be given the District Board (compulsorily, at a fair valuation).

The long pond at Craigend acting so admirably as a retaining-pond, I had no difficulty in spawning the whole of my *S. fario.* The kelts, to the number of 160, I returned to the dam at Craigend. I spawned the first Loch Leven trout on the 1st November. "Went to Kinross; got five ripe spawners near the boat-house; tried the North Queich, but only got one milter. Took a wast set at the South Queich mouth: half a dozen fish, none of them ripe; I got one spawner at the churchyard also. Got home at 11 o'clock P.M. 8100 ova." It was now evident that, if anything was to be done to re-stock Loch Leven, the fish must be caught and ready for me when I went there. I instructed the Manager to have a second safe made to ripen the fish. This safe—or more properly crate,—for it consisted only of wooden slats nailed to framework, answered well. It was weighted so as to float with its top just above the surface of the lake, to ensure the largest amount of space and the greatest amount of aëration of the water. The safe answered fully better than I anticipated. I note under November 12th :—" Had a splendid day at Kinross, the fish in the new safe having come on nicely, probably on account of its floating higher in the water. Total, 13,580 ova." The old safe floated almost level with the water; in fact, it was practically an immense cage. On the 17th I spawned at Kinross, for the last time this season, and let what fish remained unripe go, they having been fourteen days in the safe. The other two lots of *S. levenensis* ova were taken by White, the foreman of the boats at Loch Leven. The determination of the period which elapses between two consecutive spawnings of an individual trout was noted under November 25th : " Spawned

'Queichy,' it being exactly 363 days since she spawned last year. Total, 154 ova." This is absolute proof that a Loch Leven trout can spawn two successive seasons, and that a complete year does not always elapse between spawnings. I hope to be able to show that, as a general rule, Loch Leven trout spawn earlier every season, so that the oldest spawn first and the youngest last,—only as a general rule however, for by feeding certain kinds of food the trout can all be made earlier, and by withholding food trout may all be made later. There are, of course, certain yeld trout in every water; these I have almost invariably found to be females. I cannot give a reason, but possibly the fish may have not got in condition soon enough in spring to start the ovaries.

On the same day that I spawned " Queichy " I pumped the pond dry. This operation took two days and a half. Now, when all the ponds can be emptied in a few hours without trouble, merely by lifting a valve, it seems strange to look back at the immense amount of manual labour required at that time.

As soon as I was satisfied that no fish were left alive in the pond, I refilled it; and as by the 7th December the ice was causing much trouble in the 20-feets at Howietoun, I transferred about half the Loch Leven springlings to the pond in front of Craigend House (now called the upper 100-feet pond). I transferred the rest on December 14th, and also the hybrids. These seem to have been placed partly in the 9-feet plank pond, and partly in a temporary earth pond.

This season I sold for the Loch Leven Angling Association 16,000 ova (*S. levenensis*) and 1000 fry (ditto). I also liberated 22,000 in the tributaries of Loch Leven, and retained as many fry as left me 7000 springlings on the 3d of December 1876. This accounts for 46,000 of the 61,370 *S. levenensis* ova taken in the autumn. Of the remaining 15,000—4000 were lost as eggs; 10 per cent., or 4600, disappear as extra count, and the 6000 odd represents the loss in rearing the fry and springlings.

Of the whole 86,710 eggs laid down, 5777 were picked out either as white or unimpregnated—the numbers being, 2753 dead ova, and 3024 picked out clear as unimpregnated eggs. This represents a loss of only 6·66 per cent., and a hatch of 93·34 per cent. of the eggs laid down.

The *S. fario* did not fare so well, principally for want of space. Out of 13,800 ova laid down, I only had 2315 year-old trout to show. The single lot of Queichy's eggs (milted by a burn-trout) gave 1000 year-olds out of 1540 eggs.

The following notes as to the growth of *S. levenensis* yearlings occur, March 1876 :—" Loch Leven yearling died of indigestion : length, 4·13 inches ; weight, 42 ounces. Hatched January 23d, 1875." And March 31st (1876):—" Loch Leven yearling died from over-eating : length, 4·71 inches ; weight, 74 ounces."

On June 24th 1876 I began stocking the new 60-feet pond at Howietoun. I placed 180 Loch Leven yearlings into it, and on the 13th July I put in 343 more. That evening I went up to London. There was still a little water running into the pond at Craigend. On the 15th I received a telegram, that nearly all the trout in the pond in front of Craigend House were dead. I came north by the limited mail, and arrived at Craigend at 9 A.M. The temperature of the water in the pond was 72° F. I picked out 630 *S. levenensis* trout, weighing 20 lbs., or twenty-one to the pound nearly ; but as they had lain some time in the sun before weighing, it is probable that had they been weighed at once on being taken from the water, they would have run eighteen to the pound, or better. I netted out 555 alive, and transferred them to the 60-feet pond at Howietoun. I then returned to London, and next morning received a telegram to say that no more were dead, and that 335 more had been safely transferred to the 60-feet pond. The pond was emptied in my absence, and there was ascertained to be only 1210 fish. This left me with 3060 *S. levenensis* yearlings, many of whom have since exceeded 8 lbs. in weight. On the 27th July I called at 37 Albany Street, and saw Mr. Buckland. He suggested the thundery state of the atmosphere ; and I think he was right, as, if it had been over-crowding, my experience is that the loss would have been almost total. The cause of loss is not very material, as, with the water at 72° at nine in the morning, the fish must have succumbed sooner or later; and the main inference to be drawn is that ponds must be constructed in such a manner that this temperature never can be reached. This necessitates a combination of supply with depth. Shade is out of the question, at least from trees, as the decaying vegetable matter imprisons—if I may use the word—the free oxygen. Depth is governed directly by the size of the fish the pond is to be used for; indirectly, by the facility of drainage. The depth must never be such as to enable the fish to get out of control; up to this any depth may be used in earth ponds. In plank ponds, however, where the sides are perpendicular, other considerations intervene; but in earth ponds no depth can be too great if the fish are always under perfect control. If the supply is clear, deeper ponds can be used than if the water is muddy. In practice, 5 feet will be found the average limit; and $4\frac{1}{2}$ feet for muddy, and 6 feet for clear, spring water, the absolute limits for earth ponds into which feeding-fry are to be placed to grow into yearlings. With water less than 4 feet deep yearlings do not thrive, unless the current is very strong; and a strong current is too expensive to pay, and, besides, very dangerous, as the screens are much more apt to choke than with a moderate supply. A strong current is expensive, because it necessitates larger and more costly intakes and outlets; because the wear and tear is much increased, both of banks and of perforated zinc; and lastly, because it uses up water that can be much more profitably employed elsewhere. If these limits are exceeded, the fry are not under control at first. They cannot be collected for feeding, nor their numbers checked daily without drawing down the water, and the labour which this would entail renders it out of the question.

The collection of the fry for feeding, especially for the first month after they have been turned into the pond, is of great importance. It is at this period nearly the whole of the loss occurs. If the fry do not feed when first turned out, they get weak, and never afterwards pick up. This is the prime cause of fungus on three-month-old fry; some get weak, others take on cannibal instincts, and nibble the fins of their brethren and sisters. This may be mitigated in some way by filling the pond with stagnant water for three weeks before the fry are placed in it ; but the growth of *crustaceæ* is so dependent on the weather, much reliance should not be put in this method.

The depth thus being fixed, the direction of the pond must be considered. In Scotland, it is found that fry do much better in a pond which runs north and south than in one running east and west. The reason is that the east wind is the most deadly foe they have to contend with, and that of course, if the pond runs with the wind, it gets much more of it than if it runs across it. But narrow ponds, lying north and south, also keep much cooler than those running east and west, the reason being that if a pond exposes its side to the sun, the reflection heats the water more than if the end only reflected. Of course the surface of the water in a pond running north and south gets more sun than the surface of the water in a pond running east and west ; but the reflection from the sloping sides is so important a factor that it far more than counterbalances it. Heat-rays, whether obscure or luminous, are refracted in the same way as rays of light when they enter a diathermanous medium. (Ice is only diathermanous in regard to the luminous rays, it arrests the rays of obscure heat.) It is the sun's rays we have to consider in connection with placing longer axis of rectangular ponds. The slope of the sides is usually between 45° and 60°. The refraction of the water has the effect of making the heat-rays strike the side nearer the bottom than if the path of the ray was straight. The slope above the water also, when the pond runs east and west, reflects the rays back on to the surface of the water, and these rays are also refracted. The consequence is that extremes of temperature are produced in a pond running east and west, and this in itself is fatal to good work in trout-rearing, to say nothing of the danger of the limit of the temperature being reached unexpectedly.

TABLE OF OVA SPAWNED 1875-76.

Date.	S. fario.	S. levenensis.	S. levenensis (Queichy).	Totals.	Remarks.
1875.					
Oct. 28	1,160	...	...	1,160	
Nov. 1	...	7,600	...	7,600	
4	4,905	...	...	4,905	
6	...	6,325	...	6,325	
8	2,370	...	...	2,370	
12	...	13,580	...	13,580	
13	4,015	...	...	4,015	
17	...	7,560	...	7,560	
18	1,350	...	...	1,350	
25	...	...	1,540	1,540	
26	...	6,525	...	6,525	
Dec. 4	...	19,780	...	19,780	
Total	13,800	61,370	1,540	86,710	

TABLE OF STOCK ON 1ST JANUARY 1876.

Upper 100-feet, Craigend,	.	4500	S. levenensis, springlings.
Other ponds,	,, .	500	,, hybrids.
Dam,	,, .	160	S. fario, aged.

CHAPTER XV.

SEASON 1876-77.

CONSTRUCTION—HOWIETOUN.

THE hatching-house at Middlethird was no longer sufficient for the growing wants of the Fishery, so I used the sarking of which the fence round the first 20-feet plank ponds had been made to build a hatching-house at Howietoun. This house was a little larger than the one at Middlethird, and held four 7-feet hatching-boxes on each end, and the five rearing-boxes that had done duty in 1874-75 at Middlethird.

The house was placed below three of the 20-feets, and beside the fourth. One of the 20-feets was converted into a filter, and the water from the 10-inch pipe was used. The water in winter was often very dirty; and there were cattle in a field above, through which the stream flowed; the filter thus became of some importance. It was formed by fitting two divisions of flooring lengthways in the pond. These were held in their place by cross-pieces, so arranged that the water passed over and under alternately. The water thus had to pass three times the length of the pond, or a distance of 60 feet, through gravel and road metal.

The plug-hole in the pond was used to clean the filter; but it was found insufficient, and the only effectual plan was to take out all the metal and gravel and wash it. Life would have been too short if it had required washing oftener than once or twice a season. The end of the 20-feet was closed by the insertion of a plank, jointed with flannel, and a spout was fitted in this plank to convey the water from the filter to the aqueduct supplying the house.

The main aqueduct was also tapped, and a 3-inch lead pipe, bent in the form of a segment of a circle, inserted in the side. The mouth of the pipe was placed beyond the hole cut in the side of the aqueduct, so that if any débris was sucked against the mouth, the current in the aqueduct tends to clean it away. Had it been reversed, there would have been the danger of the pipe choking up, as the suction and the current would have acted in the same direction, and every blade of grass, or leaf, or bit of water-weed, however small, would have helped to gather more. I may explain that the main aqueduct was covered only by open slats, and that in windy weather, especially in autumn, the leaves occasionally blew in; and in winter the perforated zinc at the intake was replaced by wooden slats, through which small bits of weed passed. The mode of taking water by means of a pipe bent in the direction of the current may be found useful for other purposes. It would be useful in taking water from swift streams, in situations where a dam was inconvenient, and where a leaf-screen was unnecessary.

The house had three distributing-spouts. The one at the south end received the short spout from the filter, also the end of the bent pipe from the aqueduct. The old H-spout was again fitted up inside the house, to lead the water to the distributing-spout for the rearing-boxes, and a 3-inch lead pipe was fitted in the end of the H-spout underground, to take the water across to the distributing-spout on the north end of the house. A cleat was fixed in the distributing-spout at the south end, and a cross-spout was fitted to lead the water to the H-spout; this thus had the first of the water. But the spout cleat was so levelled that as soon as the water stood flush with the supply-holes to the hatching-boxes, the flow was strong over the cleat. This enabled me to regulate the supply to the eight hatching-boxes almost independently of the supply given to the five rearing-boxes. The foundation of the house was sunk, to allow the supply to be brought in as high above the floor as possible. Fortunately, the soil was hard fire-clay and boulder-clay, the latter very tenacious, and the fire-clay making the best possible puddling when worked. By cutting a drain to join the one from the 60-feet pond, ample fall was obtained, and all the house kept dry underfoot. One or two ochre holes were found in the boulder-clay, and one, about 3 feet

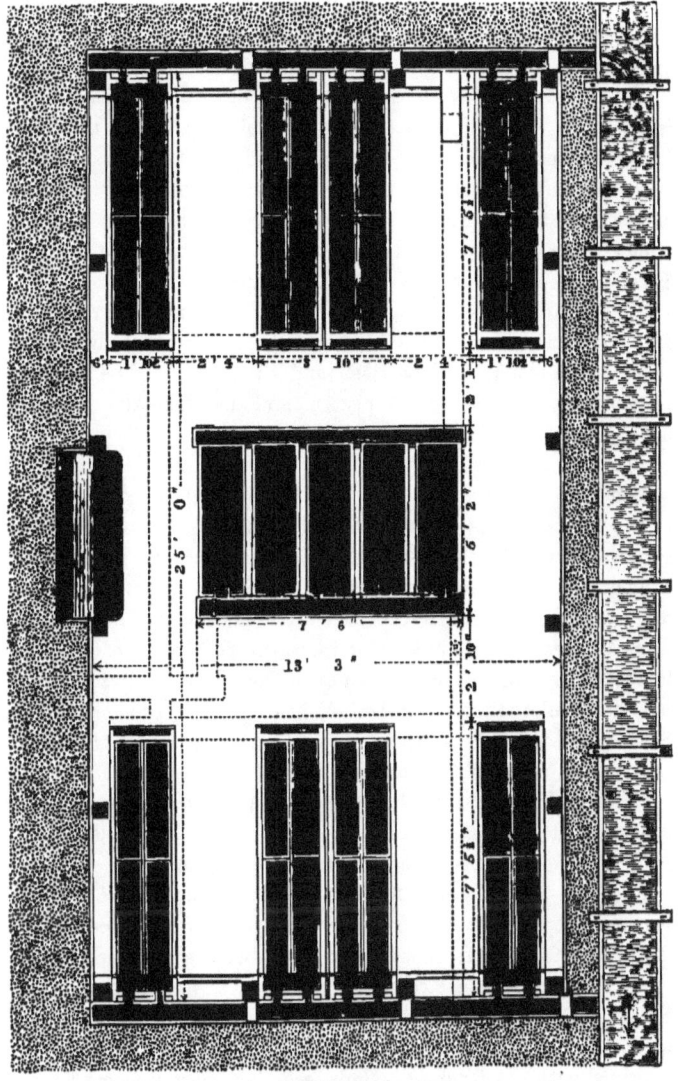

Fig. 151—scale 1/18.
PLAN OF THE HOWIETOUN HATCHING-HOUSE.

deep, occurred in the centre of the floor. I knew of this hole, and thought it was a nice trap, so I told the foreman navvy not to fill it up till the rough stones which were to form the bottom of the floor were to be put in. In a few days a very particular friend came to shoot with me, and I took him to see the new hatching-house, which was then just ready for its floor. Unfortunately, I forgot all about the ochre hole, and stepped most carelessly into it. The navvies never forgot the joke; and as yellow ochre is very tenacious, I had literally to be hauled out. Practical jokes are not necessarily fish-culture.

The drains were arranged in three lines across the house. Into the northmost drain a tap discharged from the 3-inch lead pipe, thus enabling the pipe itself and the H-spout to be run dry or flushed at pleasure. In all piscicultural operations the drainage is as important as the supply.

The hatching-house was built by driving posts into the subsoil, and binding them together by a tie running all round at the proper height to receive the ends of the hatching-boxes. A doorway was formed in the east side, with steps down to the level of the floor. Light was admitted by two windows,—one in each end; and over the one in the north end a seat under the roof was formed, open to the outside, from which the habits of the fish in the 60-feet pond could be studied. The roof was of wood, overlapping, and, though unprotected, has lasted in good condition for ten years. It is now, however, showing signs of decay. Opposite is a plan of the hatching-house (Fig. 151).

The 60-feet pond having proved a success, I surveyed the ground, and laid off three other ponds on a similar plan, only longer, some distance below. But before commencing them, I ordered the head forester to erect a fence round the ponds and house already completed. This fence consisted of larch posts sunk deep into the ground, about 5 feet apart, with a top and bottom rail, also of larch, and larch spars nailed on so near together that no one could place a foot on the rails to climb the fence; the spars terminated in a sharp iron spike, so that any attempt to cross was attended with great danger. This fence has since been continued round the ponds from time to time as the works advanced, and I have found it answer well.

No pains should be spared to keep uninvited guests out of piscicultural establishments. Nothing resents intrusion more than fish. Trout soon get to know those that feed them, and the hours at which they are to be fed; but once let strangers about them, and one or two evils must be faced: either the fish will get frightened, and soon become wild, and scatter all over the pond, and refuse to collect for feeding, which entails great waste of food, and the certainty of the uneaten food fouling the water; or the fish must be fed whenever strangers are present; and if trout are fed irregularly, disease is sure to set in amongst them. The collection of fish at regular hours for feeding is a most important factor in success in fish-breeding.

The next work was to provide a small larder to keep the meat, and to chop it up in. I laid two beech sleepers across the stream, and on them built a small wooden hut, with a convenient shelf in the window for an American chopping-machine. The one I used was the same recommended by Stone (*Domesticated Trout*, p. 215). I sent to New York for it; but Starret's American chopping-machine can now be obtained from any large ironmonger in Scotland. I cut a hole in the floor, so that meat might be kept cool in the stream below, and drawn up when wanted for cutting up. Meat keeps well in water, if the water is cold enough, *i.e.* under 50° F. In those days a horse lasted as long as it kept fresh. Trout are very particular, and their food should be absolutely untainted. Now-a-days four, and sometimes five, horses are killed, and eaten by the fish at Howietoun in a single week. No difficulty arises about keeping the flesh fresh; then it was otherwise. Everything was tried. At the very first an arrangement was made with the head keeper to let the fish have part of a horse when he killed for the kennels; but this was found to work with too much friction, and the fish had to have a horse killed specially for them. The hut was also used as a store for the grilles when not in use, its position over the stream allowing a thorough current of air under the floor, rendering it dry at all seasons.

Next in position is the dividing-box, which collects the water from the 20-feets, and from the 60-feet, and mixes it with a fresh supply from the main aqueduct. This box is built of 3-inch plank; it is rectangular, and divided into several compartments. In the first the pipes from the 20-feets and from the main aqueduct came in opposite each other, so as to mix and aërate the water, while the outlet spout from the 60-feet discharged into the same compartment through a cut in the end, thus completely mingling

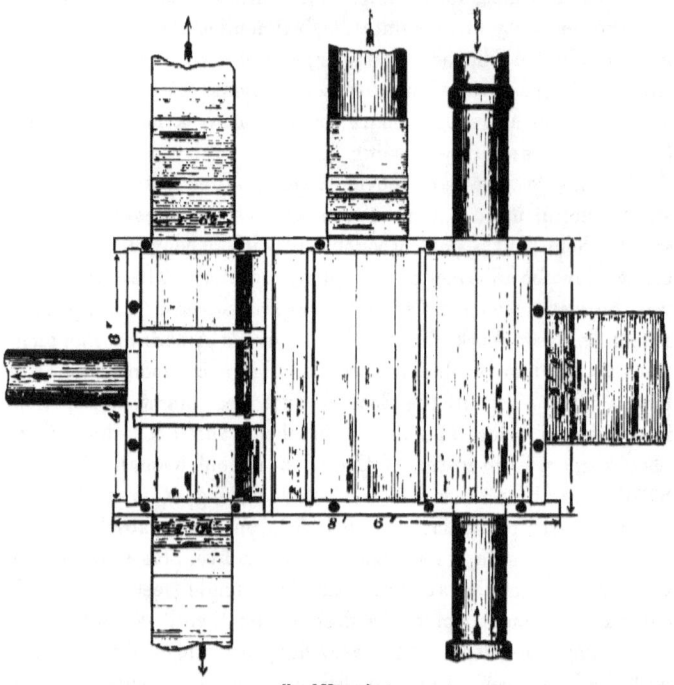

Fig. 152—scale $\frac{1}{24}$.

the whole three sources of supply (Fig. 152). A division of 1½-inch wood slid in a groove from the top of the dividing-box to within a few inches of the bottom, forming the first compartment. The second compartment was formed in the same way, a square cut being made in the side of the dividing-box for waste water. This opening was fitted with a subsidiary box, in which two grooves

Fig. 153—scale 1/12.

were cut, and from which a 15-inch sanitary spigot and faucet glazed pipe led to the stream (Fig. 153). In these grooves pieces of flooring were slipped, and the space between filled up with clay, thus making an absolutely tight valve ; and as the surfaces of the clay are protected on both sides the valve remains tight for years. A small groove was also cut in the sides of the dividing-box for a few inches in the centre of the second compartment, and a piece of 1½-inch wood slipped in while the dividing-box was in construction. This served to turn the current of the water upwards, so that it struck the second board which formed the limit of the second compartment. This board is called the dead-water board, and its duty is to receive any currents that may set up, from one

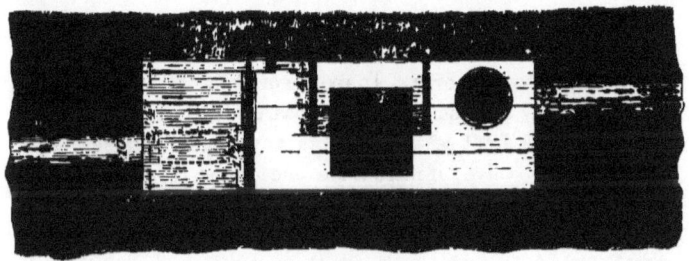

Fig. 154—scale 1/12.

spout or supply being stronger than the others. The next compartment thus received the water almost dead, rising evenly upwards from below the dead-water board (Fig. 154). This compartment was furnished with an overflow-board rising from the bottom, about half the depth of the dividing-box; and the end of this compartment is again subdivided into three,—this time laterally, by two divisions of flooring-boards held in position by a frame, in which are grooves to receive small pieces of flooring, so as to shut off any of the three small compartments, each of which communicated with one of the 130-feet ponds. Below is a section of the dividing-box, showing distribution (Fig. 155).

FIG. 155—scale 1/12.

This box passes the water to the overflow-board so dead that the division is absolutely dependent on the width of the three divisions on that board. Thus it is evident that the supply can be regulated to the three ponds in any given proportion desired, merely by contracting this width by slipping a piece of flooring into one of the grooves, so as to contract the space without altering the height of the overflow; and to isolate a pond entirely, all that requires to be done is to slip the piece of flooring (cut to the size) between two grooves. To reduce or limit the whole supply, remove the clay and the two sets of boards in the subsidiary box and replace the front set arranged to any height suitable. This acts as a safety-valve; if more than one of the 130-feets is shut off at the same time, it is almost always necessary to use the waste-pipe. The water was taken from the dividing-box and passed through screens, to prevent the upward passage of the fish from the ponds. These screens were, in fact, wooden trap-boxes, so constructed that all the sand that got into them fell to the bottom, while the water flowed through the screen without clogging it. The screens were fitted at a very slight angle, and the water rose through them (Fig. 156). This is the true principle of all inlet screens, as the trout cannot hurt themselves by jumping or falling on their tough bellies. These boxes were connected with the dividing-box—two (those for the east and west 130-feets) by a

FIG. 156—scale $\frac{1}{14}$.

short covered spout, and that for the centre 130-feet by a 10-inch pipe, the reason being that a high bank or mound lay between the dividing-box and the 130-feets, and I did not care to go to the expense of clearing it entirely away. Below the trap-box screens

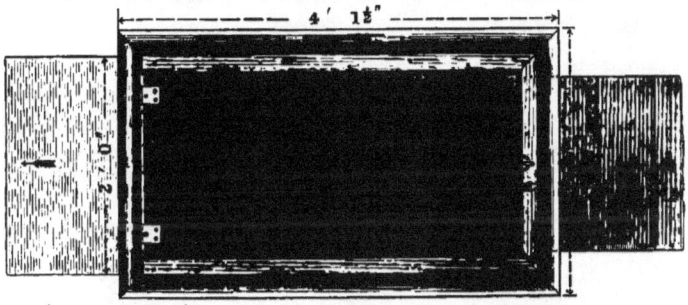

FIG. 157—scale $\frac{1}{14}$.

of the east and west 130-feets an aqueduct was formed in the ground, of cement, into which the screens discharged, by a fall of 3 to 4 inches. Fig. 157 is a diagram of the trap-box, with screen.

The screens were about 18 inches below the surface of the ground, and the earth sloped up from them at an angle of 45°, so any fish jumping too high over the screen slid back without injury. The surface of the earth was about 1 foot above the dividing-box, and retained by a wall of turf. No frost has ever interfered with the working of either the dividing-box or with the screens. These latter throw off any ice forming on them by the force of the water rising through.

The 130-feets were built all in a piece; that is to say, the skeleton was continuous. Half beech-trees were laid as anchors in the banks on either side, about 6 feet from the side of the ponds; battens were laid as sleepers in the bottom of each pond, at an unusually short distance apart, as in the 60-feet pond; from the ends of these battens others were raised perpendicularly, being nailed to the edges of those used as sleepers. The upright battens on the outer sides of the outside ponds were tied to the beech anchors; those on the inner sides were tied to the uprights of the centre pond. Thus a huge skeleton was formed, and when the battens were tied by the flooring being nailed on them, the whole formed one body, where any local strain at once distributed itself over the whole. And still further to carry out this principle, bridges were thrown across each of the ponds as ranches, as well as a convenience to the works. Below is a cross-section of the 130-feets (Fig. 158).

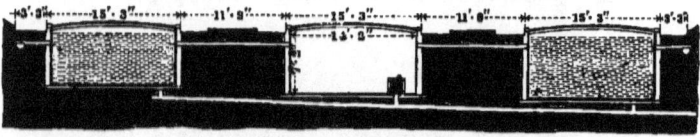

Fig. 158—scale 1/32.

The first sleeper of the east 130-feet was laid on the 29th of March 1877, and the centre 130-feet pond was in working order by the 4th of July, same year. The three were finished on the 1st October. The centre 130-feet seems to have been the only one actually completed in the season (1876-77) to which this chapter belongs, but it was more convenient to treat them as a whole.

At Craigend a small octagonal pond was dug below the lower 100-feet, into which the hybrids were placed. The hatching-house at Middlethird required no alteration; in fact, the work of the season was almost entirely confined to Howietoun.

SEASON 1876-1877.—EXPERIMENTAL WORK.

On July 25th, after I had consulted Mr. Buckland as to the causes of the loss of trout (yearling) in the pond at Craigend, he talked over the failure of the Timaru experiment, and he asked me to undertake the following experiments:—

A. When eggs arrive, say on a Tuesday, and the ship does not leave till the following Saturday, make experiments to see whether it is best to put the eggs into hatching-troughs, and pack them, say on the Friday morning, or whether it is better to pack them once for all when first received.

B. Please to try experiments on freezing eggs.

C. Try the effects of freezing during impregnation.

D. Find out whether it is advisable to pack the eggs at the river-side, or wait till next morning.

The object of all these experiments was to gain information as to the best mode of procedure in taking and packing eggs (salmon was of course understood, though the word did not appear on the memorandum Mr. Buckland gave me) for the next experiment to New Zealand.

Being much abroad this and following winters, these experiments were not all concluded in one season, but they have each been carried out since, with the following results:—

A. Eggs have been packed by me on many occasions at the time of taking. These eggs travel as well as eggs carried in water. I have handled or packed eggs each day, from the second to the thirtieth. There is always some loss, and with the water at 45° F. this loss is at its maximum on the twentieth day. The per centage of loss increases slowly from the second to the tenth day; then rises rapidly to the twentieth; then falls very rapidly, and on the thirty-first day the loss in packing, if the handling is skilful, is almost *nil*.

The answer to Mr. Buckland's first query is therefore: "Pack as soon as the eggs arrive, but so as to be able to pick out the ova killed before the ship sails, without disturbing the rest."

B. Freezing eggs I have only tried with Loch Leven ova. In all cases where the ovum has been frozen solid in water, it has turned white on being thawn out. Where the eggs have been only partially frozen, *i.e.* where a film of ice has formed on the tray and partially involved part (some) of the ova, the loss has been partial, the ova involved showing white specks—some large, and some very small indeed. All those with large white spots died in a few weeks; in the case of some with small specks, the specks enlarged, and they also died. In the case of about half the eggs involved, the development stopped; but they did not turn white till due to hatch, while some few eggs actually hatched into puny alevins. A number burst when about due to hatch, or a little before. Eggs which I froze dry in air, and afterwards thawed out in snow-brae, hatched without any obvious injury. There is room for many more experiments in freezing ova; those conducted were with eggs in which about 40 per cent. of the period of incubation had been accomplished. Livingston Stone mentions (*Domesticated Trout*, p. 146) that alevins will stand cold wonderfully; and that he had frozen them (apparently in air) so that they were glued tight on to the ice, and that he had kept these "frozen thaws" by themselves; and that they appeared to do as well as any trout of their age, and showed no signs of being injured by freezing. The result of my experiment points to the embryo being capable of standing great cold—$10°$ or $20°$ F. below freezing—without injury. But if frozen in water, the embryo is injured by the pressure of the ice, and probably by the spiculas of ice in formation.

C. I have often spawned fish in hard frost. Within ordinary limits, no evils result; the eggs take longer to adhere and much longer to free—sometimes an hour and a quarter. The eggs require to be carefully thawn, if frozen to the bottom of the spawning-dish; and my experience is that the percentage of impregnation is sensibly affected if a film of ice forms on the surface of the dish after the water is added. I have used milt after it had been exposed to 20° F. for several hours; the resulting embryos were deficient in vitality. We must, however, repeat the experiment frequently before we are justified in assuming the deficiency was due to the frozen milt. But the experiment does prove that milt may be frozen without destroying entirely its vivifying power.

D. Eggs should be packed at the river-side in preference to waiting till next morning; but they should be packed in trays in such a way that they can be picked over next day. But in 1876 few besides myself believed in packing partially-eyed ova for so long a journey as to the antipodes, and at that time I had had no experience in sending eggs long distances.

SEASON 1876-77.—FISH-CULTURE.

The stock on hand on the 1st of August this season (1876) consisted of the old *S. fario* in Craigend dam, numbering a little over 100; about 200 hybrids in the octagon (then only an earth) pond, and some 3060 *S. levenensis* (yearlings) hatched in 1875. Besides these, there were about 10,000 *S. levenensis* (fry) hatched 1876, some 3000 *S. fario* (fry), hatched also 1876, and between 1100 and 1400 of the so-called "hybrids" (fry), hatched 1876, between "Queichy" and a small burn-trout male. These springlings were distributed between the plank ponds and the rearing-boxes. The young fish were well grown. One, on the 20th August (hatched 23d Jan. 1876), measured 2·6 inches; and one (hatched Jan. 1875) measured, on the 14th September,

7·5 inches, and weighed 2·9 oz. This is good average growth in Scotland for trout seven and nineteen and a half months old respectively.

By October 20th the upper 100-feet pond at Craigend had been cleaned, deepened, and filled; and 1242 of the *S. levenensis* springlings from the centre 20-feet pond at Howietoun were brought across to Craigend and placed in it. On the following day 1540 more were brought across, and placed in the upper 100-feet at Craigend, from the same 20-feet. This was all there were, and as at least 5000 were placed in it as fry early in spring, the loss must have been nearly 50 per cent., only 2782 remaining on the 21st of October. I added 2218 *S. levenensis* from the east 20-feet (which contained many more fry than the centre 20-feet), thus bringing up the number in the upper 100-feet to 5000 trout. I then cleaned the centre 20-feet, and filled it without re-charring; and on the 22d of October I placed 629 *S. levenensis* fry into it. These were all that remained of a lot of 1000 fry I had placed in the 9-feet pond in May, the loss in this case being under 40 per cent. The next day I completed the lower 100-feet pond at Craigend, and on 30th October I placed in it 2315 *S. fario* fry from the west 20-feet at Howietoun. These were all that remained of the 13,800 ova laid down in October and November 1875, and they averaged nearly 3 inches in length.

On the same day I counted the *S. levenensis* springlings in the east 20-feet, and found there were 1279 left in that pond. These, with the 2218 already removed, bring up the number in that pond to 3497, and experience has shown that this is as large a number as can be raised up to November in the 20-feet pond without sacrificing size. I returned 954 to the east 20-feet, and placed the remaining 325 in the centre 20-feet, making 954 in each. The perforated zinc was removed, and a larger size (No. 11) substituted.

On the 31st October I took 92 *S. levenensis* springlings from some I had in the rearing-boxes, and divided them between the east and centre 20-feets, thus bringing up the number in each to 1000 exactly. The west 20-feet was fitted up as a filter for the new hatching-house, as already described. Before I touch on the spawning season, I must insert the table showing the stock belonging to the Fishery as at the end of 1876 :—

TABLE OF OVA SPAWNED.

MIDDLETHIRD HATCHING-HOUSE.					
Date.	S. levenensis.	S. fario.	Hatching-box.	Eyed.	Hatched.
1876.					
Oct. 28	12,500	...	Box 2	Dec. 1	Jan. 10
,, 28	12,500	...	,, 3	,, 1	,, 10
Nov. 2	12,500	...	,, 4	,, 7	,, 19
,, 2	12,500	...	,, 5	,, 7	,, 19
,, 3	6,250	...	,, 6	,, 8	,, 21
,, 3	6,250	...	,, 1	,, 8	,, 21
HOWIETOUN HATCHING-HOUSE.					
Nov. 3	12,500	...	Box 6	Dec. 17	Feb. 18
,, 3	12,500	...	,, 7	,, 17	,, 18
,, 13	12,500	...	,, 2	Jan. 3	Mar. 10
,, 13	12,500	...	,, 3	,, 3	,, 10
,, 15	...	9,000	,, 5	,, 5	,, 12
,, 18	12,500	...	,, 8	,, 7	,, 18
,, 22	......	3,500	,, 5	,, 12	,, 23
Total,	125,000	12,500			

The above table shows a grand total of 137,000 trout ova for the hatching season 1876-77. Of the *S. levenensis* ova, 18,500 were sold for the behoof of the Loch Leven Angling Association, Limited, and a sum of £65, 5s. was obtained for these eggs. The following paragraph occurs in the Third Annual Report of the Association, dated Kinross, 28th September 1877 :—" During the season there have been 18,500 eyed ova sold, yielding a revenue of £65, 5s., and upwards of 70,000 artificially hatched fry have been deposited in the stream running into the loch. The Directors have been enabled to do this through the kindness of Sir J. R. Gibson Maitland, Bart., in having placed at their disposal one of his hatching-houses at Sauchie. He has also borne the whole expense connected with the eyeing of the ova and hatching of the fry; and the special thanks, not only of the Directors, but also of the Association, are due to him." This accounts for more ova than Middlethird would hold. As a matter of fact, only 62,500 ova (*S. levenensis*) were laid down in Middlethird; but the same number of *S. levenensis* were laid down in the Howietoun hatching-house also, and the Association got all the ova and fry, except about 20,000, which were retained for the Fishery. Thus 108,500 out of 125,000 *S. levenensis* ova are accounted for, showing a loss of a little over 13 per cent. As the water in the hatching-house at Howietoun was occasionally very dirty, in spite of the filter, and as the boxes were exposed to a great range of temperature, and specially as I was on the Continent nearly all winter, and the care of the eggs was committed to men, however anxious, with little or no previous training, I think the result was fairly satisfactory. Afterwards no accommodation could be provided for the *S. fario* fry, and they were used to stock my own waters at Sauchie. The *S. fario* spawn were obtained by running the dam at Craigend dry. This I did on November 15th, and got 98 trout, averaging three-quarters of a lb. each. On that day I spawned 45, of which 25 were females; on the 16th I spawned 18 more, and on the 23d I stripped the remainder. All the fish were returned to the dam without injury.

On my journey down from London two nights before, when nearing Sheffield, at five minutes to 1 A.M., November 22d, the Pullman car in which I was travelling upset at Healy, and I was pitched into the lamps. I was not much hurt, only cut a little, and the skin knocked off my knees. I shot the Sauchie covers on arriving home, and, beyond limping when I walked, was none the worse. A day or two afterwards I was much amused by a stranger calling. For some time I could not guess the purport of his visit; but at last he referred to the accident. Then it dawned on me that the Railway Company were counting up the cost, and I at once relieved his feelings by assuring him that I never saw things better arranged after the smash, which I said with all the more emphasis as, shortly before, I had some experience of a break-down in France, when the delay was much more inconvenient than the accident.

But however exciting a railway smash may be at the time, especially in travelling at fifty miles an hour, as we were when the Pullman left the rails just before the signals at Healy Station, it shakes the nerves terribly afterwards. For many a month after, when travelling at night, any rough bit of the road used to wake me up if asleep. As the accident occurred on my way to Craigend to complete the spawning, I have recounted it here. I returned south almost immediately afterwards, and on December 2d I received a telegram that "the fish are all doing well." This completes my notes to December 31st, 1876, and below is a statement of stock to date.

TABLE OF STOCK ON 1ST JANUARY 1877.

100-feet	Upper	5,000	S. levenensis	Hatched	1876
20 ,,	East	1,000	,,	,,	,,
20 ,,	Centre	1,000	,,	,,	,,
60 ,,		3,000	,,	,,	1875
20 ,,	Lower	1,000	Hybrids	,,	1876
	Octagon	180	,,	,,	1875
100 ,,	Lower	2,315	S. fario	,,	1876
Dam,	Craigend	98	,,	,,	Aged
	Total,	13,593			

The stock remained as shown in the table till spring.

CHAPTER XVI.

SEASON 1877-78.

CONSTRUCTION—HOWIETOUN PONDS.

THE 130-feets were completed before 1st October 1877, as described in the last chapter, but the completion of the water-carrier or leads properly belongs to this. The centre 130-feet was supplied by a sanitary spigot pipe from the dividing-box. This pipe was led into a screen-box, similar to those already described, except that a hole was cut in the bottom communicating with a 4-inch pipe (spigot and faucet, carefully cemented), so that any drop from the board-sluice, when the water was shut off the centre compartment, could be caught before reaching the pond, thus enabling the wooden bottom to be dried before re-charring

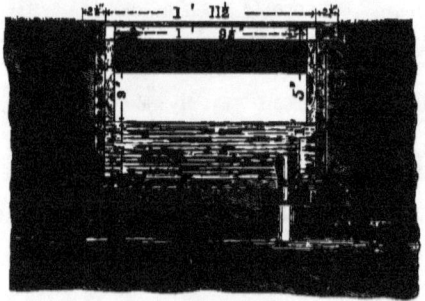

FIG. 159—scale ₁/₁₂.

when necessary. The 4-inch pipe just mentioned was led across to the old course of the burn, and a catch-box was fitted in the lead to the east 130-feet above the pipe (Fig. 159). Lengths with straight-eyes were arranged below this catch-box and below the screen-box of the centre 130-feet, and the corresponding holes stopped with long-handled hardwood plugs, so as to be capable of being fitted tightly, and still easily removed. The west end of the pipe was continued through below the centre pond's screen-box, to enable a connection to be made with the catch-box of the west 130-feet pond; but owing to the pond being wanted in a hurry, this has never been done, and the water which drips through the sluice-boards has had to be (very inefficiently) kept out by means of clay each time the pond required re-charring. The trouble and expense this has entailed has shown me the great advantage and convenience of the catch-boxes where properly drained. Fig. 159 is a section of pipe, showing connections with catch-box and screen-box.

The centre 130-feet was the first finished, being filled and stocked with the *S. levenensis* hatched 1875 on the 4th July 1877. The lead of the west 130-feet was concreted on its sides. The course was an ogee from the screen-box to opposite the centre of the pond. The moulds for the ogee were made and fixed on the 5th September, and the straight moulds for the sides of the duct were completed the following week. The concrete was made of the best Portland cement, whinstone road metal, and shivers of freestone, mixed with sharp sand in the proportion of one of cement to two of sand, and three of shivers and road metal mixed. This has stood ten winters, and can be recommended as a cheap, permanent, and safe revêtement for the sides of water-courses. A coping of double turf was laid on the top of the cement. After the *S. levenensis* (hatched 1875) were transferred from the 60-feet, the pond was re-charred and the plank cope painted, and a larger hole cut in the bottom to facilitate the pond being run dry. An iron pipe was inserted below the bottom of the pond to the plug-hole, to save lifting the flooring, and connected with the drain from the hatching-house.

The three 130-feets were emptied when required by a 6-inch spigot and faucet pipe, passing from the old course of the burn below the ponds, and communicating with each of them by straight-eyes fitted into frames of heavy wood (white pine) on which bronze plates were hinged as valves. These frames carried perforated iron plates, so that large fish could not escape when the valves were lifted. The perforated iron plates were countersunk half an inch clear of the bronze valves; and to enable me to use the ponds for smaller fish, a frame of oak was constructed, covered with No. 9 zinc, sufficiently large to allow the valve to rise freely inside; each pond received one of these frames. Below is a diagram of the screen in position, showing valve and straight-eye pipe (Fig. 160).

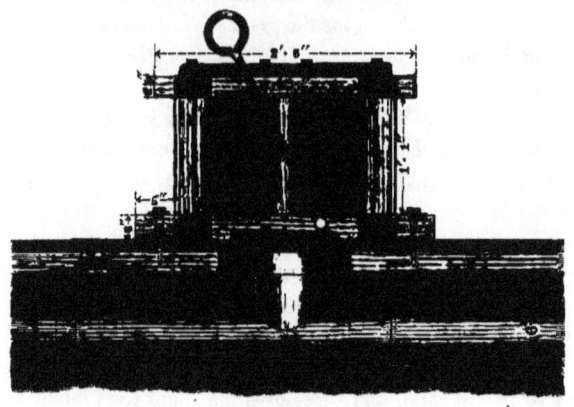

FIG. 160—scale 1/10.

The valve was provided with a rod passing through the top of the frame, which was covered by two oak boards joining in the line of the aperture through which the rod passed. This rod ended in a loop immediately above the oak cover when the valve was closed. A long rod of iron terminating in a hook was used to lift the valves, and the position of the loop being marked on the side of each pond, no difficulty is encountered in finding them. The next thing done was to put up supports for the covers of the 20-feets, so that the lids could be laid back on a fine day without straining the hinges. I find that the less trout-ponds are covered, the better for the fish; but shallow ponds must be covered at night, or rats, frogs, and birds will rapidly reduce the fry. The earth-slopes on the outer sides of the paths were turfed, and the slopes dressed uniform to a bevel. This tool has been so useful, and there must generally be so many slopes to dress in any new fish-farm, that I give a sketch. It can be used with either a level or plumb-bob, and costs about 6s. Fig. 161 is a sketch of triangle, or level and plumb.

Fig. 161—scale 1/12.

The old hut had now become too small to prepare all the food for the trout, and a new mincing-house was ordered, and built by the foresters of home-grown timber. The floor was laid with pavement, except in the centre, where two large beech blocks were bedded in concrete to support a powerful mincing-machine and deaden the jar. A boiler was built in with brick in one corner of the house, and a brick chimney led outside to the roof. Two windows were made in either end, and filled in with perforated zinc to ensure a thorough draught. Beams fitted with pulleys were placed opposite the windows, from which the horse-flesh was hung. A double-sparred door in the centre of the north side of the house completed the work. The roof was protected by roofing-felt, well tarred, and the house was painted on the outside. It was placed near the end of the east 130-feet pond, at right angles to the run of the ponds. The mincing-machine was in full working order by the 10th September 1877, and has a capacity of half a cwt. at a time. It is driven by four men, but, if not too heavily charged, can be worked by two. Some day I hope to chop all the horse-flesh required by water-power. The machine chops with knives on to a beech chopping-block, the block revolving slowly at each stroke. After the meat is all prepared for the day, if any of the very young fish are on horse-flesh diet, their proportion is placed a second time on the block, and thus the difficulty of the food being too small for the large trout is avoided. A suitable place was dug for the bones, lined with wood, and covered with a lid. The bones are all prepared by boiling, and the meat scraped off them. The boiled meat is fed to the three-year-olds and four-year-olds. Two-year-old fry do not care for it, and the older fish, if mature, are fed on clams (*Pecten opercularis*) to improve the appearance of the ova. While the foresters were finishing the mincing-house, the navvies were engaged on a drain to empty the three 300-feets, which had been surveyed and laid off about 50 yards below the three 130-feets. This drain took many months' hard work. It commenced near the old course of the burn, and ran due west for about 80 yards. In one place the bottom of the drain was nearly 20 feet below the surface of the ground, and several feet of rock had to be cut through. But at last I got the cut through, and 8-inch iron pipes laid in the bottom. Three eye-pipes were specially cast, and placed so that each eye came just clear of the bottom of the slope of the bank in the deepest part of each pond.

At Craigend, the two ponds in front of the house were emptied by the 4th October 1877, and on the 5th I emptied the octagon, in which I found 61 hybrids left; these I transferred to the Francis Box in the wood. The work of pumping the ponds at Craigend dry was so heavy that I cut a drain parallel to the 100-feets, and deeper than the bottom of each, and laid a 1-inch sanitary pipe, carefully cemented in the faucets, with a straight-eye laid level towards the centre of the lower 100-feet, and a bend leading to the centre of the upper 100-feet. From the bend straight-eye pipes led, terminating in two lengths of iron pipe, to the end flanges of which brass sockets were bolted, and elbow-joints of the same metal fitted, turning easily in a perpendicular plane parallel to the sides of the ponds. A large square stone was laid in each pond below the elbow, and in these the brass sockets were countersunk the depth of the flange. This steadied the sockets. A deep square hole was also cut in each stone, and an iron bar $1\frac{1}{2}$-inch square was dropped in after the elbows were placed in the sockets. A knob cast on the elbows rested against the iron bars, preventing the elbows from slipping forward; and lastly, copper pipes soldered on to the elbows led to a distance of some 9 inches above the water-level of the ponds when full. To empty the ponds, all that is necessary is to turn this copper upright pipe to below the water, and the pond discharges through it.

Fig. 162—scale 1/12.

Fig. 163—scale 1/12.

The advantage of this arrangement is that the pond can be emptied from the surface of the water at any rate desired; that the mouth of the emptying pipe is always in sight, and can be guarded with a perforated zinc screen if necessary. It can also be arranged as an overflow-pipe, and is thus a guarantee against loss from the pond overflowing, in case the outlet gets accidentally choked, or too much water enters the pond in a spate. By removing the iron bar and pulling forward the elbow, the last drop of water is run out of the pond,—a very great convenience when it has to be re-stocked with a smaller size of fish in a hurry; and lastly, while not very expensive in first cost, it lasts for ever.

The bottom of the pond for several feet on each side of the valve was laid with causeway, and several feet more of concrete joined the causeway to the earth-slope of the bottom. This facilitated cleaning, and ensured no live fish remaining in the mud when the pond was drawn down. It is only after counting fry from a pond in which half-a-dozen yearlings have been left that any idea of the enormous loss can be formed. It is not in numbers only, but in quality also; the yearlings so bully the fry if confined, that their growth is most unsatisfactory. Of course, in large pieces of water, the loss is less in numbers and nothing in size; but in small ponds it is very marked, and there are few large pieces of water where fry can be placed without much loss from starvation.

Before the causeway was laid the two 100-feet ponds were cleaned and deepened; the top parts of the slopes were turfed to 6 inches below the water-line. This prevents the wavelets wearing the earth away. The turfs were hung on the sides by pegs until the grass rooted through and united them to the banks.

The water from the leaf-screen had formerly flowed through a 6-inch ordinary drain-tile. The drain was reopened, and a 6-inch spigot and faucet pipe substituted. This obviated any leakage in dry weather, and, when the ground was very wet, the percolation through the soil no longer perceptibly increased the flow. The sanitary pipe ended in a wooden trough, in which a third leg was inserted. Immediately beyond the insertion a groove was cut in the sides of the trough, and 5 inches on a second pair of grooves was cut. In each of these pairs of grooves pieces of board can be slid, and, when filled between with clay, the water is completely stopped. The leg is cut by two pairs of grooves precisely similar to those in the straight of the trough. If these are filled, the water flows straight; if the grooves in the straight are closed also, the water would dam back in the pipe. This invariably makes a mess of the ground at the junction of the trough with the sanitary pipe,

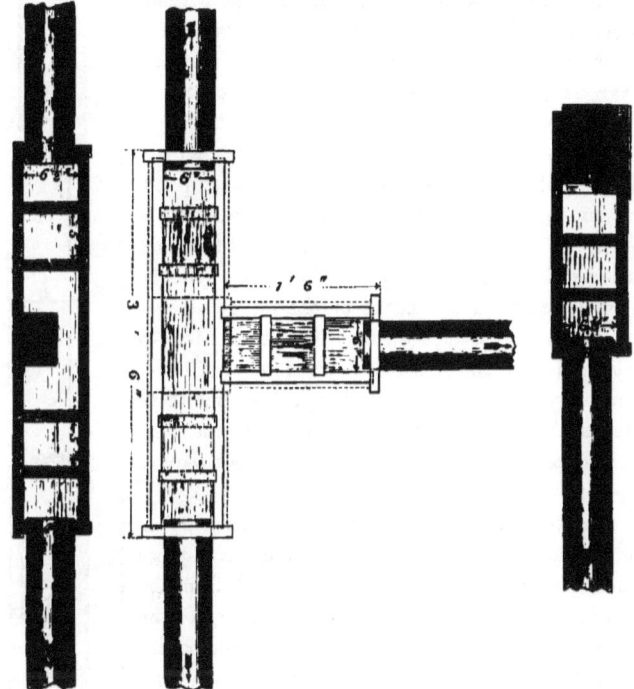

Fig. 164—scale 1/12.   Fig. 165—scale 1/12.   Fig. 166—scale 1/12.

and care should be exercised when closing the leg to see that the straight is clear, and *vice versa*. The trough was fitted at its lower end into the screen-box, which was made on the same principle as the screen-boxes already described at Howietoun, and has a very arduous task to perform, the sand, owing to the position of the leaf-screen, collecting in it in large quantities. In fact, the box requires to be emptied of sand sometimes as often as once a month in winter. Figs. 164, 165, and 166 are diagrams of the trough and leg, showing leg closed.

A 4-inch pipe was laid from the leg, running parallel to the ponds, with a straight-eye opposite the centre of each pond, rising perpendicular, so as to afford a view of the interior of the pipe without interfering with the run of the water. Between the upper and lower 100-feets a connection was laid, and a three-legged trough placed in the line of 4-inch pipes to feed this connection when required.

The outlets of the 100-feets were made by driving two substantial piles into the end of each pond, and supporting between them a frame carrying a screen-box and screen. The screens were fitted into face-checks and fastened by turn-buttons. Troughs of wood led from the backs of the outlet screen-boxes, carrying off the water. Now that between forty and fifty outlet screens are used at Howietoun, they are all made interchangeable; but these screens act well, and some may wish to adopt them for isolated ponds, especially as they do not require any masonry.

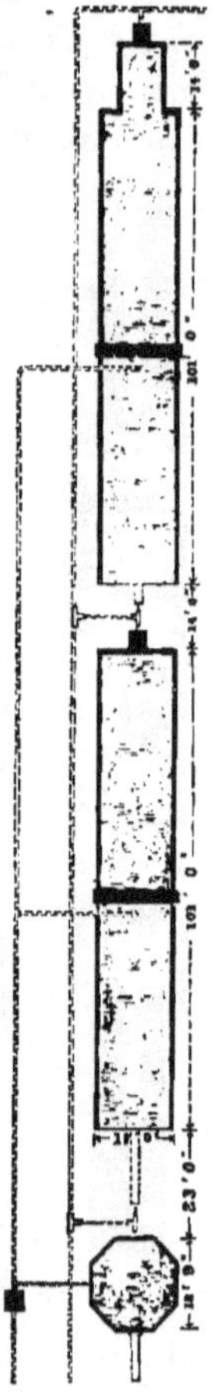

The troughs below the upper and lower ponds were connected with the 4-inch pipe by cross-pipes from the three-legged trough; and the fall from the upper pond to the lower, and from the lower to the octagon, were sufficient to ensure the temporary supply thus obtainable running the right way, and not flowing back into the pond above. Fig. 167 is a plan of the ponds, showing 4-inch supplementary and 6-inch drain-pipes.

FIG. 167—scale $\frac{1}{75}$.

From the above plan the mode of working the supply will be readily understood. Should the upper 100-feet require to be drawn, all that is necessary is to open the three-legged troughs at A and B, and stop the water off the pond at A, turning it down the 4-inch pipe to B. At B the 4-inch pipe is closed by placing in the cross-boards and filling between them with clay, while the leg is opened by removing the clay between its cross-boards, and lifting them out, thus throwing the supply into the trough running from the outlet screen-box of the upper to the inlet screen-box of the lower,—the fall in this trough being sufficient to prevent the water passing back into the upper 100-feet. The upper pond is then drawn by depressing the upright copper stand-pipe, first protecting its mouth with perforated zinc, if it is wished to retain the fish in the pond. This, however, is not now requisite at Craigend, as will be presently shown.

If the lower pond only is to be drawn, the screen of the inlet screen-box is lifted (it is hinged for convenience), and well-milled clay prepared. A thin board, fitting easily in the trough, is inserted as a face to the clay, which is next plastered in, and rammed so as to enter and fill 6 or 7 inches of the trough. A second board is then fitted, and held in position by means of a ranch driven tight against the lower end of the screen-box. This of course forces the water vented by the outlet screen of the upper pond through the connecting-pipe to the leg of the three-legged trough, through which, all clay and cross-boards being removed, it finds a free passage, past the lower 100-feet pond to the next three-legged trough, where it can be turned on to supply the octagon or to waste, as desired. Of course the screw sluice at the leaf-screen in the wood is lowered to reduce the quantity of the supply whenever any of the ponds are drawn, otherwise the 4-inch pipe would be insufficient, it being only 4-9ths of the capacity of the 6-inch. Below is a plan showing the pipes and connections of these ponds in detail.

The octagon pond was emptied, and having been useful for experimental lots, though too small for work, I increased its capacity by deepening it and building it, like the 60-feet and 130-feet, of wood. The shape was at first a difficulty, but by packing the outside tight with very wet puddle, the form of the pond enabling it to bear great crushing strain, I overcame all tendency to spread at the corners, and the pond has remained tight to this day. The inlet screen differed from those of the ponds above; it and the outlet screen were formed on the model of the outlet screens at Howietoun, although at that time the importance of all the outlet screens being interchangeable was not realised. A frame of batten was made, and fitted on to the two opposite ends of the octagon; the frames carrying the zinc slid in grooves in the batten frame. The connection with the 4-inch pipe was made as before, between the upper and the lower 100-feets; but as there was no screen-box, the connecting-trough between the lower 100-feet and the octagon was itself provided with a moveable board in the cover, below which the trough was grooved to receive cross-boards to hold clay, thus turning the waste from the lower 100-feet into the three-legged trough c, and so to waste. The screens used in the octagon will be fully discussed when the yearling ponds at Howietoun are described. Below is the detail of the octagon pond.

The trough from the outlet of the octagon discharged into an open drain. A third 100-feet was commenced, but, as will appear, was abandoned before being finished. A plug-hole was bored in the bottom of the octagon, and a spigot and faucet sanitary pipe connected by a bend led from the hole to the 6-inch pipe.

The plug was turned out of wood; hardwood is best, as it does not swell so much under water. There is no difficulty in drawing the plug, if a small portion is thickened above the hole, as a light chain, passed through a small ring attached to the end link so as to form a loop, will take a good grip of it; and by holding a pole on the top of the plug, and passing the loop down over the end of the pole, the plug can generally be involved the first try.

The 6-inch drain-pipe (sanitary) terminated in the first well. These wells are now a feature in the work at the Fishery. Without wells, much time would be lost catching the last fish in a pond; and most probably many fish would be suffocated in the mud before they could be removed, and a large number would certainly be injured in handling. All this is a vision of the past at Howietoun. The problem has been solved. Time, money, fish, and temper have all been saved, and by the most simple arrangement possible,—merely by a rectangular well! The 6-inch discharged into a well about 9½ inches above the bottom (Fig. 168). The well was of brick, and a wood batten frame was built in, 1 foot from the opposite end. In this frame a screen fitted, being slipped

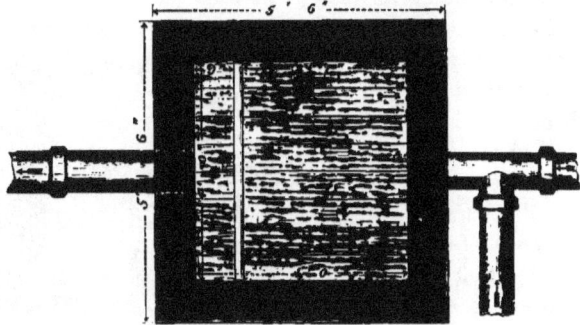

Fig. 168—scale 1/12.

between two pairs of cleats, one pair nailed on each side. A 7-inch ordinary red drain-pipe drained the well, but the connection was made by a 6-inch sanitary pipe built into the end wall, level with the floor of the well (Fig. 169). The floor was

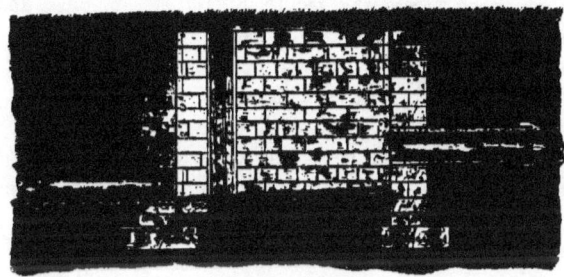

Fig. 169—scale 1/12.

laid with causeway blocks, but they were found too rough to work the net on, so a thin floor of wood was laid immediately above them.

The well is used as follows:—The screen is first slipped in between the cleats, then the pond is drawn, either by pulling up the plug for the octagon, or by depressing the upright pipe for either of the 100-feets (Fig. 170). The fish have first been netted out, so far as can be easily done; and, as a rule, not more than 500 are left in either of the 100-feets after several sweeps of the net, in the case of yearlings. The octagon, from its shape, is harder to net clean. As some years each 100-feet yields 12,000 yearlings, 500 is a fair proportion for the well to take. For some time after the pond is drawn, few fish descend, or, if they leave the pond, they remain in the pipe, swimming against the current. But after a 100-feet is down so low that the iron bolt can be withdrawn, and the elbow

FIG. 170—scale 1/14.

is drawn forward, the fish can be easily driven to the mouth of the pipe, when they quickly take refuge in its interior. A net then held in the well takes them safely; or the water, which by this time is much decreased in volume, can be heightened by placing a board across the mouth of the escape-pipe, and so deepened in the well, to assure the fish from injury. In fact, with a small board to heighten the water, a large number of trout will live for hours, and by letting a little fresh water into the 6-inch pipe fish might be left in the well all night without loss. The screen in the well should be as fine as possible—not larger than No. 9 for yearlings—so as to reduce the suction, and heighten the water in the well at first when the flow is strongest. All the sizes of the wells, pipes, and screens must be proportioned to each other. When this is the case, everything works smoothly and safely.

At Middlethird, the boxes were numbered and new zinc placed on the outlets, and the house was ready by the end of November. The hatching-boxes at Howietoun were ready by the middle of October.

SEASON 1877-78.—EXPERIMENTAL WORK.

I spent most of this winter abroad; the work under this head is therefore almost *nil*. In the statement for December 1876, two lots of hybrids appear, viz. 1000 in the lower 20-feet pond, and 180 in the octagon pond at Craigend. The former were hatched from the ova obtained from "Queichy" on 25th November 1875, and milted by a *S. fario* at Craigend dam. These I would now call a cross or mongrel, and not a hybrid at all. No other mention occurs in the note-book of this lot, so I suppose the 20-feet in which they were got frozen—which the lower 20-feet, from its position, sheltered by the hatching-house, has a tendency to do,—or that the remains of them were freed in the burn next spring, when the pond would be required for fry. The hybrids in the octagon number all left of Experiments 1, 2, 3, 5, 7, 8, 9, and 11 of 1874, which had been mixed for want of room. On 5th October 1877, on emptying the octagon pond, 61 remained. They were then two years and nine months old, and the males had milt in them; but as Experiments 1, 2, 3, and 5 were mongrels, not hybrids, and as it does not appear to what experiments the survivors belonged, no deduction as to fertility can, so far, be made.

Perhaps the most important experimental note yet made is: "13th October. Caught a male fish in the centre 130-feet pond at Howietoun. Pure Loch Leven, the milt running freely: length, 12¼ inches; weight, 12 oz. Hatched 22d January 1875, and thus thirty-two and a half months old. Noticed two rows of bright yellow spots with black centres; belly very black; under-jaw slightly hooked; hind margin of caudal convex. I sent him to be cast." Here is a trout whose parents were spawned at Loch Leven, and undoubtedly mature representatives of the *S. levenensis*, developing marks which had hitherto constituted one of the most trusted barriers of the species. In Günther's Catalogue of the fishes in the British Museum, vol. vi. p. 101, *S. levenensis* is thus described:—

" D. 13, A. 11, P. 14, V. 9, L. lat. 118, L. trans. 28, 26. Caec. pyl., normally 60-80. Vert. 59.

"Largest specimen observed, 21 inches; female mature at a length of   inches.

"Head well proportioned in its shape, and rather small when compared with the body; body much less stout than in *S. fario*. The posterior point of junction of operculum and sub-operculum is nearer to the lower anterior angle of the sub-operculum than to the upper end of the gill-opening. Præoperculum generally with a very indistinct lower limb. Snout of moderate length, conical, not much produced in the male sex, in which a *mandibular hook has never been observed*. Maxillary much longer than the snout, but much narrower and more feeble than in *S. fario* (see p. 6). In specimens 13 inches long it extends to below the hinder margin of the orbit, and at no age does it reach much beyond it. Teeth moderately strong. The head of the vomer is triangular, a little broader than long, with a transverse series of two or three teeth across its base. The teeth of the body of the vomer form a single series, and are persistent throughout life. Fins well developed, not rounded; the pectoral is pointed, and in specimens of more than 12 inches in length its length is less than one-half of the distance between its base and that of the ventral. The caudal fin always has the lobes pointed, is marginate, and appears truncate only when stretched to the utmost extent. In specimens 13 inches long, the middle caudal rays are not quite half as long as the outer ones, and in older ones they are half as long. The hind part of the body is rather slender. There are from thirteen to fourteen scales in a transverse series, descending from behind the adipose fin forwards to the lateral line.

"Upper parts brownish or greenish olive; sides of the head with round black spots; sides of the body with more or less numerous X-shaped, sometimes rounded, brown spots; dorsal and adipose fins with numerous small brown spots; extremity of pectoral light blackish; dorsal and anal without black or yellow margin.

"A non-migratory species, inhabiting Loch Leven and other lakes of southern Scotland and of the north of England."

This was the best description of *S. levenensis* until the publication of Day's *Fishes of Great Britain and Ireland* (1882).

The change of character is very marked. The black spots are found in the first generation passing to red, and showing in the intermediatory stage yellow and ocellated. It is interesting to note that this stage was manifested when the fish had assumed its bridal dress. Both before and after the spawning season the males were as silvery, and their spots as black, as in Loch Leven itself. The ocellation shows that the tendency to change was not in the first generation sufficient to overcome their normal habit; the yellowish halo only invested those spots which in *S. fario* are often, at this season, of the brightest scarlet.

SEASON 1877-78.—FISH-CULTURE.

On the 4th July I ran the 60-feet pond dry, and found that 490 of my *S. levenensis* trout hatched 1875 had disappeared since they were put in in July last year. Out of these 50 had been given away, and over 100 had either jumped out, or been taken for experiment; the loss unaccounted for would thus be under 340 fish, or 11·11 per cent. I transferred the remainder, *i.e.* 2570 trout, to the centre 130-feet pond. They averaged about 6 oz. Each 130-feet holds 11,750 cubic feet of water, equal to 73,437 gallons of water. When in ordinary work, the supply fills each pond in 1 hour 50 minutes, and the quantity running through is the same in each pond. This gives a supply of 120,000 gallons an hour to the three ponds, or of 40,000 gallons an hour to each. This is equal to changing the entire quantity of water in each of the 130-feet ponds thirteen times per diem. This is one of the principal reasons why the fish thrive so remarkably well in them. After the 60-feet had been cleaned and re-charred, on the 1st October I re-stocked it with yearling *S. fario* (hatched 1876), and I brought 1878 from the lower 100-feet pond at Craigend. There were a few more in that pond, but as they were rather larger than the others, being over 5 oz., I put them into the dam in case they had taken on cannibal habits.

On 2d October, 2021 *S. levenensis* yearlings (hatched 1876) were shifted from the upper 100-feet at Craigend to the east 130-feet at Howietoun; and on the third the rest of the *S. levenensis* from the upper 100-feet were brought over to Howietoun and added to those in the east 130-feet, making a total of 2802. The two 100-feets were then run dry, and 13 burn-trout were found to have been left in the lower pond. They were transferred to the 60-feet, making the total in that pond 1891 *S. fario*.

The lower 100-feet at Craigend had 2315 *S. fario* in it in the previous December, so, allowing for the few placed in the dam, the loss had been 320, or 13·39 per cent. The loss from the upper 100-feet is not stated in the notes. I find that over 5000 *S. levenensis* (hatched 1876) were placed in the east 130-feet pond; and as only 2000 were in the 20-feets in December 1876, it is evident that some must have been transferred from the upper 100-feet previous to the 1st October 1877 ; and that, as the whole stock of *S. levenensis* (hatched 1876) being only 7000 in December, the loss must have been under 2000, or less than 20 per cent. This is a very heavy percentage, and is probably 8 per cent. too high, as I find 5000 alive on the 31st December 1878, or fourteen months afterwards. The most of the loss would be among the fish in the two 20-feets, as these ponds, however well suited to fry, are too cramped for yearlings.

New zinc was put on the screens of the earth ponds on the 19th November, and one was filled, and stocked with *S. levenensis* springlings (hatched 1877). These had strained the capacity of the Fishery very much, as only the west 20-feet, which had been used as a filter to the Howietoun hatching-house the previous winter, had been available for fry, and all the rearing-boxes and hatching-boxes had had to be pressed into service for an unwonted time. But in spite of all difficulties, about 8000 were reared, the lower 20-feet, where the 1000 hybrids had been, being also used in spring for fry.

This was the first season ova was obtained from fish reared from eggs hatched at the Fishery. The centre 130-feet pond was netted, and 2000 trout transferred to the west 130-feet, those with ova being spawned if ripe, and, if unripe, returned to the centre pond, to be re-caught next net day. The number obtained is not recorded; but, so far as I remember, it was about 16,000, and they were laid down in boxes 1 and 6 at Middlethird. I was again abroad most of the winter, and the spawning at Loch Leven was done under the superintendence of Mr. Hall, the Manager. I believe about 150,000 ova were obtained from Loch Leven. No *S. fario* were spawned this season, and no crosses were made.

Date.	*S. levenensis* (Loch Leven).	*S. levenensis* (Howietoun).	Hatching-box.	Eyed.	Hatched.
MIDDLETHIRD HATCHING-HOUSE.					
1877. Nov. 28	12,500	...	Box 2		Mar. 7
,,	12,500	...	,, 3		,, 7
,,	12,500	...	,, 4		,, 7
,,	12,500	...	,, 5		,, 7
,,	...	8,000	,, 6		,,
,,	...	8,000	,, 1		,,
HOWIETOUN HATCHING-HOUSE.					
Oct.	12,500	...	Box 1		Feb. 20
,,	12,500	...	,, 2		,, 20
Nov.	12,500	...	,, 3		,,
,,	12,500	...	,, 4		Mar. 7
,,	12,500	...	,, 5		,, 7
,,	12,500	...	,, 6		,, 7
,,	12,500	...	,, 7		,,
,,	12,500	...	,, 8		,,
Total,	150,000	16,000			

The following is the portion of the Fourth Annual Report of the Directors of the Loch Leven Angling Association, dated Kinross, 2d October 1878, referring to Howietoun : "Through the kindness and liberality of Sir J. R. Gibson Maitland, Bart., the Directors have again been enabled, without expense to the Association, to sell 19,000 eyed ova and fry, yielding a revenue of £42, and to deposit in the streams running into the loch about 95,000 fry; and the cordial thanks of the Directors and of the Association are again due to him."

Unfortunately, the lake reaped only half the benefit it should have got, as, owing to some of the consignments of fry being, in my absence, too much crowded in the carrying-tanks, a large number were lost *en route*, and I doubt if more than 45,000 effective fry were turned into the streams running into the loch.

35,000 fry were retained at the Fishery, which makes the loss during hatching and rearing the fry till they were turned out about 20,000 out of 150,000, or 13·33 per cent. The loss on the young eggs of my own trout (*S. levenensis*) was very great; only some 5000 survived to be placed in the lower 20-feet in summer, or a loss of 68·75 per cent. All subsequent experience has confirmed this experiment, and I am now convinced of the folly of breeding from young fish. These trout were well grown, as on the 7th March one (hatched 1875) jumped out of the pond. Some animal ate the tail half, and the remainder weighed over 1 lb. Another jumped out on the 7th July, and measured 14·6 inches, and weighed 1 lb. 5 oz. The average of the large trout netted in Loch Leven in 1878 was 1·755 lbs. Size, therefore, does not necessarily imply maturity for breeding purposes, and the idea that the development of ova implies it, must be abandoned—at least as regards *Salmo*.

On the 1st July I counted the *S. levenensis* (hatched 1875) in the west 130-feet pond, and found 1776 remaining,—a loss of 224 since they were counted in last November. But the pond was so near the fence, it could be easily fished, and, from information received, most of these must have been stolen. I took certain personal steps in the matter with a heavy six-shooter, and have had no reason to suspect any loss from theft since.

On next page is the table of stock at the end of the year.

STATEMENT OF STOCK ON 31ST DECEMBER 1877.

100-feet Upper,	4,000	*S. levenensis*	Hatched	1877
100 ,, Lower,	...	Under alterations		
20 ,, West,	...	Used as a filter		
20 ,, Centre,	1,000	*S. levenensis*	,,	1877
20 ,, East,	1,400	,,	,,	,,
20 ,, Lower,	1,200	,,	,,	,,
60 ,,	1,880	*S. fario*	,,	1876
130 ,, West,	2,000	*S. levenensis*	,,	1875
130 ,, Centre,	500	,,	,,	,,
130 ,, East,	5,800	,,	,,	1876
Dam, Craigend,	125	*S. fario*	,,	Mixed
Octagon,	61	Hybrids	,,	1875
Total,	17,966			

CHAPTER XVII.

Season 1878-79.

CONSTRUCTION—HOWIETOUN PONDS.

This season was occupied in making the 300-feet ponds. The ground was surveyed, and the cubic yards of excavation and of banking calculated and balanced; a small surplus was found, and a fourth pond laid out, so that the surplus might be used to form its banks. The size of the ponds made the old method of navvying on a barrow road impossible. Light rails were bought, and wagons, holding half a yard each, were made by the estate carpenter. As the road got longer, it was found cheaper to run the wagons by horse; and an old animal was bought, who spent the rest of his days on the tram. One very wet day, however, on being led out after his noon feed, he slipped into the drain cut for the pipe which empties the 300-feet ponds. We tried to get him out, but the drain was some 12 feet deep at the place, and the clay so slippery, he could not rise, and I could not get ropes under him; so at last I ordered *le pauvre bête* to be pole-axed. This is the only accident which occurred at the works during the ten years of construction.

The bottoms of all the three 300-feet ponds were found to be rock, and many hundred cubic yards had to be quarried. The formation is sandstone, lying immediately above the coal, and some large fossil plants were found. The rubble quarried was saved for walks. The banks of the ponds were all dressed to 3 over 2, and a seat 1 foot wide was cut, on which the turf rested. Turf is the best finish for ponds of this sort; laid a few inches below the water-line, it protects the whole bank, the wear and tear being just at the line betwixt air and water. The turf can be fixed without the seat, but the pegs which must then be used to hold it catch the nets when the fish are being caught, and cause much delay and annoyance.

The outlets of the ponds are of masonry, and a frame is built in to hold two screens. The screens are similar to those used in

Fig. 171—scale 1/12.

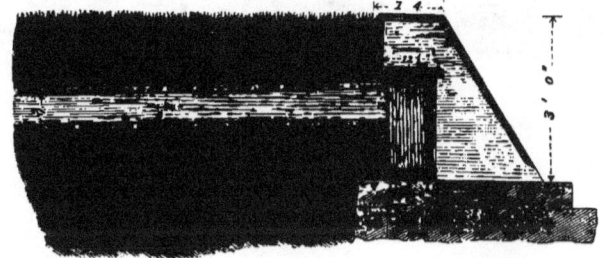

Fig. 172—scale 1/12.

the 130-feets and other ponds; and a covered trough, which carries off the water, is fitted in the centre of the outlet frame. A plan and sections of the outlet of a 300-feet pond are here given (Figs. 171-173).

The valves of the ponds are all of brass, simply closing on a wooden seat. This seat is formed by the top of a frame enclosing a straight-eye branch on the 8-inch iron pipe which runs below the

FIG. 173—scale 1/12.

300-feets. A large ring is riveted to the valve, and so placed as not to catch the net when the pond is drawn (Fig. 174). To lift

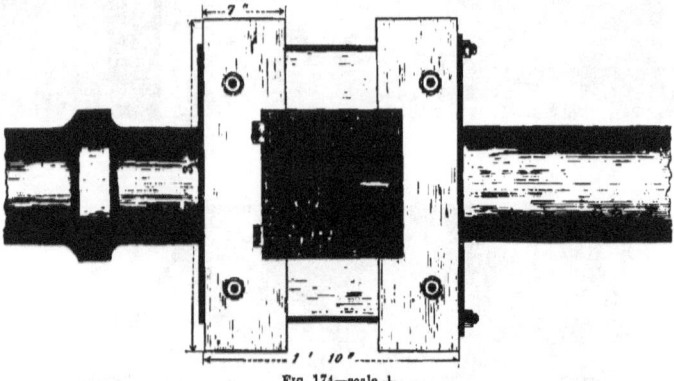

FIG. 174—scale 1/7.

the valve a light flat-bottomed boat is employed, and a rope passed across the pond and fastened to the boat holds it in position over the valve. An iron rod, terminating in a hook, is used as a probe, and the brass valve thus easily found, its position being roughly determined by marks on the bank. The hook is inserted in the ring, and the rope slacked from the boat, and made fast to the rod. Three men on the bank can then lift the valve. I at first guarded the pipe by means of an iron grating fitted below the valve, so that no fish could go down till the grating was removed; but experience has shown this superfluous, and its only action was to delay the emptying of the pond; the gratings are now removed (Fig. 175). As a matter of fact, few fish descend the pipe till the pond is so nearly empty that the grating would have been removed as a matter of course; and secondly, if any fish do go down the pipe, it is of no consequence, as they are in practice as safe in the pipe as in the pond or well. No one who has not witnessed the slow and

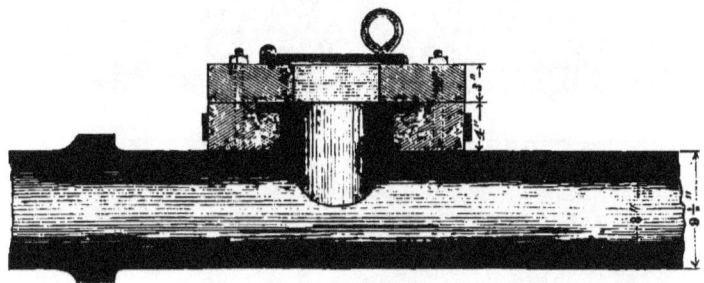

Fig. 175—scale 1/12.

leisurely way fish descend a pipe, tail first, through which water is rushing at a speed which apparently carries all before it, can

Fig. 176—scale 1/12.

believe the absolute immunity from injury enjoyed by trout under the circumstances. But of course it must be borne in mind that

HOWIETOUN PONDS.

at Howietoun the size of the fish in each set of ponds is carefully proportioned to the depth of the ponds.

FIG. 177—scale $\frac{1}{71}$.

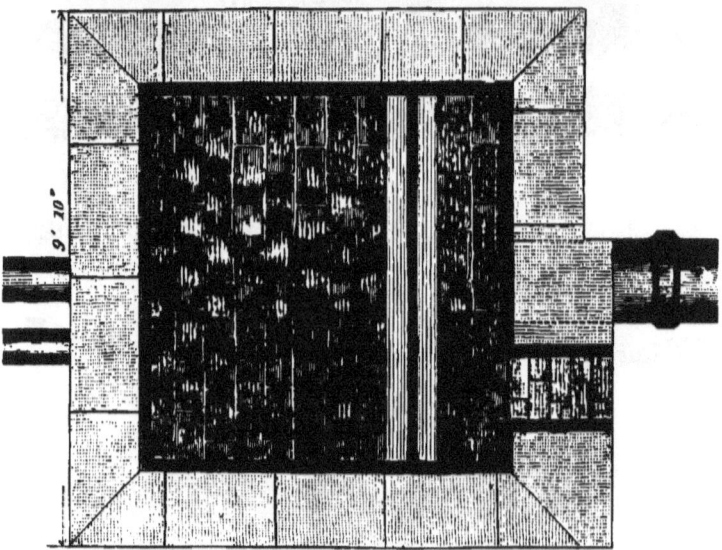

FIG. 178—scale $\frac{1}{71}$.

The pipe discharged into a well on the same principle as the one already described at Craigend (p. 244), only larger. This well is situated at the side of the old course of the burn, which is the lowest point where drainage could be secured in all weathers. A plan of the well is all that is necessary.. Figs. 180-182 are plans of the well for the 300-feets, showing sizes.

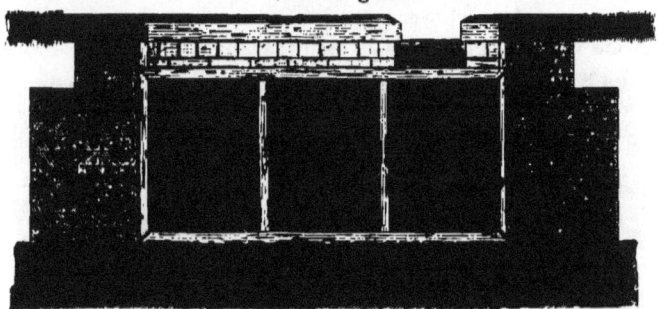

Fig. 179—scale 1/12.

Fig. 180—scale 1/12.

Fig. 181—scale 1/12.

Three bridges were built over the water-courses feeding the three 300-feets. These bridges really formed the ends of the course, and a short arm of the ponds ran up to the bridges. In netting the ponds this short arm is particularly useful. There is usually over 1000 fish in each net, and if the net is hauled into the arm a good current of water flows through it, and the operators are not so much hurried over the spawning process. Too great haste means bad impregnation as certainly as too little speed, and, what

FIG. 182—scale $\frac{1}{18}$.

is worse, might mean insufficient care in the selection of breeders, especially if the fish-culturist was short of ponds, and had neglected segregation.

The water-courses of the 300-feets were laid out with the view of exposing the water which had already passed through the 130-feets to the atmosphere as much as possible. With this object the longest path was chosen for the two outside ponds, and a diamond was left in the centre as an island, round which the water flowed to the centre 300-feet. The sides of the water-courses were built of brick, and coped with black and white bricks on edge, placed alternately. The plan is curvilinear, and wells, which the fish freely use as sanatoriums, are inserted, one in each water-course (Fig. 183).

The dividing-box was made on the pattern of the one already described (see p. 221). The water from the three 130-feet plank ponds was brought in in three covered troughs, and the wastes were led to the old course of the burn.

On the 27th March 1879 the water was turned through the

dividing-box on to the east 300-feet pond; and on the 21st May

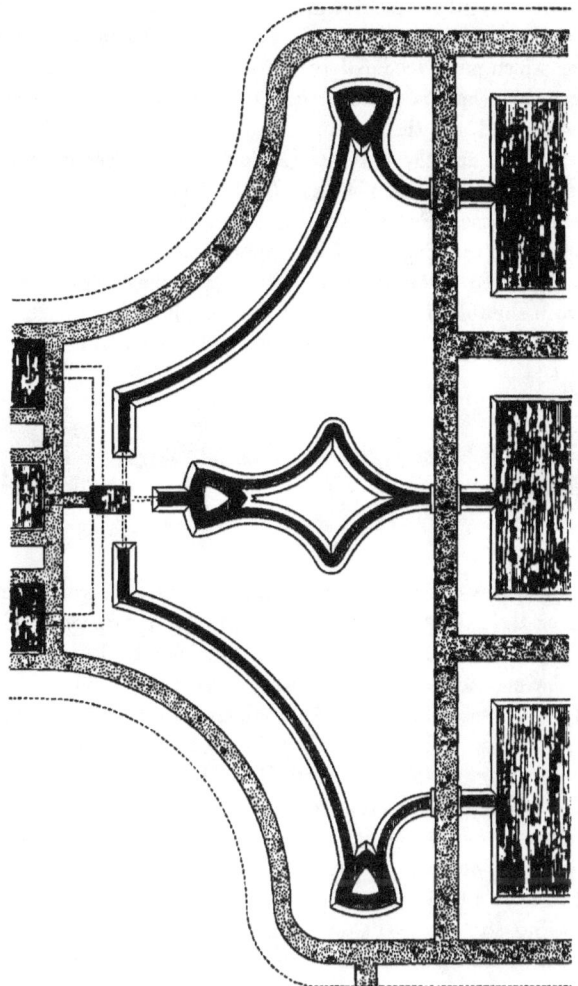

Fig. 183—scale 1/111.

the water was turned on to the west 300-feet, the centre 300-feet pond being completed last, and filled early in August 1879.

HOWIETOUN PONDS.

The feeding of the fry in the 20-feets still required much attention. In all the ponds the fry scattered, as only fry can; and it took an hour of patient coaxing to collect them for feeding, during which much food fell to the bottom, and lay unconsumed, necessitating the ponds being frequently brushed out. The feeding-jars were tried, but the area of each pond was too large for them to cope with; and the old man who helped me to feed did not see so well as once, and did not then (he has improved since) make a successful nurse. So at last I made a water-wheel, and placed it in the trough carrying the main supply to the ponds; on the axle a small grooved wheel is placed, and copper pins driven into the groove at suitable distances. Over the trough feeding the 20-feets, a driving-shaft was fixed, carrying two eccentrics, and at the end a

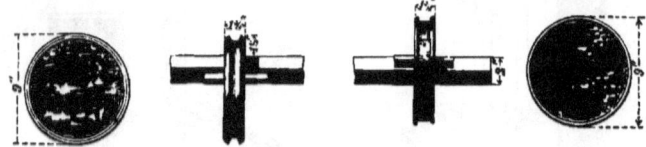

FIG. 184—scale $\frac{1}{12}$.

studded wheel driven by a chain passing over the small grooved wheel on the axle of the water-wheel (Fig. 184). Spoons made of perforated zinc, and attached to short but flexible handles, bored near the end to receive a pin, were constructed, and steel pins fixed in the sides of the 20-feets, about 5 feet from the upper ends; 9 inches further iron rods 6 inches in length were pivoted. Below are diagrams showing details (Fig. 185).

The *modus operandi* is as follows:—Collars of copper wire are fitted, one on each eccentric. From these collars strings lead to the four rods, one on each 20-feet pond. These strings are adjusted so as to have 4 to 6 inches of slack. A lead weight depends from each string, and is placed so as to travel freely between the rod and the handle of the spoon round which two or three turns of the string are next wound. Balls of finely-chopped meat are made, each ball the size of a large walnut, and two or three balls are dropped into each spoon. The chain is then passed over the driving-wheels,

and the spoons move to and fro with a sharp jerk. As each
eccentric is moved back, the handles of the two spoons connected

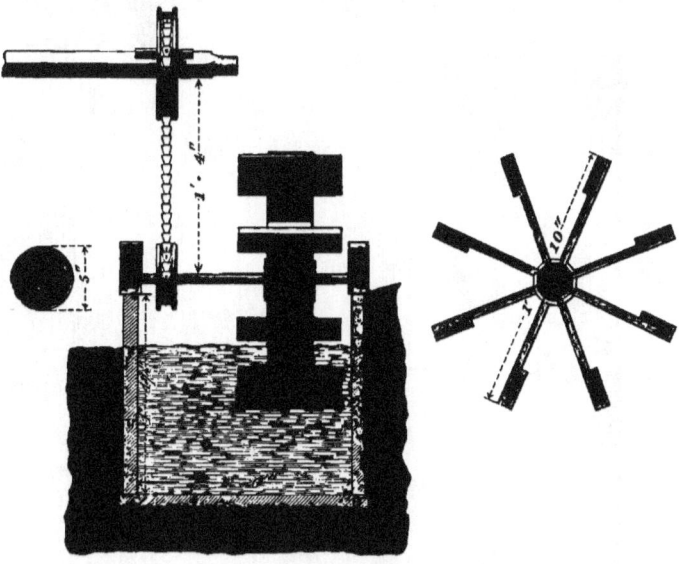

FIG. 185—scale 1/12.

move forward, and their spoons descend the pond; and as the
eccentric moves forward the back-weights jerk the spoons up the
ponds, scattering the meat very evenly and at regular intervals.
The amount of motion is regulated by the position of the rod, or,
in other words, by the amount of slack between the handle of the
spoon and the end of the rod. Thus each of the four 20-feets can
be fed at a different rate with any alteration of the number of turns
of the shaft. If it is wished to increase or decrease the power, it
is easily done by altering the depth of the immersed portion of the
water-wheel. For this purpose grooves are cut in the sides of
the trough behind the wheel, and boards are slipped in to deepen
the water, which can thus be dammed back on the floats of the
wheel to any desired depth. I should have mentioned that the
wheel is undershot. The advantages of this invention are great.

HOWIETOUN PONDS. 263

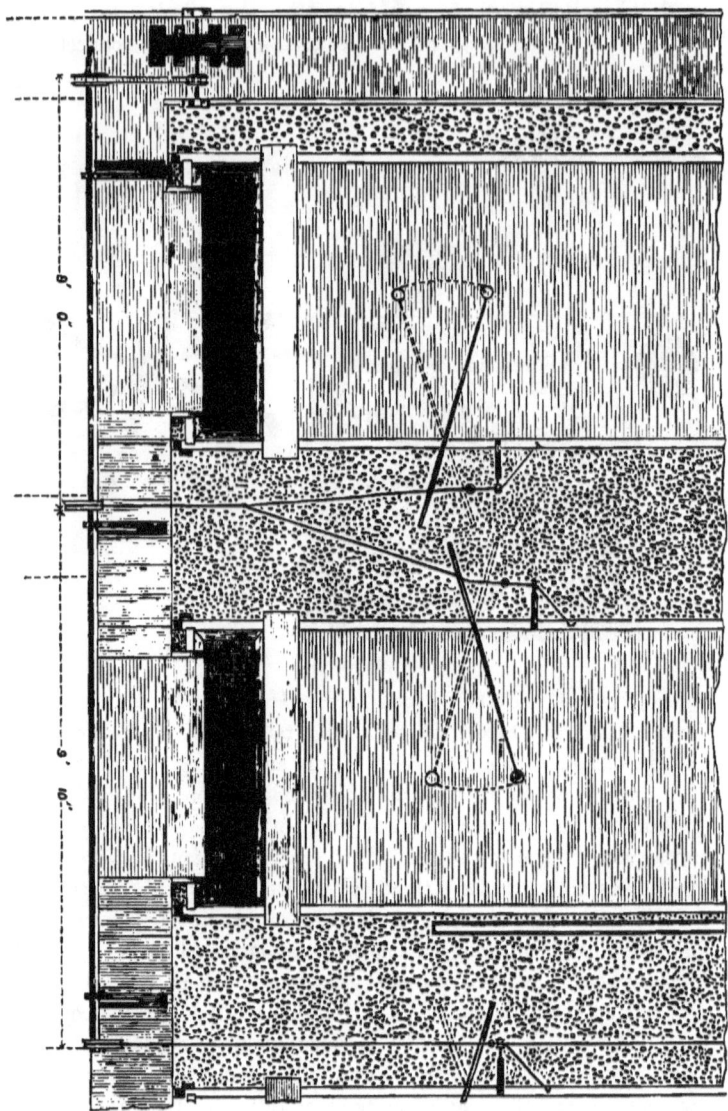

FIG. 186—scale 1/14.

In the first place, the meat never becomes sodden, as in all other machines,—in itself a recommendation; fry will not eat white, washed-out food. The ball entirely protects the meat, and the rolling contact with the perforated zinc sides of the spoon disengages fresh particles every time. Secondly, no deaths from choking ever can occur, and this prolific source of loss amongst young trout is eliminated. No unsuitably-sized particle can escape through the perforations. Of course the size of the zinc must be regulated to the age of the trout fry; No. 8 is the smallest size and No. 10 the largest suitable to mechanical spoons. Compact-

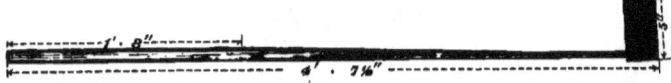

FIG. 187—scale $\tfrac{1}{1}$.

ness of the fish for feeding is the next advantage. They soon collect in a crowd, and follow every motion of the spoon. As those nearest get gorged they fall back, and others take their place. Little or no food falls to the bottom, and, if any, it is not allowed to rest, as the concentrated swarm of fry continually agitates any particle of fallen food, and aids in its consumption. It is only when fed too much at a time, or too often, that any waste occurs. Lastly, a continuous flow of meat being secured for from twenty to thirty minutes at a time, and many times a day, all the fry get an equal chance, and the result is more uniform than by hand-feeding. These spoons have been used in the four 20-feets every season, and up to date (December 1885) show no signs of decay. I still find them the best and most economical feeders. Of course, as the demand for yearlings is now over 100,000 per annum, other ponds have been made where mechanical feeding is out of the question, and, where the fishery is on a very large scale, unnecessary, as two girls, following each other at a distance of ten minutes with long-handled spoons, give excellent results. But at least 40 per cent. of the fry die of starvation before they understand hand-feeding, and this must be allowed for in turning in the fry from the hatching-boxes. The loss with healthy fry in the 20-feets, when fed by the mechanical spoons, is almost *nil*. After August the spoons are removed, and hand-feeding substituted without difficulty. The worst of the 20-feets is the small number they can accommodate in winter—not more than 1200 each—without dwarfing the fish; and it is advisable to thin them very considerably in September. However, we find that where the fry are intrinsically valuable—as hybrids for experiments, or foreign fish for acclimatation—the 20-feets, with mechanical feeding, give by far the best results, supplying as they do a constant flow of fresh food in any desired quantity.

The lead to the east 130-feet pond, which had been stocked in October 1877 before the lead was finished, was concreted this summer (1879), and the water turned in again on the 7th June. A box of wood, with No. 14 perforated zinc, was supported on piles in the heart-shaped well of the centre 300-feet pond, and filled with earth, in which water-cress was planted. The water-cress soon filled the whole well, and now forms a striking object in summer, growing as it does luxuriantly out of apparently deep water, no part of the box being visible. Water-cress so planted is a great assistance in a fishery, as it not only improves the water by removing the fishy taint, but also forms a nursery for all sorts of water-snails and *Entromostricæ*, which would otherwise be unable to freely reproduce their species. This applies also to the *Crustaceæ*, especially to *Gammarus*, of which the trout are so fond, that in a plank pond above the Fishery—although the stream swarms with them—none are ever found.

The five rearing-boxes in the hatching-house at Howietoun were fitted with deep hatching-trays; but as the results were far from encouraging, their use has been discontinued, and they fall more properly to be considered under the next head.

SEASON 1878-79.—EXPERIMENTAL WORK.

The experimental work this season was undertaken chiefly with a view to economise space in hatching. Most fortunately, the winter was a very severe one—so severe, indeed, that 20,000 trout ova laid down in the Howietoun hatching-house on the 8th November did not hatch till the 16th April, the incubation lasting 160 days. As eggs will stand much more crowding in cold than in comparatively warm water, I could not have had a better opportunity to experiment. At this date nothing was known of the power the pisciculturist exercises over the vitality of the embryo, nor was the large amount of space demanded by the alevins as a condition to their future existence recognised.

I made deep boxes to fit into the 4-feet rearing-boxes; a level 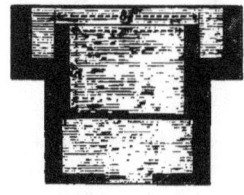 trough was built on to the deep box, and a lead pipe fitted into the trough. The edge of the deep box was kept under the top of the trough; a false bottom of wood and perforated zinc admitted the water into the deep box; some inches higher a grille was fixed to carry the eggs. A board was next fitted with flannel across the end of the rearing-box, 2 or 3 inches above the outlet screen. Water was admitted to the rearing-box, and the deep box floated to its level. A hole was then cut in the board to fit the lead pipe, which, when passed

FIG. 188—scale ¼.

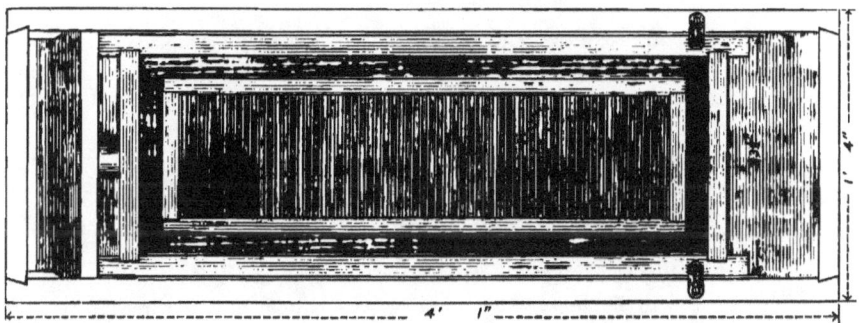

FIG. 189—scale ¼.

through, held the end of the deep box in its place; the other end was next carefully levelled, and two turn-buttons screwed on to the sides of the rearing-box, against which it floated. When the water is turned on to the rearing-box it falls clear of the end of the deep box, and rising through the false bottom, it passes through the grille, and upwards through the eggs, and, falling over the edge of the deep box, is collected in the trough, and discharged by the lead pipe into the outlet end of the rearing-box, from which it passes through the conducting-spout into the drain. The great length of the overflow of the deep box, it being equal to the perimeter of the sides, seemed to ensure an even upward current through the eggs, while the box itself being held in position by its own buoyancy acting against fixed supports, it appeared that any sediment could be removed by simply depressing the box and allowing it to rise slowly to its place. On page 266 is a sketch of the deep hatching-box (Fig. 189).

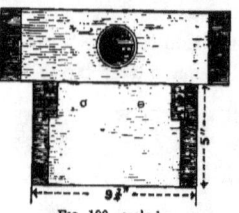

FIG. 190—scale ⅛.

I also built a large hatching-box, on the same principle of an upward current, but so arranged that it could be used with a downward current at the same time, and the results compared. This I named the

QUADRUPLE HATCHING-BOX.

It consists of a box 5 feet 4½ inches long, 3 feet 8¾ inches wide, and 3 feet 2 inches deep over all. It was built of 2-inch plank, as it was intended to use it out in the open; the planks jointed with a slip feather as in the 20-feet ponds, and held together by iron bolts tightened by nuts against a runner laid on the bottom. Five grooves were ploughed in each side, three being stopped 6 inches from the bottom, and two 4 inches from the top. In these, five divisions of flooring were fitted with red lead, so that all the joints were water-tight, and a fillet was nailed with its upper edge touching the bottom of the three divisions (Fig. 191). A pipe was fitted into one end near the top to carry off the water, and the supply was obtained by another pipe, not shown in the drawing, discharging into the opposite end compartment. Grilles were placed on the fillets to

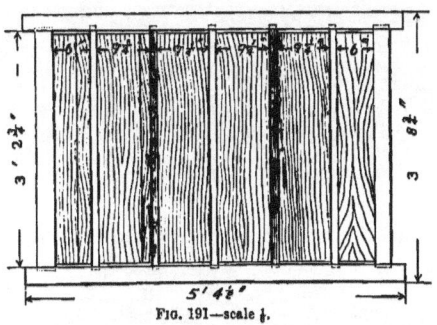

FIG. 191—scale ⅛.

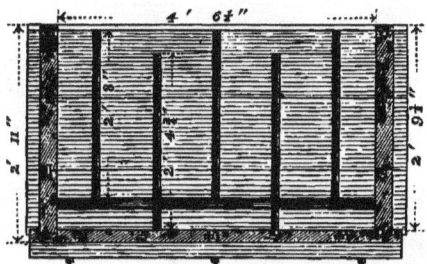

FIG. 192—scale ⅛.

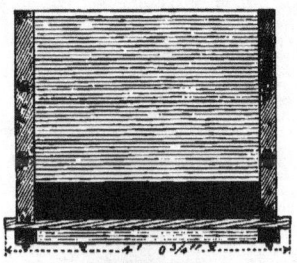

FIG. 193—scale ⅛.

carry the eggs, and the water, entering the first compartment, passes under the first division; rises (Fig. 192) in the second compartment; and falls over the second division, passing under the third into the fourth compartment, where it rises over the fourth

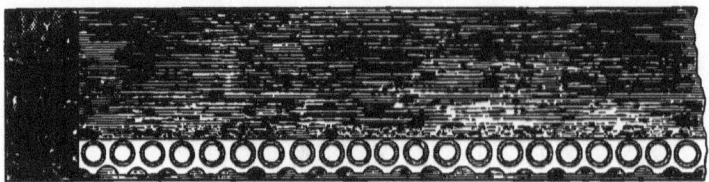

Fig. 194—scale ¼.

division into the fifth, and passing below the fifth division into the

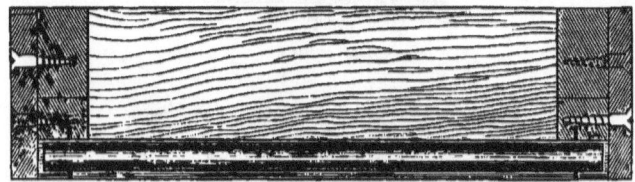

Fig. 195—scale ¼.

last compartment, it rises to the pipe, through which it escapes.

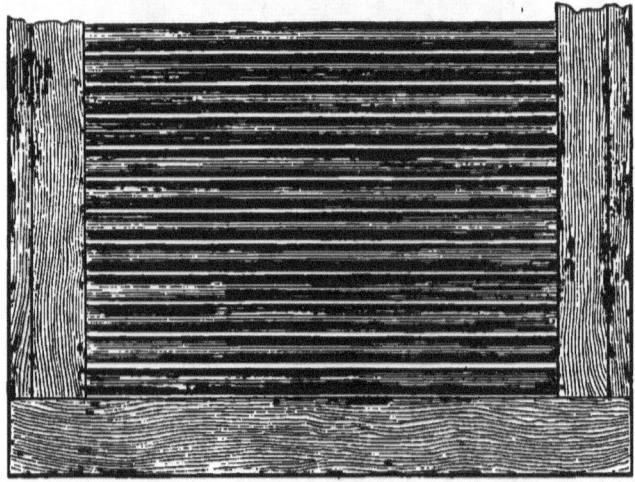

Fig. 196—scale ¼.

To take full advantage of the quadruple hatching-box I designed a grille specially for it. The plan was similar to the ordinary grille used in the 7-feet hatching-boxes (Fig. 69), only the glass tubes were rather thicker, the hole in the strip of perforated zinc being enlarged to bring the tubes closer together. This will be easily understood from the longitudinal section (Fig. 194). The two pieces of wood into which the zinc was fixed were slipped into the frame, and held with four screws, so as to be easily removed should it be necessary to replace a glass tube. The sides were made sufficiently deep to allow four or five layers of salmon ova to be placed on each grille; although two layers, or about 7000 ova, were considered a fair stocking. The experiments with this box were not satisfactory, the compartments being too large to ensure an even distribution of the current through the whole horizontal section, but I am of opinion that they indicated that, so long as the ova are subjected to an even, uninterrupted flow of pure water, the direction of the current is immaterial, and if the water contains sediment, it will be deposited on the shell of the ovum opposite to the direction of the current; that is to say, that an upward current keeps the lower portion of the shell clean, and deposits sediment on the upper, while a downward current keeps the upper portion of the shell clean, but deposits sediment, though only to a very slight extent, on the under portion of the egg; the adherence is probably due to the absorption of water through the pores of the shell.

On the 17th March 1879 I experimented with various sizes of zinc for screens, using *S. fontinalis* alevins. The result was that the alevins passed through No. 9 perforated zinc with great ease. I found No. 8 perforated zinc perfectly secure, and No. 7 dangerously small, as it not only was apt to clog and cause an overflow, but the increased suction due to the increased depth of water caused by the smaller hole, held the fish so tightly against the screen, that many of them were unable to leave it if they once touched.

I also experimented on the quantity of water required to carry trout. I netted the east 130-feet wooden pond, and selected one hundred Lochleven trout, weighing 80 lbs. These fish were barely three years old, and very good specimens for their age for this part of Scotland. I despatched them in four of the conical yearling tanks, with 15 gallons of water in each. The temperature of the air was 34° F., and the temperature of the water 38° F. The fish were despatched in the middle of the day, and the length of the journey was a little over four hours.

On the 18th March I received a post-card from Lord Balfour that the fish had arrived without loss or symptom of distress at Tulliallan.

Next morning I despatched a second hundred of the same sized trout by the 11.30 A.M. train from Stirling, but one tank sprang a leak shortly after leaving the Fishery, and the trout were divided into the three remaining tanks. These fish also arrived at Tulliallan without any loss. This was the first important consignment from Howietoun, and I considered, as the result of the experiment of sending successfully 200 thirty-five months' old trout to Tulliallan, weighing 160 lbs., that 24 lbs. of trout can exist with safety in 12 gallons of water for four hours, provided the temperature is under 40° F. Therefore 2 lbs. of trout can exist in 1 gallon of water for four hours, or 1 lb. of trout can exist in 1 gallon of water for eight hours. Therefore an *hour-gallon* can support 8 lbs. of trout.

Or, to put this in its simplest mathematical form, $g = \frac{wt}{8}$, where g = number of gallons, w = weight of trout in lbs., and t = the time in hours occupied in the journey. For example, suppose it is required to send trout a sixteen-hours' journey from water to water to know how many trout can be sent in an ordinary 40-gallon tank; here $g = 40$, and $t = 16$, therefore from $g = \frac{wt}{8}$, $\therefore 40 = \frac{16w}{8}$ $\therefore 40 = 2w$, $\therefore w = 20$ lbs. of trout,—that is to say, 20 trout of 1 lb. each, or 80 trout of ¼ lb. each, or 100 trout of five to the lb., 200 trout of ten to the lb., always provided that the temperature of the water does not rise above 40° F.

On the 3d April 1879 I experimented by placing 100 yearling trout in a conical tank, with 12 gallons of water, at 4.40 P.M. At

7 the following morning only 5 survived; they were of all sizes, including one of the smallest and one of the biggest, measuring 2½ inches and 6 inches respectively. I weighed the remaining 95, and found them to be 23 oz., therefore the 100 yearlings would weigh almost exactly 1½ lb. The 6 largest weighed 4 oz., and were all over 5½ inches long; the 8 smallest weighed 1 oz., and were from 2½ to 3 inches long.

The temperature of the air at the commencement of the experiment was 40° F., and fell below freezing during the night. The water was not aërated artificially. According to the foregoing formula, 7 lbs. weight ought to have survived for the period of time occupied, according to the hour-gallon formula. It is possible the formula does not hold good for very small trout, say under 4 inches in length, but the absence of any aëration of the water, and the formation of a thin skin of ice on the surface in the morning, are sufficient to account for the unsatisfactory results. At 11 A.M. I repeat the experiment, placing 100 yearling trout from the centre 20-feet pond (No. 2) into a conical tank, with 12 gallons of water; at 7 P.M.—that is, after eight hours—they were all lively. The temperature of the water during the experiment was about 40° F. At 11.20 A.M. I placed 7 four-year-old Lochleven trout, weighing 12 pounds, and each fish between 15 inches and 16 inches in length, into a conical tank with 12 gallons of water, temperature 40° F., the same as in preceding experiment. At 2 P.M. one fish showed symptoms of distress. I removed it, and then aërated the water with a syringe. At 3 P.M. I aërated the water by lifting some out with a jug and pouring it back. At 5.30 P.M. I again aërated the water with a jug; the fish were then much more lively than at 2 P.M. At 7 P.M. all the fish showed symptoms of distress, two being very sick, but on aërating the water with the jug, they all recovered. I then returned the fish into the centre 130-feet pond (No. 7). 10½ gallons of water would have been sufficient, according to the hour-gallon formula, and with a little earlier and more frequent aëration, it certainly appears it would have been ample.

By the formula $g = \dfrac{wt}{8}$ here, one fish weighing 1½ lb. was removed after 2½ hours, and the remaining 6 fish were left for five hours longer, so let $w't'$ represent the weight and time until the removal of the fish—that is for 2½ hours—and $w''t''$ represent the conditions from then until the end of the experiment, then $wt = w't' + w''t''$ (2), but $w' = 12$ lbs., and $w'' = 12$ lbs. $-1\frac{1}{2}$ lb. $= 10\frac{1}{2}$ lbs., and $t' = 2\frac{1}{2}$ hours, *i.e.* from 11.20 A.M. to 2 P.M., and $t'' = 5$ hours, *i.e.* from 2 P.M. to 7 P.M.; then substituting the value wt in (2), we get from (1) $g = \dfrac{12 \times 2\frac{1}{2} + 10\frac{1}{2} \times 5}{8}$ (3), therefore $g = 10\frac{1}{4}$ gallons nearly; and the experience of subsequent years has proved that this calculation is sufficiently accurate for all practical purposes.

SEASON 1878-79.—FISH-CULTURE.

On the 1st July I counted the three-year-olds in the west 130-feet wooden pond, and found 1776 trout remaining. A good many had jumped out previously. I transferred the fish to the centre 130-feet wooden pond, in which 500 of the same lot had been left from last year, making probably about 2200 trout in the pond. They averaged just over 1 lb.

On the 2d July I moved 424 Lochleven yearlings from the upper 100-feet earth pond at Craigend to the west 130-feet wooden pond at Howietoun, and on the next day I moved 2709 Lochleven yearlings from the upper 100-feet earth pond at Craigend, and 957 Lochleven yearlings from the lower 100-feet earth pond at Craigend to the west 130-feet wooden pond at Howietoun; and on the 19th August I emptied the ponds at Craigend, and found 548 Lochleven yearlings in the upper and 743 Lochleven yearlings in the lower. These I also transferred to the west 130-feet wooden pond at Howietoun, making 5381 in all.

On the 7th July a three-year-old Lochleven trout jumped out of the centre 130-feet wooden pond at Howietoun. It measured 14·6 inches, and weighed 1 lb. 5 oz. I consider this a very important record, as the fish could not have been more than forty-two months old, although I have reason to believe it was by no means the largest fish in the pond, as I find on the 7th March 1878 a note regarding the same lot: "Some close on 2 lbs. One jumped out the night before last, and a cat ate the tail half. The part left weighed over a lb."

The fry for the Craigend ponds were turned out in August, and about 30,000 were placed in each of the 130-feet ponds. These were fry from eggs obtained at Kinross. The east and centre 20-feet plank ponds at Howietoun were also stocked from the same source, while the lower 20-feet was stocked with *S. levenensis* from my own fish, being the first generation from parents bred in confinement.

On the 8th November 1878 I commenced to spawn the Lochleven trout in the centre 130-feet wooden pond at Howietoun, and obtained a large number of eggs from them.

I also spawned the *fario* in the 60-feet wooden pond on the 30th November, and obtained 50,000 eggs. These *fario* were a year younger than the Levens in the centre pond.

I placed the eggs in two of the deep boxes in the Howietoun hatching-house. They eyed on the 15th March, that is to say, a few of them did, as the deep hatching-trays were not a success, having killed almost every egg intrusted to them by the 8th February. In the beginning of January I purchased 10,000 *S. fontinalis* eggs from Mr. Capel of Footscray. They arrived in very good condition, and their descendants have now thoroughly established themselves at the Fishery. This was the coldest season I have experienced at Howietoun, none of the eggs in that hatching-house hatching in less than 157 days. On the 13th January I removed the grilles from the boxes in the hatching-house at Howietoun, and washed them in air by means of a watering-pot with a very fine rose. This made the eggs beautifully clean, and killed very few, although they were not nearly eyed,—in fact, the earliest did not eye for more than five weeks afterwards. The temperature of the air at the time was 33° F., but next morning I found a considerable difference in the boxes.

In Box VIII. I found I had killed about 1000 eggs. This box, from being one of the outside boxes, was the coldest and considerably the most backward. The eggs were spawned on

November 13th. In Box v., on the contrary, which was in the warmest situation, and at least a week more advanced, partly on account of temperature, and partly on account of eggs being taken three days earlier (November 10th), there were only about 100 eggs killed. As there were about 20,000 eggs in each box. the loss represented 5 per cent. in the one case, and a half per cent. in the other. If we apply the table of percentage of incubation, page 206, and suppose it applies equally below 40° F., as between 40° and 50° F., the extraordinary deduction occurs, that the temperature of the water averaged 28° F., which is absurd. There must, therefore, be some point—probably between 33° and 34°—where incubation almost, if not absolutely, ceases, and it would be very interesting to determine the exact percentage of incubation per diem between 33° and 35°. Unfortunately, the temperatures of the water for this season at Howietoun were not kept.

The *fontinalis* eggs commenced to hatch on the 17th January, but not more than 2000 had hatched up to January 29th. On that day I put down the remaining 8000 to hatch, and by the morning of the 31st they were nearly all hatched out. The alevins were dark, firm, and their yolk-sacs were well-shaped, but very sluggish, the temperature of the water being only 36° F.

By the 8th February the frost had entirely gone, and both the streams at Middlethird and at Howietoun were in flood. The leaf-screen at Middlethird gave way under the spate, as did the inlet-screen of the 60-feet wooden pond at Howietoun; and the inlet-screen of the upper earth pond at Craigend was torn completely off its hinges, and many fish escaped up the supply-pipe. A leak also sprang alongside the outlet-pipe of the lower earth pond at Craigend, and some 30 yearlings escaped. Similar disasters will always occur to young fish-culturists, but after a little experience, the risk of re-occurrence may be reduced to infinitesimal proportions. Misfortunes in fish-culture seldom come alone, and on the same day I found that most of the eggs in the deep hatching-trays had died.

I packed and sold 31,000 Lochleven eggs, and sold 1250 yearlings this season, which was the first return made by the Fishery, all former sales being of eggs obtained at Kinross and disposed of on behoof of the Lochleven Angling Association.

TABLE OF OVA SPAWNED, SEASON 1878-79.

| \multicolumn{7}{c}{MIDDLETHIRD HATCHING-HOUSE.} |

Date.	S. levenensis.	S. fario.	S. fontinalis.	Hatching-box.	Eyed.	Hatched.
Nov. 13	10,000	...	...	Box 1	Jan. 17	Mar. 19
,, 13	25,000	..	...	,, 2	,, 17	
,, 13	20,000	...	...	,, 3	,, 17	
,, 13	20,000	...	...	,, 5	,, 17	Mar. 19
,, 13	10,000	...	...	,, 6	,, 17	,, 19
Jan. 7	...	...	10,000	,, 4	?	Jan. 30

| \multicolumn{7}{c}{MIDDLETHIRD—SECOND STOCKING.} |

Mar. 18	10,000			Box 1		June 15
,, 18	20,000			,, 2		,, 15
,, 18	10,000			,, 6		

| \multicolumn{7}{c}{HOWIETOUN HATCHING-HOUSE.} |

Nov. 8	20,000	...	...	Box 1	Feb. 20	Apr. 17
,, 10	20,000	...	...	,, 2	,, 23	,, 18
,, 10	20,000	...	...	,, 3	,, 23	,, 18
,, 10	20,000	...	...	,, 4	,, 23	,, 18
,, 10	20,000	...	...	,, 5	, 23	,, 18
,, 13	20,000	...	...	,, 6	,, 25	,, 19
,, 13	20,000	...	...	,, 7	,, 25	
,, 13	20,000	...	...	,, 8	,, 25	Apr. 20
,, 13	20,000	...	...	a		
,, 13	15,000	...	...	b		
,, 13	10,000	...	...	c		
,, 30	...	25,000	...	d		
,, 30	...	25,000	...	e		
Totals,	330,000	50,000	10,000			

On February 19th I brought a grille of eggs over from Middlethird, but the weather having again become very cold, they were frozen to the grille when they arrived at Howietoun. I placed the grille in water, and next morning the eggs had thawn out, and appeared to have perfectly recovered; and up to the 1st March only 50 of these eggs had died, and on the 3d April they hatched remarkably well. The number would be about 5000, as the eggs were very small. This shows that partial freezing after the egg is eyed is not necessarily fatal if the eggs are frozen in air.

The eggs in Box I. at Howietoun, which had been spawned on the 8th November, eyed on 20th February, being 104 days. These eggs afterwards hatched on the 17th April, being 160 days. This is the longest record in my experience, and the eggs hatched uncommonly well, being almost entirely hatched out on the morning of 18th April, sixteen hours after they were laid down to hatch.

On the 22d February I put the first advertisement of the Fishery in the *Field*. (See Appendix.)

This spring herons began to be very troublesome, and, in spite of guns and traps, their numbers have increased steadily with the extension of the Fishery. By the 6th March the *fontinalis* alevins were all herding together, forming one of those useful co-operating breathing societies in which the combined movement of thousands of pairs of pectoral fins induce a current through the whole mass. On the same day I drew the valve of the east 300-feet earth pond (No. 10), and it took five hours to empty. In spite of the cold winter, the two-year-olds were well on the feed, and I killed the second horse for the season. On the 12th March I observed several large trout spawning in the feeder to the east 130-feet wooden pond (No. 6), and on the 18th March I netted the pond, and obtained 50,000 *S. levenensis* ova. The eggs were slightly smaller than those obtained in October from the three-year-old *S. levenensis* in the centre 130-feet wooden pond (No. 7), but were of a richer amber colour. Milt was easily obtained, and of the consistency of thin cream. The temperature of the air was about 40° F., and deep snow formed a very convenient carpet to turn out the landing-net on. The trout were about thirty-six months old, and some of the males scaled fully 1½ lb. Most of the eggs were sent to Middlethird hatching-house, as a second stocking, and they hatched on June 15th, probably the latest date on record in this country. On the 25th March I corrected proofs of the first price list of the Fishery. (See Appendix.) On the 2d April I tested the size of the fish in the various ponds, and found the two-year-olds (about twenty-six months old) measured from 7 to 9 inches. The three-year-olds averaged ¾ lb., and the four-year-olds averaged 2 lbs., from which I gather that the fish were fed considerably heavier previous to 1879 than they have been since.

On the 16th April I emptied the east 130-feet wooden pond, and transferred 4398 three-year-old trout to the east 300-feet earth pond. The largest fish measured 17 inches. I also brought the *fontinalis* alevins from Middlethird to Howietoun. On the 18th April I sent 250 fifteen-month-old trout to Carnarvon. The journey occupied about twelve hours. No ice was used, and there was no loss. The fish were carried in three tanks, with 14 gallons of water in each. On the 29th April the young *fontinalis* commenced to feed, and on 11th May they were transferred to the east 20-feet plank pond (No. 3). On the 21st May the water was turned on to the west 300-feet earth pond (No. 12), and next day the four-year-old *S. levenensis* were transferred from the centre 130-feet wooden pond (No. 7). They numbered 1914 in all, the largest being between 5 and 6 lbs. in weight. On the 7th June the sides of the feeder of the east 130-feet wooden pond (No. 6) were concreted, as the earth-banks had not stood the test of the severe winter; and on the 9th I commenced to restock the pond with yearlings.

STATEMENT OF STOCK ON 31ST DECEMBER 1878.

100-feet,	Upper	(Craigend)	17,000	*S. levenensis*	Hatched 1878
100 ,,	Lower	(,,)	16,000	,,	,, ,,
20 ,,	West	No. 1	used as a filter		
20 ,,	Centre	,, 2	2,500	*S. levenensis*	,, 1878
20 ,,	East	,, 3	1,000	,,	,, ,,
20 ,,	Lower	,, 4	2,500	,,	,, ,,
60 ,,	Plank	,, 5	1,500	*S. fario*	,, 1876
130 ,,	East	,, 6	5,000	*S. levenensis*	,, ,,
130 ,,	Centre	,, 7	2,150	,,	,, 1875
130 ,,	West	,, 8	5,400	,,	,, 1877
Octagon,	Craigend		9	Hybrids	,, 1875
	Total,		53,059		

www.ingramcontent.com/pod-product-compliance
Lightning Source LLC
Chambersburg PA
CBHW021958220426
43663CB00007B/872